Dusty
Springfield

Dusty
Springfield

in the middle of nowhere

Laurence Cole

Middlesex
University
PRESS

First published in 2008 by Middlesex University Press
Copyright © Laurence Cole

ISBN: 978 1 904750 41 3

A CIP catalogue record for this book is available from
The British Library

Cover photo: Getty Images

Design by Helen Taylor

Printed in the UK by Ashford Colour Press

Middlesex University Press
Tel: +44 (0)20 8411 4162
Fax: +44 (0)20 8411 4167

www.mupress.co.uk

THANK YOU

to Clive Bloom, Celia Cozens, Richard Firth,
Paul Howes, Matthew Skipper and
Helen Taylor for your help and support

There was an excitement in her voice… a singing compulsion, a whispered 'Listen', a promise that she had done gay and exciting things just a while since and that there were gay, exciting things hovering in the next hour… a stirring warmth flowed from her, as if her heart was trying to come out to you concealed in one of those breathless, thrilling words… that voice… couldn't be overdreamed – that voice was a deathless song.

F. Scott Fitzgerald, *The Great Gatsby*

People either know the name but they can't think of what I sang, or they know the record but they go, 'Now who was it who sang that?'

Dusty Springfield

Not wholly this or that,
But wrought
Of alien bloods am I…
Nor this nor that
Contains me…

'Cosmopolite' by Georgia Douglas Johnson

Dusty Springfield blurred the distinctions of race, gender and sexuality just as she did those between life and art and those between reality and artifice.

Patricia Juliana Smith in
'"You Don't Have To Say You Love Me":
The Camp Masquerades of Dusty Springfield'

Contents

The door was opened by this fresh-faced farm girl who'd obviously just been out milking the cows... and I almost said, 'Is Dusty in?', and I sort of realised it was Dusty.

Derek Wadsworth, *Living Famously*, BBC TV, 22 January 2003

Preface

'High in the sky there's a bird on the wing', sang this heart-stopping voice in the middle of a group close-harmony record I had, until that moment in December 1962, been doing my best to ignore. 'Please carry me with you'. Well yes, indeed, I would – and for the next 45 years! But though I think I knew then and there, aged 18, that I had fallen instantly and irretrievably in love, I was as bewildered as I was smitten. '"Island Of Dreams" by the Springfields', said the man on the radio. But wait a minute, Mr DJ, could I have heard right? Weren't the Springfields that bland and boring folksy trio I'd half watched on TV and dismissed as even more corny and dull than Frank Ifield and Adam Faith, and most of the other British pop stars of the day? What was going on? The voice sounded like a woman's but I couldn't be sure, and if it was a woman's, then it had to belong to the blonde beehive who'd been bobbing about between two smarmy-looking blokes in ties and jackets – and anyway, she was white and British and clad in a soppy gingham frock and sang all whiney and nasal and pseudo-country, and this was a black American voice – well, wasn't it? – and I was only really interested in black American music, and…? No, there had to be some mistake. Even when I saw her a few days later singing 'Island Of Dreams', I remained unconvinced, for this sound, this voice should not – could not! – be coming out of this mouth from a woman looking this white and frowsy and, well, what my mother would call 'common'. It was all totally confusing and I could make neither head nor tail of it.

Not until a subsequent Springfield's single, 'Say I Won't Be There', with the same thing happening on the middle bridge – 'Bring me back my darling, be my friend for life' – did I begin to come to terms with the improbable and unpalatable truth. Dusty Springfield – for that was the girl's name – forced me to reconsider my preconceived notions of what a woman (as opposed to a man), a white (as opposed to a black), a Brit (as opposed to an American) should, or could, sound like when they sang. Intuitively too, I'm sure, I tuned into someone so oddball and idiosyncratic that, despite being the 'wrong' gender for the aspirations of my queer sensibility, I felt she would do nicely as the only girl to play more than a bit part in my dreams.

Despite other moments of pop epiphany, and other vocal loves, Dusty Springfield remains the only singer who can sing _anything_ to me and do any number of things to my heart according to what mood she is in. Hers was –

and is – the most beautiful, sensual and fascinating voice I have ever heard or can conceive of hearing, and the one voice which I have been in love with all my adult life. I cherish it, above all perhaps, for the generosity with which it shares its difficult experience as a flawed and wounded human being, and leaves me feeling just that bit less stranded.

Her voice has been my most loyal and faithful companion for almost half a century. A one-way love in flesh-bound reality but surely not unrequited in most other ways when she has given so much of herself. She may not have saved my life but she has certainly enhanced its quality.

This book is a small gesture of gratitude.

Introduction

A Fab Funeral

When I was growing up in the Sixties, Dusty was the very essence of fabness… She was fab and, because of her music, she always will be.

Neil Tennant at Dusty Springfield's funeral

For a late-1990s celebrity funeral, the one which took place in Henley-on-Thames♮, Oxfordshire on a wet and chilly Friday in March 1999 was a relatively quiet affair – at least compared with the supersonic roar of a funeral for a princess 18 months earlier. This deceased too was female and, like the princess, had regularly been dubbed an icon♮. But in terms of final send-offs, there are, of course, icons and icons. This icon was well-enough known to warrant TV cameras outside the church but not inside to broadcast events live as they unfolded, as with the royal one; a sound system relaying the service to the immediate locality had to do instead. The venue was an imposing early-thirteenth-century church called St Mary the Virgin which, after midday on 12 March, accommodated about 300 people. Although Westminster Abbey would have been more upmarket and spacious for a cake-throwing, crockery-smashing tribute to the deceased, who was almost as famous for her food and plate demolitions♮ as her singing, the building was not made available and an opportunity for funeral frolics sadly missed. The display of wreaths offered nothing in the way of competition. For one thing, there were too few of them to turn grassy parkland into a vast cellophane dustbin; for another, their location at the back of a small-town church lacked the prestige and tourist draw of the forecourt to a central London palace.

The occasion could still have snatched a mention in a piece on flashy funerals for the famous had the dead woman's brother conducted himself more becomingly for the occasion. Though not an earl, he had the right credentials. Not only had he grown up with the deceased and known her since childhood but he'd invited her to join his music group, the Springfields, at a time when he was the one in the family taking the musical initiatives. A celeb of sorts

♮ Throughout the book, the presence of an endnote will be indicated by the musical natural sign (♮). Endnotes may be found beginning on page 115.

himself in the early Sixties, he might have been expected to seize the limelight, dish the dirt and stir things up a bit for press and paparazzi. Instead of which – apart from leading 'the mourners as the Rev. David Pritchard paid tribute'[a] – he maintained a low profile[a], keeping to himself any resentments he might have had about his sister's treatment at the hands of the media, record companies and ex-lovers. All rather unsuitably restrained in the circumstances, and leaving the mourners with no option but to clap the ceremonial music rather than a tetchy tirade, applause at funerals for the famous now, of course, considered good form rather than an optional fashion accessory.

Others who turned up on the day, both inside and outside of the church, were similarly half-hearted and unrehearsed in histrionics. But then, not even the recent royal goodbye had come up with a 1990s equivalent of Pola Negri, an actress who, at the 1926 funeral of silent screen heartthrob, Rudolph Valentino[a], had collapsed in hysterics while hovering over the coffin, thereby setting the standard by which future farewells to the rich and famous would be measured. The boyfriend of singer, Alma Cogan[a], had certainly come up to scratch in 1966 by trying to throw himself into the grave along with the coffin, but perhaps in the Nineties such overexcitement was reserved for the football pitch.

As it was, the dead woman's friend, singer Madeline Bell, showed promise by bursting 'into tears almost as soon as she walked in'[a] but seems to have lacked the stamina for sustained weeping and wailing while another singer, Lulu, could only manage to make her voice drop 'away as she fought back tears'[a] during her tribute speech, and at no point was reported as giving up the fight entirely. The 'hundreds of fans [who] lined the main street to pay their respects'[a] did what they could to pass muster – indeed many of them were reported as 'weeping' like an older woman on the TV news that day – but even if 'the whole town was out in the street crying'[a], as one of the deceased's ex-lovers, Carole Pope, claimed, this would have totalled a mere 10,646 souls[a] – about the number sobbing before a single giant Hyde Park screen when the royal funeral was relayed from the Abbey in the summer of '97. Whatever way you look at it, for overkill and excess, the Henley funeral tried hard, meant well but fell short.

Some effort had certainly been made by the woman at the centre of things to stage a suitably glitzy final performance for herself. The horse-drawn carriage which took her coffin through the Henley streets and down the aisle of the church with the name 'DUSTY' wreathed in pink and white flowers on the sides, had been her idea. So too, apparently, had the choice of hymns – 'Love Divine, All Loves Excelling' and 'Jerusalem' – though whether she orchestrated a succession of Dusty Springfield recordings to accompany her coffin into the church and out again to a private cremation is questionable. Since she had always insisted that most of her records fell short[a] of how she would have wanted them to sound, why would she wish to 'inflict' them on those paying homage after she was dead? She had, it seems, done her best to ensure she would go out in style and can't be blamed if neither the samba band nor the Irish tenor she'd requested[♮] were present as the final credits rolled. As it was, the playing of hits like 'You Don't Have To Say You Love Me' and 'Goin' Back' provided the Disneyland visuals of horse-drawn glass-sided carriage, coffin wreathed in flowers, stained glass windows and lachrymose mourners with a suitably resonant soundtrack, and informed the Henley residents that an occasion, even an event, was happening in their midst.

Having a minor-league celebrity funeral may have its compensations. The crowd weeping may fall short of mass wailing and your brother may fail to laud you as a martyr, but you still get to have a song about the wind sung to send you off. Perhaps in mock imitation of 'Candle in the Wind' at Diana's do, Dusty requested 'The Wind Beneath My Wings' for her parting piece. If, however, she had expected her friend, Elton John, to sing the honours, she was out of luck. Elton was on tour in the States and unavailable not only to sing but to put in an appearance, and she had to make do with another friend named Simon Bell (no relation to Madeline) – a man who'd not only been one of her backing singers but had looked after her during her final months. Not having Elton resurrect in tribute to you a song he'd written years ago in memory of someone else called Marilyn may not be such a bad thing after all, especially if, like Dusty, you get a yellow heart-shaped bouquet from him and partner, David, eloquently proclaiming, 'To The Greatest'. He didn't sing, he didn't come but he did send flowers. Who better than Elton to set the celebrity pecking order?

At the top end of the Britpop Fame Academy – at least the pensionable branch – were the Rolling Stones, Rod Stewart, Tom Jones and Paul McCartney, plus a more provincial variety of English celeb, Cilla Black. Like Elton, they all sent flowers in lieu of themselves. In anticipation perhaps of Dusty's later metamorphosis into a Brighton bus[♮], Sir Paul's card expressed pleasure at having called her a 'classic' a few weeks earlier while Mick, Keith, Charlie and Ronnie wrote cryptically, 'With fond memories'. Another British female singer from a later time, P.J. Harvey, sent a single rose. American pop luminaries like Carole King, Burt Bacharach, Diane Warren, Ellie Greenwich and Dionne Warwick also sent cards or messages to give a dash of international clout to the proceedings, though with flowers from the likes of Gary Glitter and the Alma Cogan Appreciation Society, not to mention Debbie, Andy and the Dogs, to remind us of Dusty's showbiz roots in post-war British variety[♮], such attempts at globalisation made little impact.

But what A-list celebs actually showed up in person? Despite the OBE which she'd recently bestowed on Dusty[♮], the Queen was not thought likely to wish to commemorate a woman who'd insulted her sister Margaret nearly 20 years earlier[♮] by referring in her presence to all the queens in the audience at her concert that night. And anyway, what incentive was there to appear this time round when crowds had singularly failed to clutter up her back yard by demanding she stop sulking and show her face? Nor, as with Pavarotti over eight years later[♮], did either the Prime Minister or the Pope feel moved to put in an appearance – in the latter's case a particular disappointment considering Dusty's natal credentials on the Saints' Roll of Honour as Mary Isobel Catherine Bernadette O'Brien. Did she remain excommunicated after her heretical suggestion of 30 years before that good Catholic preacher men might have sons strewn around? Failing royalty or ecclesiastical bigwigs, Robbie Williams might have been expected as he is rumoured to have Dusty on his Ipod[♮]. But in 1999 Robbie had notched a mere ten million sales worldwide[♮] and was not yet Supermega; even had he attended, his 'listing' would have been a lacklustre 'A minus'.

So, in addition to Lulu, the celebrity clatter came from Elvis Costello and the Pet Shop Boys – Neil Tennant and Chris Lowe – none of them, with their lowish international profiles, exactly 'A' listing but ranking above fellow guests like Kiki Dee, Rosie Casals, Lionel Blair, Nona Hendryx, all of whose stars had shone briefly but dimly in earlier eras and were hardly the stuff of legend. If Greater and Gooder than these were present, they kept quiet about it. The four young women[♮] spotted in dark glasses and headscarves bobbing in the back pew to 'I Only Want To Be With You' certainly resembled the Spice Girls, but were more probably the granddaughters of the Lana Sisters[♮] – the first group Dusty sang with professionally – snuggling together against the draught.

* * *

Dusty Springfield's funeral, then, went off with enough fanfare to make the British national papers and feature on the television news, but fell short of bringing a country or city to a standstill like those of earlier female icons, Marie Lloyd, Edith Piaf[♮] or Princess Diana. Neither did it inspire a spate of suicides and attempted suicides like those in the wake of Valentino's demise[♮] in the Twenties. This was partly because her death from breast cancer was not unexpected, partly because, at nearly 60, she had not died young and in her prime; but much more because the celebrity status which had been almost on a par with the Beatles and the Stones during the Sixties, at least in Britain, had grown blurred and cobwebbed with the years. If she was an icon, she was an obscure one whom a lot of people knew little or nothing about. The 'almost but not quite' pomp and ceremony which the funeral provided fitted the impulses of the woman in the coffin who could never make up her mind whether to revel in her fame and stardom or flee from it; claiming her 'rightful' place centre stage as a diva and an icon jostled with attempts to be as inconspicuous as her brother. In death, as in life, Dusty Springfield was full of contradictions.

She had reportedly said that she wanted to die as anonymous Mary O'Brien[♮], her real name which, as she got older, meant privacy, integrity and reserve – all the things which the Dusty Springfield star persona part of her was not. At the funeral the rector of St Mary's Church referred to her as 'a private person. It was hard for her being in the public gaze.'[♮] If this were so, she could, like film director Stanley Kubrick[♮] whose funeral took place on the same day, have employed staff to keep details of the service secret and security guards to prevent fans from coming anywhere near it. Or, as with John Lennon[♮], she could have dispensed with a funeral ceremony altogether.

Yet there she was, stopping traffic and riding through town in a flower-strewn horse-drawn carriage, her coffin emphatically proclaiming that DUSTY resided within and not the woman birth-named Mary that now, in death, she supposedly wished to reclaim. Raised as a Catholic[♮] and unable, quite, to shake off the influence of that religious denomination, she chose an Anglican church for her funeral ceremony. The Mary part of her had given a hard time to the voice which came out as Dusty; but as we've seen, the funeral was very much a celebration of that voice. Considering how much she'd polluted her body with drink and drugs, and slashed it with scissors and razors[♮], her death from natural causes could be considered rough justice or at least something of a delayed surprise. Equally unexpected was her bravery and stoicism during her last illness. The most moving tribute at the funeral may have come from a neighbour – a retired civil servant named Gibb Hancock who knew little about her pop singing career yet testified to her complete lack of anger or self-pity: 'She never once asked "Why me?" She fought so bravely, she was one of the bravest I have ever known'[♮]. Presumably, the fortitude witnessed by Mr Hancock was Mary O'Brien grit and guts rather than Dusty Springfield drama and ditziness.

Perhaps the most ironic funereal feature of all was its location. Dusty had ended up living in the tiny village of Harpsden Bottom outside Henley-on-Thames and had died there on 2 March. So the medieval church in the centre of Henley was not an unexpected choice for her funeral, especially as she is said to have sought solitude there towards the end of her life[♮]. But what brought her to Henley in the first place? She had often blamed her middle-class upbringing[♮] in nearby High Wycombe for the fears and inhibitions she felt had always dogged her, yet here she now was living near one of the most solidly prosperous middle-class towns in the country. More to the point, Henley-on-Thames has a whiter population[♮] than many towns and cities in England, and Dusty Springfield had often seemed ill-at-ease with her own whiteness[♮]. More than any other female performer of her generation, she had repeatedly championed black American music; had been heard herself as black, or not-quite-white; and at one stage during the Sixties had claimed she felt more comfortable[♮] in the company of black people. Like so much else about Dusty Springfield, the conundrum is not easily resolved[♮].

The doubts and discrepancies continued after the funeral. With some of her ashes interred in the grounds of St Mary's, Henley, and the rest scattered by her brother Tom over the Moher mountains on the west coast of Ireland, the division between public Dusty and private Mary was bequeathed to the hereafter. Both her Henley memorial stone and blue musical heritage plaque in Notting Hill, London are small, simple and easily missed. It's as if her spirit wants you to know that she was once around and made her mark but half hopes you'll walk on by and not notice her. The company she keeps in both spots is worthy. Behind her in St Mary's churchyard is a stone to a certain 'Ann, Wife of S. Mortlock' who was the same age as Dusty when she died in 1866 – 59 – but, as a mere wife with 'attention to the wants of others her daily charge', sits behind Dusty's stone like a reproach from her Catholic conscience. The house she lived in briefly in Notting Hill – 38 Aubrey Walk – stands almost adjacent to Aubrey House where a larger, more conspicuous plaque than Dusty's announces that an 'art lover', two 'philanthropists', a 'Lady Mary Coke, diarist' and 'Edward Lloyd Richard, 1st Earl Grosvenor' were once in residence. In her Henley and London memorialised lives, Dusty has acquired pillars of the community for neighbours; however nomadic and defiant-of-convention she was in life, in death she has settled down with the respectable.

A final irony concerns the original dating on the London plaque. 'Dusty Springfield, OBE, Singer, 1939–1999, Lived here, 1968–1972' the plaque now informs the rare passer-by in Aubrey Walk. When it was first unveiled in April 2001, the wording read '1966–1972'[1] and was subsequently altered. Surely, you exclaim, the Heritage Foundation should have got this right? If a plaque was thought worth putting up in the first place, wasn't it a simple matter to check the dates which would go on it as a historical record? What an insult to Dusty that no-one could be bothered to do this for her!

On reflection, though, the lack of attention to dates seems a fitting memorial to someone as restless and unanchored[1] as Dusty Springfield. You can hardly make out the plaque anyway, especially in springtime when it's likely to be covered by wisteria, so what does a year here or there matter when the woman's residence was probably tentative and sporadic whatever years she 'lived here'? The birth and death dates are correct, however, both here and on the stone in Henley, as is the OBE which Dusty was awarded just before her death and now, in death, on both memorials, seems the most substantial thing about her. Recognition from the monarch sits below her name as if to give her life credibility and authorise her right to have existed. A third memorial to Dusty is in Kew Gardens – a Japanese cherry tree. There is no memorial stone and the tree is part of a group of similar trees. Dusty often said how she liked to be part of the surrounding musical ambience[1], so perhaps being one unmarked tree amongst others is where she rests most comfortably.

***

At her funeral tribute Lulu spoke of how Dusty 'allowed me to get close to her'[♮]. Close to who or what? we may ask. Dusty's personal assistant, Pat Rhodes, who was a steadfast friend for most of her adult life, said elsewhere that however well you thought you knew Dusty Springfield, you didn't and couldn't because she always kept some essential part of herself back from other people[♮]. She believed that no-one knew Dusty Springfield, no-one knew Mary O'Brien. Not Lulu, we might surmise, and not the woman herself.

This book is not concerned with the futile task of tracking down the 'real' Dusty Springfield, or the 'real' Mary O'Brien. Indeed, the human being who went by those names features obliquely rather than centrally, and those who seek biographical information will access it more directly elsewhere[♮]. The book's subject is more the *idea* of Dusty Springfield or Dusty Springfield as cultural icon – partly promoted by the woman who went by that name, partly interpreted down the years by newspapers, magazines, television, books, websites and, of course, myself. The main thrust of the book is descriptive – to track the cultural reception of Dusty Springfield when she was alive and since her death. What has been said and written about her music, appearance and celebrity will be reviewed with the intention of building a picture of one figure's place in Anglo-American culture. Although neither history nor biography in any conventional sense, the work may be viewed as containing historical and biographical features, as it narrates a life-in-text across nearly half a century, occasionally straying further back in time to Dusty Springfield's 'real-life' childhood. With other people's comments integral to the writing, the book contains a number of quotations; the notes on sources are therefore extensive, and include information which sets the text in a larger cultural context.

Central features of the material presented are the boundary-blurring, category-evading aspects of Dusty Springfield's iconography whereby binary positions like male–female, black–white and straight–gay were, and are, undermined, and assumptions about class, celebrity, even identity are questioned. As a cultural reference point, what Dusty Springfield has in common with Princess Diana is the multiple interpretations you can give her and the way she will constantly slip away from any attempts to pin her down. Thus, her idea or sign has a postmodernish, shifting and indeterminate quality as relevant today as when it first surfaced nearly 50 years ago. If the song she chose for her funeral, 'Wind Beneath My Wings'[♮], was the woman's sense of her provisional, contingent place in the scheme of things, the title of her 1965 top-ten hit 'In The Middle Of Nowhere' was where she was, is and probably will remain in British culture. This book is about that paradoxical position.

The material is organised into three main sections. The first deals with the way Dusty Springfield's voice has been constantly referenced in terms of skin colour and why people might have needed to do this. The second is concerned with

Dusty developing a look and persona to negotiate a man's world, and how these have been received and interpreted. The third section concentrates on Dusty's standing as a 'gay icon' and queer cultural figure, and the implications of her outsider sexuality for understanding her performance strategies.

PART ONE

My Colouring Book

For those who fancy colouring books, and lots of people do
Here's a new one for you.
A most unusual colouring book – the kind you never see
Crayons ready, very well – begin to colour me...

'My Colouring Book', song by Ebb and Kander,
recorded by Dusty Springfield in January 1964

It's odd to think that the finest white soul voice of the 20th
century wasn't from Memphis, Chicago or New Orleans, but
West Hampstead.

Phil Jupitus, *Radio Times*, 11–17 November 2006

There's always been this big fascination about a white woman
who can sound like a black woman. What's that all about?

Alison Moyet, *Brit Girls: Cilla*, Channel Four, 11 April 1998

Chapter one

White Negress

 In discussing recordings by Jerry Lee Lewis and Mick Jagger where they present themselves 'slurring' like black men, Simon Frith wrote, 'No listener could have thought either Lewis or Jagger was black; every listener realised that they wanted to be'[ц]. Most white singers who came to prominence in the late Fifties and early Sixties whose vocal styles owed much to black American music – Cliff Richard or Cilla Black for instance – were not described in terms of their black/white vocal textures or aspirations; or if they were, as with Elvis Presley or Tom Jones[ц], the association between white skin and black-sounding voice did not become attached to the singer like an ID card. Elvis may be 'The King' but there's no 'white' affixed to his sovereignty; and Tom Jones as 'White Soul Brother Number 1' has yet to enter common parlance. Generally speaking, whether or not white singers sang as if they wanted to be black as Frith suggests of Jerry Lee and Jagger, they were rarely heard to *be* so – least of all by black American musicians. One such – Charlie Foxx – liked the Rolling Stones but thought they 'still have an English accent… They say "yeah"… and it don't sound like an American Negro group'[ц]. The Stones sounded who they were – British and white, their music obviously not black, and born in the USA only through inspiration.

With Dusty Springfield it was, and remains, different. A considerable number of writer–listeners – black as well as white – have either thought she sounded black and American or made a point of saying she did not[ц]. If they have done neither, they have mentioned her unusual proficiency, as a white woman, with black-associated musical forms. In this regard, she is considered to have stood out by forging her own path through the racial divide in music. Journalist Simon London's view in 1989 that 'she was just another name in a long list of white singers who became the acceptable face of black music'[ц] is shared by virtually no other commentator – and whatever other names were on this 'long list', hers would head it for longevity and frequency of colour inscription. Indeed, the racial references became more regular with the passing of the years so that when she died in 1999, few obituary tributes failed to mention her in terms of black or white[ц], apparently assuming that colour was an integral part of her artistic and personal identity.

With numerous current references to her as a 'white soul singer'[♮] or 'a white woman with a black woman's voice'[♮] and their variants, the association continues to this day[♮]. To such an extent, in fact, that Dusty Springfield is likely to have her skin colour alluded to more than any other British white cultural figure, whatever their gender or profession. In this sense she is a 'marked' woman, since in western Europe where the majority of the population is white, black as the minority colour may be used as a marker of identity but not white, just as white is the 'marked' sign in, say, Nigeria or the West Indies. Even 'odder' than the fact that Dusty and her voice hailed from West Hampstead is that commentators on the subject have broken with convention so regularly across 45 years that calling Dusty Springfield 'white' seems perfectly normal[♮]. Imagine David Beckham famed for being 'the white soccer hero' or Margaret Thatcher repeatedly called 'the white Indira Gandhi', and it is clear that the ongoing attribution of 'white' to Dusty is a reversal of linguistic usage[♮], and one worth discussing. In the normal course of things, 'we don't', as Richard Dyer states, 'mention the whiteness of the people we know'[♮]. What, then, is the history of Dusty Springfield's white marker and what meanings accrue to it?

Surprisingly perhaps, the whole thing seems to have started with Cliff Richard – hardly known for setting trends, especially of the transgressive kind. Although the not-quite-conventional quality of Dusty's voice[♮] was commented on in the music press during 1962 once she had left the Lana Sisters and was featured upfront in the recording mix of the Springfields, it wasn't until April 1963 and an article in *Record Mirror* that Dusty Springfield and colour made their first appearance as a duo. '"THE WHITE NEGRESS – THAT'S WHAT THEY CALL ME"[♮] – DUSTY SPRINGFIELD' screamed the headline. 'They' were Cliff and his then backing group, the Shadows. Since they had performed on the same bill as the Springfields, Cliff and the boys were presumably acquainted with Dusty as performer and person, and the description may have had as much to do with her aspirations as her voice. Whatever the circumstances giving rise to it, the tag quickly gained cultural acceptance largely due to its repetition by journalist Peter Jones[♮] in several editions of that year's *Record Mirror*. Indeed, on the announcement of the Springfields' break-up in September, Jones may well have been the first in print to add 'soul-stirring' to the whiteness[♮].

The word combination 'white... soul-stirring... negress' was thus up and running when Dusty was still a member of a group and predates her career as a solo performer. This is remarkable because unlike, say, Shirley Owens with the Shirelles, Dusty had sung solo on a few bars[♮] of Springfields recordings without ever carrying a whole song, and often adopted an embarrassingly phoney country-and-western accent in keeping with the group's idea of 'down home' folksiness. Any hint of 'black' vocalising would have been confined to a few bars here and there and not easily detected. But, according to Shelby Singleton, who worked with the Springfields on their early 1963 Nashville album, *Folk*

Songs From The Hills, she had already 'become more "black" with her voice'[ ] during the recording. Certainly her brief solo flights on album tracks like 'Settle Down' and 'Midnight Special' and hit singles like 'Island of Dreams' and 'Say I Won't Be There' signalled a disruptive presence at odds with the pseudo folk 'n' country material and straining for musical release. In the autumn of 1963, something urgent this way headed which, bucking the trend, could not be contained within the confines of a group, particularly one with her brother at the helm. Before she had released a record as a solo singer or fully fashioned her glamorous star persona, Dusty was called white by Cliff Richard and the Shadows to suggest that her affinities or aspirations lay in directions other than white. Britain in early 1963 was certainly not Mississippi but the so-called discriminatory colour bar of 'I'm not prejudiced but...' was still socially prevalent, and a term like 'white negress' carried hints of taboo-breaking which Dusty no doubt enjoyed and exploited.

Shelby Singleton heard 'black' in Dusty's voice from the perspective of nearly 30 years later. At the time he would have heard 'coloured', since it wasn't until the late Sixties with James Brown's anthemic 'I'm Black and I'm Proud' that 'black' was used in any but a pejorative sense, at least by whites. Soon after she became a successful solo singer, 'white' was not applied to Dusty as much as 'coloured'. She is thus unusual not only for being a white cultural figure repeatedly described by her skin colour but, even more confusingly, for having a skin colour she did not possess assigned to her to convey the same idea of racial transgression. By early 1964, mere months after her solo debut, comments on the 'coloured' sound of her voice seem to have become commonplace. In a February interview she mentioned that 'people started saying I sounded as if I were coloured'[ ], confirmation of which came three months later when Paul Jones, lead singer of British group, Manfred Mann, named her as a rare British singer 'to capture the real r-and-b sound' of black Americans: 'Dusty gets it. We don't know if she means to but she does get it'[ ].

'Get it' she was certainly heard to do by other singers during her first full year as a solo performer when several British and American artists, black and white, described her voice in terms of colour. John Lennon included her second British single, 'Stay Awhile', amongst a collection of black American records because 'she gets a real coloured sound in her voice'[ ] while both Dionne Warwick[ ] and Mary Wells thought she was one of their own, the latter commenting, 'No white person ever sounded so coloured. It's frightening'[ ]. Martha Reeves took things a step further by suggesting that backstage in the wings at New York's Brooklyn Fox theatre when she, Dusty and the Vandellas were backing Marvin Gaye 'you couldn't tell the difference between her voice and mine'[ ] as the black–white musical seams were so flawless. When virtually all the Britgirl singers of the early-to-mid-Sixties – Cilla Black, Lulu, Marianne Faithfull, Sandie

Shaw, Helen Shapiro, Mille Small – named her[♮] as a favourite singer, she was often the only white performer to feature in a list of black Americans.

Where performers and music critics led, the public followed. At the end of 1964 in the pages of *Melody Maker*, two readers had a disagreement regarding Dusty's by now famous 'coloured' sound. On 12 December a certain Anne Marfurt wrote protesting, 'Why doesn't Dusty Springfield leave the "coloured sound" alone?'[♮] There were 'already excellent coloured singers… without people like Dusty making silly attempts to capture their warmth and sincerity'. Not only, as we shall see, did this reproach prompt Dusty to reply herself but a Barbara A. Reid rushed to her defence two weeks later by asserting, 'Dusty Springfield comes as near as possible to the coloured sound for a white singer'[♮], and, anticipating Phil Jupitus 42 years later, dared someone to 'show me another girl from West Hampstead who can sound like a Negro from New York'. Thus, when Mike Ledgerwood suggested in *Disc* at the end of 1964 that Dusty Springfield's voice was 'closely identified with that of coloured singers in the States'[♮], he was merely stating the obvious. In just under two years the link between singer and skin colour was regularly made in discussing Dusty Springfield. Hardly mentioned were more general issues such as what kinds of connection there were between vocal texture and skin colour, or why, in 1960s pop music, blackness or 'coloured'ness gave a white person like Dusty status[♮] whereas in virtually any other area of life, it would have been a social stigma.

Considering the fact that nine out of the twelve tracks on her first album, *A Girl Called Dusty*, released in April 1964, were covers of songs first recorded by black Americans and that she was regularly including Motown and R 'n' B material in her live performances, Dusty certainly invited, even encouraged, comparisons with the (to her ears superior) original singers. Provided, that is, you had heard them, or even heard *of* them. If either Anne Marfurt or Barbara A. Reid were familiar with the likes of Baby Washington or Charlie and Inez Foxx, they were very much in the minority in Britain at that time. For, as Dusty herself said in the late Seventies, 'At that time in England we did not have the black music[♮] that was here in the fifties and early sixties', and thus when she 'used to steal from everything I could', few would have heard the American versions usually sung by young black performers.

In the post Little Richard and Fats Domino Britain of the early Sixties, black pop voices hardly appeared at all in the best-selling charts; and when they did, they usually featured a diluted strain of black musical passion such as: novelty falsetto hits[♮]; smooth mainstream romantic ballads[♮]; showbiz cabaret-type numbers[♮]; dance tunes in the then-popular Twist idiom[♮]; or revivals of songs from earlier musical eras[♮]. Even black innovators like Ray Charles and Sam Cooke[♮] were mainly known to the British public via songs that had 'countrified' or 'poppified' their jazz, blues and gospel roots – although admittedly the timbres and inflections of those musical styles could be heard in their voices. In those years it was primarily left to young females such as Little Eva with 'The Locomotion' and groups such as the Shirelles, the Chiffons and Phil Spector's Crystals and Ronettes[♮] to present commercialised black pop vocal sounds to British ears – before, in 1964, Dionne Warwick's 'Walk On By', Mary Wells's 'My Guy' and two Supremes hits joined Dusty's records in the charts.

Generally speaking, the music critics' tendency to dismiss Tamla Motown acts[♮] like the Marvelettes, the Miracles and Martha and the Vandellas as not commercial enough to appeal to the British market was reflected in these artists' low sales figures. By making cover versions of songs originally recorded by black singers, Dusty, like the Beatles at the same time[♮], was not 'stealing' their material because few people in the country would get the chance to hear it anyway. Also, unlike in the late Fifties when white Americans like Pat Boone and Georgia Gibbs had big hits covering records by Little Richard and Etta James, she regularly acknowledged and promoted many of the original singers, and only once, in the early-to-mid-Sixties, released a cover version as a single in Britain ('I Just Don't Know What To Do With Myself'). Rather than exploiting black musicians, she can be seen as building bridges and 'weaning' the British public on to certain black American vocal styles they were either unfamiliar with or resistant to[♮].

Elvis may have 'all shook up' the black–white musical boundaries in 1956/7 but it took a good ten years before British ears fully tuned in to the cross-fertilisation process which had been taking place across the Atlantic. 'The sense of isolation in which British culture was immersed in the immediate post-war years is often forgotten'[♮], says Iain Chambers, adding that British rock 'n' rollers like Tommy Steele, Marty Wilde and the young Cliff Richard had no lived experience of the racial tensions behind the 'multiplicity of cross-cultural musical influences' which had created rock 'n' roll in the rural southern states. 'As for the transatlantic harmonies of street corner "doo-wop"'[♮], Chambers continues, 'or the black music of Fats Domino, Little Richard, Bo Diddley and Chuck Berry, it was completely beyond their ken'. In such a context, because of her increasing popularity and recognition as a high-profile black-affirming and sounding white performer with gravitas and credibility, Dusty Springfield had a vital musical–educational role to play.

As if music alone were not sufficient statement of racial intent, however, by the end of 1964 Dusty gave her growing reputation as a breaker of colour codes a pronounced political dimension. With her name in the headlines of most of the nation's newspapers, only hibernating members of the British public, musically informed or otherwise, could have failed to link Dusty Springfield with racial politics. The matter which made it known that she harboured strong views on black–white relationships was South Africa and its policy of apartheid. Served with a deportation order after ignoring two official warnings to stop singing before multi-racial audiences during her December tour, Dusty and her backing band, the Echoes, arrived back in London on the 17th to intense press attention and headlines including: 'POP STAR IN COLOUR BAR ROW', 'DUSTY: NOW FOR A BOYCOTT?' and 'DUSTY ORDERED OUT'. For two or more weeks at the turn of the year, the name Dusty Springfield was in the news on an almost daily basis as a debate ensued regarding the rights and wrongs of her actions.

Her stand against apartheid[a] became something of a cause célèbre, discussed as it was by the actors' union Equity, and British and South African politicians. However much she might protest, 'I know nothing whatsoever about politics. I have no political views'[a], her actions spoke louder than words and associated her with attitudes towards race different from other British entertainers. When South African Jan A. Jordaan praised white performers like Frank Ifield, Russ Conway, Vera Lynn 'and a host of other truly great entertainers and non-"rebels"'[a] for not creating 'trouble when they were over here' and suggested that Dusty would now 'be accepted by coloured American artists like Ray Charles, Belafonte, Miriam Makeba[a], Armstrong, Ellington, Ella Fitzgerald and others', he unwittingly put his finger on something. Dusty Springfield had stepped across an invisible but highly contentious colour line and trod on territory where she did not conventionally 'belong'. But then the woman who earlier that year had been the only white solo performer on a New York R 'n' B show[a] and who, only a month before, had told Ray Coleman in *Melody Maker* that she not only had 'a real bond with coloured artists in the States'[a] but felt 'more at ease with them than I do with many white people' was unlikely to worry much about adhering to socially acceptable behaviour in racial matters. Indeed, her statements and actions suggested that, over and beyond mere lack of prejudice towards non-whites, she actually aligned herself with them, or at least with black Americans. 'I wish I'd been born coloured'[a], she said in interviews on at least two occasions in 1963, and, to Coleman the following year, 'we talk the same language'[a]. Although she was probably referring to musical affinities[a] (plus making unconscious links with others whose lifestyles she perceived as socially marginal), such statements are likely to have encouraged young white readers in the 'colour bar' Britain of the early Sixties to sit up, take notice and ask some pertinent questions about issues broader than the merely musical.

During the mid-Sixties at the height of her fame and success, comments in the press on Dusty Springfield's black–white singing style gained momentum. Her status as a white British singer who could hold her own with black American performers was boosted at the start of 1965 when *Disc*'s Peter Thomson acclaimed her for 'showing the world that Britain can produce a girl singer with enough "soul" to be able to sing with the world's best coloured artists and acquit herself with distinction'♮. Six months later articles in *Record Mirror* and *Disc* stressed the high regard in which she was held by black American female singers like Martha Reeves, Dionne Warwick and Doris Troy; the latter wrote of her 'legendary popularity in America among coloured artists'♮ while *Record Mirror* suggested that 'the Tamla crowd dote on her'♮ to such an extent that, in Dusty's case, 'a contradiction of the usual run of events' had resulted in black musicians extolling the virtues of a white performer. This, the writer Peter Jones added, 'is worth stressing over and over again' as an unusual phenomenon.

In April 1966 Barry Pritchard, of the pop group the Fortunes, expressed annoyance by 'this talk about Tom Jones and Dusty Springfield sounding coloured'♮. This was perhaps due to the regularity with which critics emphasised her 'seemingly authentic gospel approach'♮, her 'real Negroid feel for a song'♮, the 'natural coloured sound of her voice'♮, her 'better [performance] than many coloured American soul singers'♮ and her 'intense gospel and soul inspiration'♮. So closely was Dusty identified with a skin colour she did not possess that, on seeing her in action at the 1964 *Ready Steady Go* New Year's Eve party, a *Melody Maker* writer stated 'she even dances like a coloured girl'♮. Until then, what you heard was at odds with what you saw; but apparently there was a sort of congruity if the girl shook herself about a bit.

No-one voiced their uncertainty over Dusty's musical colourings with more confusion than her brother Tom who, in his 1968 *NME* review of the album *Dusty… Definitely*♮, made explicit the colour divisions he heard operating in his sister's vocal stylings and musical choices but unwittingly also blurred them. Deciding that 'side one is meant to be black and the other side white', regarding her voice as 'a little too forward in places on the coloured side' and calling 'Ain't No Sun Since You've Been Gone' 'a typically Dusty "white-coloured" type song', he declared his preference for the white side, containing, as it did, Johnny Mathis type material: 'and it works'. Presumably, Tom Springfield thought of the black Mathis as a 'white' performer, as he mostly sang smooth romantic ballads: his white sister could record this black man's white-vocal type of material and sound white; and another black man's material – on this album, Jerry Butler's 'Mr Dream Merchant', say – and sound black. So – Tom seemed to be suggesting – it was the song and musical idiom rather than any intrinsic quality in a singer's voice which gave any particular track its colour coding. On this occasion at least, Dusty had pleased her brother more with her 'white' than her 'coloured' inclinations; the 'white' side was 'more melodic and has better songs' and, by implication, was more mature than the 'black' side which 'will appeal more to younger fans'. Tom Springfield may have dug himself into a bit of a hole in this review but at least he inadvertently raised questions about racial shadings in music such as: what is 'black'? what is 'white'? and how can you hear the difference?

What of Dusty's own comments on the black–white aspects of her vocals? As we have seen, she expressed a wish to be coloured, but did this mean she deliberately set out to sound black and pass for something other than white in her recordings and performances? And whatever her motivations, did she hear herself as black or, at least, debatably white? Unsurprisingly, she was inconsistent on these matters, though straightforward enough regarding her early wish to sing in black-associated musical idioms. Seven months before she departed the Springfields, her statement to Mike Hellicar in *NME* that her 'interest in rhythm and blues meant [she] was continually buying and listening to records that were not commercial'[h] took an autobiographical perspective when, as soon as she went solo, she said that she had wanted to be a blues singer since childhood[h]. As an older woman, Dusty repeated this story[h], and on one occasion, in the early Eighties, said her blues ambitions meant 'black': 'I was fascinated with black faces and black voices'[h], thus reinforcing the image of a girl who, in choosing a black-identified music to work in, was willing to juggle with her white identity and disrupt other people's assumptions. Another type of black music – gospel – replaced blues as her aspirational style when she told June Harris in late 1963 that she was 'praying that one day I can make a real gospel type wild rocker that will… burst the roof off the top of the charts'[h]. Whether or not she aspired to sound black, or thought that she did, she certainly identified with the music – was, in Jerry Wexler's word, 'mesmerised'[h] by it – and wished to put her own stamp on some of its forms.

Once established as a singer, she conceded in the mid-Sixties that she had 'started out copying every coloured voice I heard'[h], an admission that she elaborated on during interviews in later life. For instance, she told Sharon Davis that she 'knew exactly how to sound like a Vandella and a Shirelle'[h] and had 'slavishly' copied their vocal styles and inflections. There can be little doubt that the prime inspiration behind her first year or two as a soloist was black, largely female, American pop. She often told stories in later life[h] about being stopped in her tracks by records like the Exciters' 'Tell Him'[h] and Dionne Warwick's 'Don't Make Me Over'; even though turned into convenient moments of musical epiphany, the narratives are no doubt essentially true to the facts. So too are accounts of Dusty's championing of Motown music and artists, plus her adoration of the Shirelles and Phil Spector's black girl group records, as well as such impassioned gospel groups as the Original Five Blind Boys of Mississippi[h]. But her views on whether she believed that she sounded as 'coloured' as she was constantly being informed she did were inclined to vary.

Within a few months in 1964–5, she both shrugged off any suggestion that she sounded coloured – 'No matter what people think, I don't sound coloured'[h] – and expressed the view, unsolicited, that her 'singing, I think, has a "coloured" feel'[h]. Although generally Dusty was at pains to acknowledge the origins of the music she loved and had a self-deprecating approach to her singing whenever comparisons were made with black American performers, the comments she made about her voice's racial textures remained ambivalent. Thus, in one interview, she insisted she sounded more white than black as when she told Peter Jones in 1964 that the 'important word' in Cliff Richard's 'white negress' description was 'WHITE, not Negress'[♮] and that 'the most sensible thing said' on the subject had been when Phil Spector had called her first single, 'a good "WHITE" sound'. Yet only two months later she seemed to be bracketing herself with the likes of Mary Wells and Stevie Wonder as a singer of 'gospel-influenced music with a commercial slant'[♮]. When, in 1985, she contradicted her assertion of 20 years earlier – 'I only sound vaguely coloured to white people'[♮] – by informing Jean Rook of her cross-over credentials: 'I used to be called the singer even blacks thought was black'[♮], she certainly gave no impression of wishing to reaffirm her voice's 'white sound'.

Perhaps the most sensible – and heartfelt – view she ever expressed on the matter was in the letter she wrote to *Melody Maker* after Anne Marfurt criticised her for imitating coloured singers. 'I never claimed to sound coloured'[♮], she wrote. 'I said I was influenced by coloured artists. I try for their sound because I enjoy it. Obviously I can't sound entirely coloured because I'm not… I wasn't claiming to be one of them'. There is, after all, a difference between 'sounding' coloured and having a coloured 'feel', and, in the end, Dusty would probably have reluctantly settled for the 'feel' of coloured simply because there was no way she could *be* it. 'I want to do things the coloured singers do'[♮], she wistfully said in 1965, 'but they have the right sort of voice and range'. And if she felt that 'inside this white body is a black person trying to get out'[♮] as she said on German TV in 1990, the poignancy of the mismatch would have been apparent every time she looked in a mirror.

As both person and musician, Dusty Springfield could have shared Eric Clapton's self-description in 1970: 'I'm split half down the middle. Half of me is black and half is white'[♮]. She seemed to feel neither wholly one nor the other, and kept slipping and sliding between whatever images and associations each colour threw up for her at any given time. Perhaps recognising – or even proclaiming – her ability 'in those days [to] sound fairly daring for a white singer'[♮], she later described her singing voice as 'inherently brown'[♮], thus adding another colour to her collection. Elsewhere, she suggested she had been 'split up all over the place' with all the 'schizophrenic vocal changes'[♮] she had put herself through. 'Part of me wanted to be Peggy Lee, part of me would like to sound like Ella Fitzgerald'[♮], she said in the Nineties. Although she had 'always liked black singers more than white singers'[♮] and had 'soaked… in' black influences, she had, of course, 'never been black'. 'I wanted to be a cross-section of it all and never quite managed it'[♮], she said on another occasion. This sense of fusing both and neither into an idiosyncratic hybrid that was not-this and not-that is perhaps the key characteristic of Dusty Springfield's music.

Chapter two

White Soul Queen

Interestingly, considering her general disdain at the time for white covers of black material, Dionne Warwick seems to have been the first in print to associate Dusty Springfield with the word 'soul' in its musical sense. 'I like singers with soul'[♮], she said in 1964. 'I like Dusty Springfield. She sings with "soul"'.
At the time these words were said, 'soul' was a relatively new term in music[♮], evolving over the previous four or five years to describe the secularised brand of gospel which refocused the good news of divine salvation from sin onto the indulgence of that same sin to its carnal limits. The same black Americans who had sung gospel in the early Fifties – Ray Charles, Sam Cooke, Little Willie John, James Brown, Clyde McPhatter and Jackie Wilson, amongst others – were singing soul a decade later. The music and vocalisations were essentially the same and the passion and anguish undiminished but the love object was human, not divine. 'The story of soul music', says Peter Guralnick, 'can be seen largely as the introduction of the gospel strain into the secular world of rhythm and blues'[♮].

Although from the early days of its usage, the word 'soul' was mainly associated with black musicians, Dusty was not the first white singer to have 'soul' attached to her by a black American performer. In 1960, when the term was still free-floating and incubating, pop star Jimmy Jones thought Doris Day had as much soul as Ray Charles[♮]. And although Little Richard seems to have been the first performer to declare himself a soul singer – 'In America I'm known as the nation's soul singer'[♮], he announced with characteristic modesty in 1962 – a now largely forgotten white Italian–American woman named Timi Yuro was probably the first artist to be promoted by a record label as a 'soul singer'. Indeed, her 1962 album dared to entitle itself simply *Soul*. Although the term had yet to be coined in the early Sixties, on heartfelt singles like 'Hurt' and 'What's-a-Matter, Baby?', Timi Yuro impresses as, perhaps, the first 'white soul' singer.

Unlike Little Richard or Timi Yuro, however, Dusty did not regard herself as a soul singer. She informed journalist Cordell Marks that 'she didn't like the term "soul singer"'[♮] because 'it is a horribly overworked word'; and when David Franklin called her one in 1969, she responded so emphatically that he capitalised the words, 'I AM NOT, AND HAVE NEVER BEEN A SOUL SINGER'[q]. Others thought differently. By the time Penny Valentine used the soul word in 1967 when writing of the driving, up-tempo single 'What's It Gonna Be?' – 'unless you knew better you could be forgiven for thinking you were listening to a top American coloured soul singer'[q] – the connections between 'soul', 'coloured', 'American' and 'Dusty Springfield' were well-enough established for Valentine to have been blasé rather than amazed. But the first three words made an uneasy fit with the fourth, and Valentine continued to express bewilderment by what she heard. At the end of the decade, and despite often interviewing Dusty and praising her work, she sighed almost in exasperation, 'Oh the confusion!' because the song 'Am I The Same Girl?' sounded like 'the very best soul record to come out of America… but it isn't, it's British through and through'[q]. Familiar though she was with Dusty Springfield's work, Valentine occasionally forgot that the performer she was dealing with defied the usual rules of the game and relished incongruity. And by now a new term was being coined for what she heard in Dusty's vocal stylings – to the 'soul' add 'white' and what do you get? 'Soul white' which, for some reason, needed to be reversed before catching on.

Considering how stubbornly it has clung to her down the years, the term 'white soul' seems to have become associated with Dusty in the early Seventies – a few years after its first appearance. Penny Valentine appeared to be searching for such a term in late 1969 when it was just about surfacing to fill a gap. It was a compromise solution to a question regularly – and often heatedly – discussed in late Sixties music papers: could whites have 'soul' or be 'soul singers'? The question, of course, presupposed that 'soul' had been defined; but although even more space had, and has, been devoted to this subject than the question of who possessed it, the answers given in 2007 by Beverley Knight ('Soul is an attitude') and Solomon Burke ('It's coming from the soul… what makes you a soul singer')[q] are no clearer than those of 44 years earlier, when Ray Charles dubbed it 'a feeling you can only acquire from some sort of depression'[q], or Aretha Franklin's late-Sixties 'Soul is a feeling… a lot of depth… it's the emotion and how you sing it'[q]. From the time it first emerged as a musical possibility, soul seemed to float above and around songs, singers and music generally like ectoplasm; it had an absence and elusiveness about it as if it was always on the point of materialising into substance without ever quite doing so. It was hardly surprising, then, if critics preferred to side-step definitions by assuming that soul was singing with a whole lotta feeling, and left it at that. Attention could then be turned to the 'who' rather than the 'what' of it.

As we have seen, discussion about Dusty Springfield in her early-to-mid-Sixties heyday – the years roughly between 1963–7 – centred around her 'white'ness or 'coloured'ness. 'Soul' began to be applied to her in the last two years of this period but only – as in the case of Penny Valentine – with a degree of uncertainty. This is largely because, once the word 'soul' had been through its Doris Day 'teething' period, it was assumed to 'belong' to black people. Perhaps regretting her earlier appropriation of the word for her album, Timi Yuro stated in 1968: 'Negro people use the word, and I think it actually belongs to them, to the Negro race only'[q]. This was a tentatively phrased opinion compared with journalist Val Wilmer's 'right on' declaration of the following year: 'Soul (with a capital S) is, was and ever shall be, the exclusive prerogative of the black American, and if you're going to try claiming the tiniest helping of it for other races, don't try to discuss it with him'[q].

More commonly, though, the general view of both races was that whites were capable of soul as long as they were aware it was not their music, and that their soul performances could only be considered second best on an 'ain't nothin' like the real thing' basis. The redoubtable Nina Simone affirmed 'it was Negro music first': 'although white musicians are trying to get the same feeling', they should know their place in the pecking order, as 'we are the originators and we should be the critics'[q]. Following Nina Simone, the word 'soul' used on its own came to be understood to refer to black American and British singers, and their music. 'Black soul' as a designator had a tautological sense about it[q], the 'black' being redundant in terms of conveying meaning. But since whites were capable of soul too, albeit of an inferior quality, the term 'white soul' had a descriptive role to play. Returning to my earlier point about Dusty as an unconventionally 'marked' white woman, 'soul' was, and is, the 'unmarked' term or standard and is assumed to be a black frame of reference, with 'white soul' the 'marked' or subsidiary 'other'[q].

Although Penny Valentine did not mention the words, the term 'white soul' had been applied to Dusty Springfield by Peter Noon of Herman's Hermits as early as 1967 when he heard her 'doing a bit of white soul'[q] on her single, 'I'll Try Anything'. This seemed to be a 'one-off', though, and he described what he heard her doing rather than what she or the music were. Others were called 'white soul' singers before Dusty. Among the first was American Laura Nyro[q], whose 1968 *Record Mirror* description suggested that something exceptional had arrived on the music scene. As if to prove how needed the term was, the following week in the same paper, the Bee Gees were hailed as 'the first white soul group'[q], and soon afterwards Chris Farlowe was appreciated as 'one of Britain's most admired white soul singers'[q]. And then there was the woman called, after one of her performances, 'a phenomenon. She is white soul'[q]. Not Dusty but Janis Joplin.

Although Joplin had been well known for fewer than two years before she died in 1970 and only once scraped into the British charts (posthumously in 1971), her reputation as a woman who transgressed musical and racial boundaries is such that, even more than Dusty, 'white' accompanies her name in printed reference as a sign of crossover identity. Hers is a fame and standing that have grown over the years. In the late Sixties when she made her first British public appearance at the Royal Albert Hall, only *NME*'s Jan Nesbit and *Melody Maker*'s Tony Wilson took much notice; but by describing her respectively as 'a white woman with a black woman's voice'[q] and the 'phenomenal… white soul' mentioned above, they set the terms of reference for the next 40 years. As with Dusty Springfield, 'white' shadows Janis Joplin, but unlike Dusty, Janis rarely wears a crown as 'queen', nor is 'soul' as familiar a label as 'blues' or 'rock'. Thus, the *Encyclopaedia Britannica*'s current entry – 'the premier white female blues vocalist of the 1960s' – or Stuart Maconie's 2008 *Radio Times* description – 'the greatest white female rock singer of her generation'[q] – are more typical than Barney Hoskyns' 'the ultimate white soul mama'[q] or the *Faber Encyclopaedia*'s 'the finest white blues and soul singer of her generation'[q], where she eclipses virtually all similarly complexioned vocalists of that era, whatever their gender, nationality or black-affiliated musical styles. However, despite sharing the 'white' music marker, Janis Joplin was a very different singer/performer from Dusty Springfield. As a fairly crude and limited screamer, she was not given the time to develop Dusty's versatility, subtlety and sensitivity; and anyway, her vocal timbre was entirely different, as is demonstrated by listening to their respective versions of 'Take Another Little Piece Of My Heart'. But inasmuch as she is a female singer whose white skin colour has been mentioned across decades to signal her accomplishment in black musical forms, she is Dusty's closest cultural associate[q].

Dusty's current reputation is firmly based on her 'white soul' credentials, yet it seems the words were not applied to her as an artist until a year or two after Janis Joplin or Laura Nyro. There is an irony that the album recorded on the famed Atlantic label in Memphis and New York in late 1968, released in the UK in April the following year and regularly described today as 'one of the finest white soul albums of all time'[q] or a 'landmark white soul session'[q] should not have been heard as 'white soul' at the time. This is not to suggest that *Dusty In Memphis* was unappreciated or poorly received. Paul Sexton's contention on Radio 2's 2006 celebration that the album was 'largely overlooked at the time'[q] is correct in terms of sales in the shops but not where the music critics were concerned. Several reviewers not only paid it considerable attention but praised it as 'a stand-out album judged by any standard'[q], 'her best yet. Eleven great tracks… the recording is superb'[q] and 'every single track is a perfect little masterpiece'[q]. The reviewer in *Disc* – Penny Valentine? – even had the prescience to enthuse, 'If ever there was a history-making album in one girl's career – this is it'[q]. However, although the word 'soulful' was used by more than one reviewer, and Allen Evans of the *NME* thought the record of equal stature to Aretha Franklin's *Soul '69* album released the same week[q], there seemed to be no description of the music as 'white soul' or Dusty as a 'white soul singer'.

It was not, then, in contemporary reviews of ...*Memphis* that the label 'white soul' was first attached to Dusty Springfield. Nor is it certain that the co-producer of the record, Jerry Wexler, can take the credit for naming her 'the queen of white soul'[q], as he often claimed in recent years on film and in print. True, it has probably been Wexler's frequent application of the phrase or its variations to Dusty that has made it stick – for instance during his November 2006 tribute at her UK Music Hall of Fame 'induction' – but if he talked about her in these terms in the late Sixties or early Seventies, he seems to have gone unrecorded. Surprisingly, then, the 'white soul queen' tag probably made its printed debut with neither Jerry Wexler nor *Dusty In Memphis* but with RW (presumably Richard Williams) of *Melody Maker* and the lesser-known or discussed 1973 album, *Cameo*. Perhaps in imitation of Aretha Franklin's by-then established epithet, 'Queen of Soul', RW called Dusty 'the queen of white soul singers'[q], thus initiating 35 years of cultural reference with Wexler as advocate-in-chief. At the same time, describing the same album, *NME*'s Charles Shaar Murray thought she had 'a convincing claim to the title of Britain's first good white female soul singer'[q]. Within a week or so in early summer 1973, Dusty's 'white soul' credentials were laid down.

Dusty's low-to-zero professional profile during the mid-Seventies meant that she provided critics with few opportunities to use Williams' or Shaar Murray's words to describe her or her music. The influential 1976 *Encyclopaedia of Rock*'s assessment of her as 'among the most funky and mellow of white soul singers'[q] set the tone for the reception of two attempted 'comeback' albums[q] and their associated publicity during 1978 and 1979. It was in these years when Dusty reappeared in public after a lengthy period of Californian seclusion and was in a position to distance herself, to a certain extent, from her fame and image of ten years earlier, that she began being regularly referenced in the 'white soul' terms used by RW. She continued to have a skin colour other than her own applied to her (though now it was 'black' rather than 'coloured', as in Anny Brackx's 'an effortless "black" voice'[q] or Dennis Hunt's 'the white girl with the black voice'[q]), but on her brief return to public view, it was as a 'white soul' singer that she often appeared in print. Moreover, the territory she ruled over as queen had expanded. 'The best white soul singer in the world'[q], enthused the still awestruck Penny Valentine while for Barbara Jeffrey in the *Sunday People* and Thomson Prentice of the *Daily Mail*, Dusty was respectively 'the best white woman singer in the world'[q] and 'arguably the finest white soul singer in the world'[q].

Variations on the theme occurred in the early Eighties once Dusty had withdrawn again and nothing was heard of her. 'Arguably the greatest white soul singer ever to emerge from the United Kingdom'[q] was how Chris North put it in the part series, *History of Rock*, while Fred Dellar[q] wrote the same sentence as Prentice with 'greatest' instead of 'finest' – and no 'arguably'. In her 1980 book on pop women in American music, Aida Pavletich skipped the soul but called her 'a singer's singer, a superlative'[ ] and could easily have thrown in 'beloved by the critics' for good measure, since whenever she was mentioned – which admittedly was not often – it was with respect amounting to regret at a great performer seemingly lost to music. As with the ...*Memphis* album ten to fifteen years earlier, however, the more the critics raved, the more the general public, who had once bought her records in droves, turned their collective back on Dusty and could not have cared less about her or her music. One of the many ironies concerning Dusty Springfield is this dissonance between mass popularity and critical appreciation. As a Sixties 'white negress' she had been feted and adored as one of the half dozen or so most popular and famous women in Great Britain. She had, of course, also been a favourite of the critics and reviewers from the start but the public didn't need the press to tell them how good she was, they knew. But now that she was dubbed a 'white soul singer' par excellence, the *only* people remotely interested other than her die-hard fans were those who earned their living by writing about pop music. A new generation was buying records who most likely had never heard of her. 'White soul queen' Dusty may have been – but who were her subjects?

For a few years in the late Eighties and early Nineties, courtesy of the Pet Shop Boys, the situation changed, and Dusty (unlike an equally magical and reclusive performer of an earlier era, Greta Garbo) did emerge from seclusion and successfully re-establish herself with new work. She sold records again both with the Pets[ ] or under their sympathetic guidance; a repackaging of her Sixties hits also made the charts. But though her name became familiar once more – and was still frequently accompanied by such remarks as Jeff Tamarkin's 1988 'the finest white female soul voice of all time'[ ], or Tom Hibbert's 1989 'the imperishable white soul voice of Dusty Springfield'[ ] – it was far from a household name. If it was a comeback, it was a muted one – and, with cancer setting in not long afterwards, destined to be short-lived. At least in the flesh. The moment Dusty died, the attention she received in terms of newspaper and television tributes was considerable.

As stated earlier, central to the establishment of Dusty Springfield as a posthumous cultural artefact was the constant referencing of her in a colour or 'soul' context, with scarcely a newspaper or TV homage failing to do so. On the day her death was announced, *BBC1 News* referred to her as being 'dubbed the white queen of soul' while *ITV News* called her 'the white girl with a black girl's voice'. Over the next few weeks, there were as many variants on these phrases[ ] as there were printed or media tributes. In the first decade of the twenty-first century the situation remains unchanged, with the same phrases regularly trotted out, the words changed here and there, when the name Dusty Springfield is mentioned. 'Britain's greatest white soul singer'[ ], 'the greatest white soul voice of all'[ ], 'a great soul singer hidden inside a white British pop queen'[have been a few of the many, so that long before ITV's *South Bank Show* homage[in April 2006, 'the white queen of soul'[/'white lady of soul'[phrases printed in that week's TV magazines had become so clichéd that they were almost written in the same literary breath as the words 'Dusty Springfield' themselves.

As if 'white', 'black', 'brown' and 'coloured' were not enough shadings to have thrown at you, one more colour needs to be added to Dusty's colouring book before it can be closed. The blues may have been what Dusty as a girl had wanted to sing, but it is as a singer of 'blue-eyed soul' that she came to be feted. The term is used more in the US, and means much the same as 'white' soul; so when Los Angeles newspapers called her 'the once reigning queen of blue-eyed soul'[and, again, 'the original blue-eyed soul singer'[, and Lucy O'Brien described her as thinking 'she could break America with her brand of "blue-eyed soul"'[, they had the States as reference points. The 2003 edition of the authoritative US-published *All Music Guide to Soul* includes a section on 'Blue-eyed Soul' as a distinctive category within Soul music. 'Blue-eyed Soul', we are told, 'refers to soul and R&B music performed and sung by white musicians'[, and this is clearly the term chosen in preference to 'white soul', which has no section of its own. In the book, Dusty is called in different places 'the best female blue-eyed soul singer of the sixties'[and 'the finest white soul singer of her era'[. Not only had she shown a clairvoyant streak when she sang 'My Colouring Book' early in her solo career but, in a line in a little-known song from the late Seventies, 'Bits And Pieces', she seems, unsurprisingly, to have a sense of colour overload: 'the colours splash and repaint your sky'. And this is just the sound of her – hair shades have yet to be mentioned.

Perhaps, if her spirit had been eavesdropping on earthly doings in 2005, she would have been relieved to hear her friend Madeline Bell tell Mike Mansfield that she had 'a very, very soulful voice with no colour'[at all, thereby rendering the various attempts to box her into black or white or brown or blue futile and silly. But a colourless voice would be devoid of individuality or interest – not at all what Madeline Bell was implying. A no-colour voice that was colourful? Even when Dusty Springfield is stripped of her colour associations, she seems doomed to get them back again. Small wonder, then, that when she was asked in the Nineties to name her favourite colour, she told Dawn French with mock trepidation: 'Vodka'[.

Chapter three

The Sounds of Colour

 But what does all this mean? How can a person's skin colour be deduced from the sound of their voice?[♮] Or at least from their singing voice? Surely the body's complexion is something you see, not hear? As Chris Farlowe asked in 1966, 'What has race got to do with voices?'[♮]

The occasion for Farlowe's question was Dionne Warwick's assertion the previous week that a song like 'Shout' was 'a ridiculous song for a white person to sing… only a Negro can really feel it'[♮]. The music paper debate of the late Sixties and early Seventies as to whether or not white people could perform soul music had a sense of déjà vu about it. Similar points for and against were made as had previously occurred with jazz, where the question as to what was black jazz and what was white[♮], or even if such a thing as 'white jazz' could be said to exist at all, had raged for much of the century. Jazz, however, was predominantly instrumental, not vocal, music. That a voice too, like an instrumental style or presentation, could sound black or white – or any other colour for that matter – was a relatively new notion. In a tradition going back over a hundred years[♮], whites had blacked-up on stage as negro minstrels – indeed were still doing so throughout the Sixties in the phenomenally successful BBC TV series, *The Black and White Minstrel Show*[♮] – but there was little suggestion that their voices had the textures of the blacks they were imitating and caricaturing. Nor is it probable that such a designation was sought, or would have been welcomed.

As if to confirm the onset of a revolutionary development in popular music during 1963, no less a figure than Little Richard was probably the first black American to recognise, with some considerable astonishment, that British white men could sound like one of their own. Referring to the Beatles, he announced on a visit to the UK, 'If I hadn't seen them with my own eyes, I'd have thought they were a coloured group from back home'[♮]. His disbelief at what he heard was subsequently expressed by others with other singers. With the advent in Britain in the Fifties of weekly record reviews, music journalists were often put into positions where they had to comment on singers without knowing anything about them. Pop celebrities were also invited to give their opinions on the latest releases, without being told who was singing. Frequently, as with Dusty, 'coloured' might be applied to a white singer, though the reverse process hardly occurred at all.

Timi Yuro, Del Shannon and Jimmy Beaumont of the Skyliners were wrongly colour-coded[♮] at the time they were being heard and written about, while several singers, later discovered to be white, were described in retrospect as having sounded 'coloured' or 'negroid' – rarely 'black' – to the listener on first hearing. The list included[♮]: Tom Jones, the Righteous Brothers, Georgie Fame, the Four Seasons, Long John Baldry, Chris Farlowe, Joe Cocker, Stevie Winwood, Cliff Bennett, Janis Joplin, Eric Burdon, The Rascals, Delaney and Bonnie and (to the ears of Cilla Black and *1-2-3* hitmaker Len Barry respectively) Neil Sedaka and Sandie Shaw. Indeed, Sandie was heard by Len Barry as sounding more coloured than Dusty Springfield and by Georgie Fame as 'coloured trying to sound white or white trying to sound coloured'. Elsewhere, John Fogerty and Creedence Clearwater Revival were heard as black by Paul McCartney: 'When I found out they were white chappies, I was most amazed'[♮]. Black performers like Nat 'King' Cole, Lena Horne, Sammy Davis Junior and the earlier-mentioned Johnny Mathis[♮] were often regarded as singing in white mainstream idioms but were not generally commented on as sounding white. Nor – in a reversal of the prevailing racial hierarchy in Anglo-American culture – would a remark to the effect that Cole or Mathis sounded white have done much for their musical credibility with the Sixties generation.

Perhaps what most of the white-heard-as-black voices had in common was a fervour or passion often lacking in white popular singers. Was the coloured quality detected in their vocalisations due to their sounding as if their very lives depended on the release[♮] of whatever feeling they were experiencing at that moment? Certainly, as we have seen, soul, if it meant anything, was about feeling and its expression. But the coloured-referenced Georgie Fame was laid-back cool, not a cat on heat; whereas the emotive no-holds-barred likes of Judy Garland and Ethel Merman were not thought to sound black[♮]; and a similar female belter, the mixed-race Shirley Bassey, was initially assumed to be white[♮] by her Las Vegas audience. An outpouring of emotion did not, it seemed, necessarily signal 'black' to musical ears. Despite working with the 'white soul'-designated Bee Gees, the powerful-voiced Barbra Streisand is not thought of as a black-sounding singer. Much, of course, had to do with the material[♮] as intimated by Tom Springfield about *Dusty... Definitely*. Both Garland and Merman sang the Great American Song Book, and represented in mid-century what Bassey came to stand for later – schmaltzy showbiz survival – which seemed (and seems?) incompatible with 'soul'.

Aspects of this trooper–survivor melodramatic tradition also came to be associated with Dusty. Yet unlike either these theatrical showbiz ladies, or the contemporaries whose vocals were once thought to cross racial lines, and regardless of the musical field in popular music she strayed into, Dusty Springfield has been heard for almost half a century as having a singing voice that belied her ethnicity; as much now as when it was first heard, her voice is referenced in terms of colour. What, then, is it about that voice which can be heard as racially deviant? Writing about Johnny Cash, Ian Sansom said that the single most important thing about him – the voice – 'is of course the most difficult thing to write about and try to describe'[1]. He also said something as relevant to Dusty as Johnny: 'What actually made him great was the simple quality of his voice, without which none of the rest of it would have mattered'[1]. Not the beehives or the panda eyes or the gowns or the woman-in-charge-of-her-music or the iconicity, gay or otherwise, or the 19 nervous breakdowns or wayward celebrity. None of it. I shall attempt to isolate some of the qualities in Dusty Springfield's voice people might have heard – and may still be hearing – as 'coloured' or 'black or 'white soulful'. 'Blue-eyed' as a voice descriptor might prove too anatomically confusing.

Of the 25 tracks on her first two albums, *A Girl Called Dusty*, released in April 1964, and *Everything's Coming Up Dusty*, October 1965, 18 had originally been recorded by black American performers[1] – firm evidence of Dusty's identification with a culture and country other than her own. Her second single too – 'I Just Don't Know What To Do With Myself' – was a cover of a black original. Many of the songs had been written by white composers such as Bacharach & David and Carole King & Gerry Goffin, and had involved white musicians and producers; but what matters here is that the vocalisations were black. With Dusty Springfield being heard as 'coloured' so early in her career, a notion of what 'coloured' sounded like must have been around in the British public even if many of these particular tracks had not themselves been much heard in the country at the time. It may be helpful to try to outline some of the voice qualities and stylistic approaches to be heard on the original records and compare these with Dusty's cover versions. It is on these tracks, after all, that The *Mojo Collection* suggests 'Dusty's reputation as Britain's great soul voice was born'[1]. Leaving aside for the moment the central, all-important matter of voice timbre, what did 'coloured' sound like in pop music when it was sung by coloured people themselves? and how closely did Dusty resemble it?

Unsurprisingly, the original black vocal approaches vary. Those of, say, Dionne Warwick ('Wishin' And Hopin'') or Maxine Brown ('Oh No, Not My Baby') are detached and demure with a touch of sweetness about them and a sense of not wanting to draw attention to themselves. They are pleasant, even graceful, voices but without much strength-of-feeling in them. Baby Washington's rich, warm, deep-toned voice on 'Doodlin'' and 'That's How Heartaches Are Made' is similarly restrained and devoid of vocal flourishes, but here the honey-toned, deep resonance of her voice creates an impression of warmth: you feel she could be a 'soul mama'[q] if she let herself go a bit, but there's still some way to go. Mitty Collier, however, whose vocal texture is similar to Washington's – rich and mellow – has the assurance and authority to turn 'I Had A Talk With My Man' into a declamatory outpouring of fidelity. Her voice is more fluid and inventive than the other women's, and sweeps and sours around the melody to bring out its intrinsic dignity and poise. She uses a vocal device called melisma, associated with gospel singing, whereby a single note or syllable is turned into two, three or more – 'my blu-u-u-u-ues got bri-i-ight' and 'star of the sho-o-o-o-o-ow'. (There may be more syllables: they are run into each other at such a rapid pace that they are hard to count.) Some notes are extended beyond their normal length as in 'l-o-h-n-e-ly would I be' and 'n-e-e-d nobody else' while other phrases are run together and given equal stress – 'hetookmeinhisarms' – and yet others are repeated 'oh yes he did, yes he did, yes he did'. Whereas the singers in the other songs sound mildly affected by the situations they are narrating, Collier's use of melisma, extension, run-on lines, repetition, and the swirls and swoops of her delivery creates the impression of emotion in excess of what she can convey.

And Dusty in comparison? The general impression of listening to her after Maxine, Dionne and Baby Washington is that in all three cases she emphasises the melodic line, heightens the drama and, from the very first note, gives the song a clarity and purpose it lacks in the others' versions. 'Oh No, Not My Baby', in particular, replaces the unassuming, even polite, tones of Maxine Brown with an altogether more assertive and forceful approach. She gives melismatic touches to words like 'toys', 'hearts' and 'fling' which are more noticeable than with Brown, and, unlike her, repeatedly says the southern 'mah' rather than 'my' on repeating the title line and 'ah didn't listen', 'ah kept raht on sayin''. This is diction that should sound as phoney as on many of the Springfields' outings, but it now goes almost unnoticed because so integrated with the rest of her sound. And when Dusty is up against as accomplished and gospel-inflected a singer as Mitty Collier, it's as if she rises to the challenge and comes into her own. All of Collier's vocal techniques are employed and, apart from omitting the third verse, she follows the original singer's inflexions and phrasings to the smallest detail as if she knows they can't be improved on. Yet astonishingly, far from sounding imitative, Dusty's version is every bit as effective and powerful as Collier's, with additional undercurrents of desire captured in the rise and fall of her voice which the black woman seems not to know about. As Robert Gallagher says, 'she surpasses Mitty Collier's sultry original with fluid phrasing and exquisite breath control'[q]. Technically, the versions are equal; emotionally Dusty's has the edge.

The way in which Dusty heightens the drama implicit in the black original is best illustrated perhaps in comparing her versions of three ballads first sung by male singers. She follows the vocal approaches of Jimmy Radcliffe on 'Long After Tonight Is All Over' much as she does with Mitty Collier but, because he is a less impressive singer, she improves on his phrasings and turns his gruff shouts into clarion calls of desperation. For instance, Radcliffe's melismatic volume rise on 'I'm yours' towards the end is intensified to such an extent that by fade-out time, Dusty draws on all the force and power she is capable of, repeating, in a gospel style which Radcliffe strains to achieve but doesn't manage, 'Long after... after it's over and done, yeah yeah yeah'. Interestingly, none of the songs by black singers covered by Dusty has the sort of call-and-response, hand-clapping fade-out which pop borrowed from gospel in tracks like the Crystals' 'He's A Rebel'[or 'Quicksand' by Martha and the Vandellas; but whenever it suited her to use or adapt them, Dusty did – usually, as here and on Tommy Hunt's 'I Just Don't Know What To Do With Myself', to exciting effect. Whereas little of Bacharach's beautiful melody[or Hal David's sensitive lyrics are to be heard in Hunt's plodding, pedestrian singing, Dusty shakes the entire edifice of the song to its foundations and turns it into an existential psychodrama. The song begins as quietly as Hunt's version but becomes, by the bridge, a roller coaster of rising, soaring emotion which is maintained for the rest of the record. Demonstrating that she loved gospel-styled repetition of words and phrases, Dusty turns Hunt's polite 'proper' ending into a rousing fade-out, 'No no no no, I don't know what else to do, no no no'.

A much more accomplished singer than Hunt or Radcliffe, Garnet Mimms, sounds uncharacteristically subdued on 'It Was Easier To Hurt Her' and takes the ballad at a jaunty, almost jerky rhythm in the chorus. Dusty approaches it with a slower and heavier vocal and, as with 'Long After Tonight Is All Over' and '...Do With Myself', builds up the volume gradually so that, whereas Mimms merely raises his voice on these lines, by the end she is hurling 'what could I do?' and 'I should have known better' at and above a more 'churchy-sounding' backing chorus[than supports Mimms. On all three cover versions, Dusty Springfield sings with a power, drive and energy greater than anything displayed by any of the men, and either adds to or enhances elements in their vocal styles which stress the intrinsic emotional qualities of the music.

Another male whom Dusty covered was Charlie Foxx, whose duet with his sister Inez, 'Mockingbird', was a US Top Ten hit early in 1963. Adapting the call-and-response chanting of the gospel church, the record features Inez hollering the nursery rhyme lyrics above her brother's low echoing repetition of certain 'key' phrases such as: 'If that mocking bird don't sing, he's gonna buy me a diamond ring'. As if to demonstrate that Dusty can not only do without her brother[but actually *be* him, she sings both parts, high and low, and in the process enacts a multi-textured mockingbird parody of black 'n' white song styles. Inez sings with the sort of vocal techniques mentioned already – melisma, lengthening and shortening of syllables – but sounds like a peeved teenager imitating a mature, wordly wise soul mama, and, by fade-out time, she's beginning to tire with the effort. Dusty sings with similar phrasing to Inez for much of the track but with far greater attack, intensity and dynamic shading so that the sulky girl is now a wild wailing woman who seems to think buying a mockingbird is a matter of life and death. In an ironic reversal, it is Inez Foxx rather than herself who comes across as an imitation of 'the real thing'[♮]. Likewise, Charlie's casual and rather off-key mumbling becomes, in Dusty's pseudo-baritone, a cool but determined counterpoint to the strident main-voice melody line – containing it, grounding it, undercutting it – in the way that many white listeners sought to do with what they heard as black vocal excess. However, the effort is doomed to failure for, in this fade-out, the upper register departs with as little decorum or reserve as she entered. No matter how insistently the lower part intones and repeats, this mocking-shrew will not be tamed.

Dusty could not be mistaken for any of the singers mentioned so far; there is no similarity between her voice's texture and theirs. However, with Shirley Owens, the lead singer of the Shirelles, the situation is different. On both versions of 'Will You Love Me Tomorrow?' and 'Mama Said', the vocals sound nasal, with a boyish sweet-and-sour sound and minimal differences in timbre or voice quality. Although Dusty did not, as she suggested, 'slavishly' copy Shirley Owens's delivery – she takes 'Mama Said' at a slightly slower pace, altering the rhythm in the last verse; and '…Tomorrow?' is full of added 'oh's and 'no's – she came as close to demonstrating her skills of mimicry as she ever did. Maybe because she realised their voices could be made to sound alike, she put more of an effort into integrating a black vocal into her own[♮] and thus failed to pay her customary attention to production values, backing group and, what makes most of her versions superior to the originals, the melodic and dramatic possibilities of the song. At any rate, these two Shirelles covers lack the magic of the original records.

The other singer whose voice textures the young Dusty had most in common with was not covered by her on the first two albums. In fact, she released only one track previously recorded by Martha Reeves – 'A Love Like Yours' – but not until the late Seventies. However, although she did not record any Martha and the Vandellas songs in the Sixties, she sang 'Heatwave', 'Dancing In The Streets' and 'Nowhere To Run' live on various occasions, and, on the 1965 *Sounds of Motown* TV Special, duetted with Martha[♮] on 'Wishin' And Hopin''. Not only, as Martha indicated, do their voices blend perfectly, but the televised Springfield versions of the Martha and the Vandellas hits have a similar dynamic resonance and overall sound to the originals, and are equally compelling. Although the voices of Shirley Owens and Martha Reeves do not particularly resemble one another, the youthful Dusty Springfield could, when she wished, capture essential aspects of each woman's vocal quality and stylistic approach, then use these basics as starting points to explore the potentialities of her own very different and more flexible voice. Whatever Paul Sexton had been listening to when he suggested Dusty's early Motown covers were 'a bit too polite – dare I say a bit too "white"?'[4] could it conceivably have been her televised performances of 'Heatwave' and 'Nowhere To Run'? If so, he'd be advised to take a hearing test.

A final track for discussion from the second album – 'I Can't Hear You' – was also one of the three songs Dusty sang on *The Sounds of Motown* TV show in 1965. Without her enthusiasm or agreement[5] to introduce the show, the programme might not have been made, for at the time the Supremes were the only one of the five acts featured who were known to the British public by way of chart hits. In a by-now-familiar environment where she was the one white performer present, Dusty stood out not because her singing style was notably different from the others but because it enhanced or exaggerated elements in the vocal approaches around her. This was most striking on 'I Can't Hear You', which had originally been recorded by sweet-voiced Betty Everett in 1964 and sung by Dusty herself on live BBC radio sessions before being included on *Everything's Coming Up Dusty*. Her treatment of a song which she clearly thought ideally suited to her voice and style was similar each time she sang it – raw, full-throated, raucous, frenetic. Whereas Betty Everett was mildly displeased with her cheating lover, Dusty left him in no doubt that her pot was boiling over and he'd better get away from the heat. On the programme, her arrival to send him packing comes halfway through – and nothing that has preceded it, even her irreverent and ground-breaking duet with Martha and the Vandellas on 'Wishin' And Hopin'' (had a white woman ever shared a song on British TV with three black women before?) prepares you for the onslaught. The famed gospel influence behind Motown music is here heightened and taken to extremes barely hinted at earlier in the programme and in evidence again only at the end with Smokey Robinson's rousing, call-and-response 'Mickey's Monkey'.

Two years before Aretha Franklin broke through into public awareness with the first of her stunning soul mantras, Dusty Springfield, a British white woman let loose amid a rostrum of pop-gospel's black American elite, can be seen on film getting on down with the best of 'em. Employing the vocal techniques she has by now assimilated from gospel and rhythm 'n' blues via the singers she has covered on record, stage or screen, and clearly revelling in the performative opportunities afforded her by the all-black Earl Van Dyke Motown house band, she rides on and over the driving rhythm to whip up the sort of musical excitement few women of *any* colour or nationality outside a bout of religious ecstasy would have been capable of imagining, let alone creating. In this young black American pop-gospel environment, Dusty Springfield is simultaneously at home and abroad. At home because she is surrounded by the musicians and singers she idolises, and sings with textures and inflections congruous with the occasion; abroad not just because of the glaring whiteness of her skin colour, hair and clothing, but because she amplifies and enriches the song styles of her fellow performers and thereby empowers them to be more than they originally were. In Martha Reeves's words, she 'glorified' the music[b] by taking it to new and unexplored heights. She is a part of the same musical inspiration and ambiance but also apart from it – in a perverse way, more black-sounding than the others, as even some of the Motown artists recognised[b], in the sense that she can push her *idea* of vocal blackness to its limits and thus, paradoxically, sound like an alternative or extreme version of 'the real thing'. Or at least the 'real' Motown thing.

And what of Tom Springfield's implication that Dusty singing a showbiz standard sounded more white than black? Listening to her 1968 version of 'Second Time Around', what she calls 'typical of Hollywood-type ballads' on the sleevenotes to *Dusty… Definitely*, one is struck by the extent to which her vocal performance draws on the sort of gospel music phrasing noted earlier. The track starts traditionally enough with strings but as soon as Dusty intones the words 'Love is lovelier', caressing each of the five syllables as if not wanting to let them go, you prepare yourself for a not-quite-straight handling of the song. Soon afterwards, the first two words in 'just as wonderful' are given equal stress, 'time' is pronounced 'tahm' and the six-syllabled 'you hear your love song sung' becomes nine syllables with 'you', 'song' and 'sung' each given a touch of melisma. Without subjecting Dusty's reading to a detailed note-by-note analysis, suffice it to say that as she proceeds, more of the 'straight' melodic line is 'bent'; and to the rousing finale she adds reproachfully 'I wanna ask you' as if momentarily forgetting the showbiz idiom she and the song are supposed to be in. Although Lucy O'Brien hears the track as 'threatening to lapse into gooey hotel foyer musak'[b], the fact that it only threatens this demonstrates how musical aspects of the gospel tradition she had begun by admiring and adopting had, by the late Sixties, been so successfully incorporated into her singing style that she flavoured even a cheesy ballad previously sung by Bing Crosby and Frank Sinatra with black music ingredients. These melismatic, emphatic touches and general reshaping of the song through additional phrases and alterations to the basic melody are presumably what listeners heard as 'soulful'. When Paul Howes, for example, suggests that Dusty 'even manages to "soulify"' the song'[b], 'My Colouring Book', the near-standard ballad on her first album, he is presumably referring to the way she introduces these flourishes from the gospel church into material originally conceived as supper-club fare for white audiences.

How 'white' or 'black' a voice is received as being depends, of course, on the context it is heard in, and this includes what the voice is being measured against and who is doing the listening. If the urgent and volatile powerhouse singing of

Atlantic-period Aretha Franklin had made its mark earlier in the Sixties, perhaps Dusty would less readily have been dubbed 'coloured'. It surely was not a coincidence that the only Aretha track Dusty recorded was the fairly light and rhythmic 'Don't Let Me Lose This Dream' – darker, heavier material might have invited unfavourable comparisons. Certainly, set alongside what Ian Hoare called the 'spine-chilling… histrionic desolation'[5] of Linda Jones's 1971/2 version of Goffin and King's 'I Can't Make It Alone', Dusty's wounded pride on the earlier …*Memphis* recording of the song sounds sober and subdued – vulnerable certainly but, in the context of this torrid 'one woman vocal hurricane'[6], more 'white' and 'polite' than on the Motown covers Paul Sexton referred to. This degree of gospel-drenched ecstatic beseeching seems to lie outside white experience or potential, Dusty included. The knowledge that when Linda Jones sang the lines, 'won't you reach out for a dying girl and let her live again?', she meant them literally, and was soon dead, aged 28, from an extreme form of diabetes, adds an existential dimension to the desperation of her singing. You can hear the death rattle in her voice, and it makes for uncomfortable listening. Whatever colour shading you give Dusty's subtle interpretation of 'I Can't Make It Alone', it lacks the black textures of Linda Jones's reading; her stripped-down poise bears little resemblance to the heart-screaming fervour of the Jones recording. But next to the massive attack of Linda Jones, even Aretha can sound bland, while Diana Ross has the aural presence of melting vanilla.

Ultimately, what a singer does or does not do with their voice provides less information about their distinctive vocal identity than that voice's texture or what Roland Barthes called the 'grain' of the voice[7]. Even when Dusty Springfield sang a song straight, the quality of her voice transformed the base material of schmaltzy showbiz sentiment into the gold of a personal emotional statement; artifice would pass for authenticity for as long as it took her to sing the song. Thus, 'light entertainment' cabaret-type ballads like 'To Love And Be Loved' and 'I'll Never Stop Loving You', which she performed on her Sixties BBC TV shows, sound as sensual and impassioned as any of her more famous arias. Because of the voice quality, something alternative seeps through which doesn't quite fit the type of nightclub venue these songs were usually sung in. It was this indefinable hint of 'elsewhere' about Dusty's voice, and neither what she sang nor how she sang it, that incited comment in terms of colour. Many other singers – George Michael, Petula Clark and Robbie Williams, to name but three – have used black textures and intonations in their singing styles without being heard as black or, at least, regularly referenced in colour terms. Although Dusty Springfield certainly wove into her vocal tapestries the phrasings and stylings from the black American gospel music she loved, it was essentially the timbre of her voice, its 'grain', which marked her out as sounding black or coloured. And as stated earlier, 'grain' or timbre is heard and felt at non-verbal levels[8], and eludes written description.

Even from a technical perspective, Dusty's voice is hard to define. In terms of pitch, she is an alto or contralto yet her dense and steely intensity lacks the creamy bloom which characterises operatic altos like Kathleen Ferrier or Janet Baker. On the male range her voice is neither tenor nor baritone, and though counter-tenor gets nearer, it isn't that either. Does Camille Paglia come closer when she describes the voice as 'a castrato'[4]? – a vocal texture which falls within the female frequency range but has male precision and power. The answer is impossible to give because we don't know how the great eighteenth century castrati sounded[5]. But the fact that the question can be asked about a woman at all without it sounding ridiculous attests to the fact that Dusty Springfield did indeed, as Paglia adds in unconscious agreement with the singer's self-assessment, have 'a very strange voice'[4]. Although, as we have seen, it could assume 'mockingbird' qualities and convincingly mimic other people's vocal characteristics, it was and remains an instrument like no-one else's – as unique, inimitable, 'one off' and, what matters most, aesthetically pleasing – as another twentieth century woman's voice which has no antecedents or descendants, Billie Holiday's. And could it be that at a time when black voices in modern pop music were little heard and often considered disconcerting or alien, words like 'white negress' and 'coloured' were used as exotic synonyms for 'odd' or 'not quite of the fold' to convey the quality of 'otherness' people detected in Dusty Springfield's voice? Even, let us not forget, when she was still part of a trio of voices, hers was the one which was heard and commented on – the one which, despite brief and infrequent solo flights, commanded attention.

The regularity with which she is called a 'soul' singer or not a 'soul' singer[4], and heard as singing in a black American framework, fails to prevent Dusty from posing a challenge to those trying to fit her into a particular musical style or cultural perspective. Her voice and approach ultimately resist categorisation. This was made evident in a 2007 BBC 4 documentary, *Soul Britannia*[5], where an argument is made for the roots of white British soul as essentially male and working class, and grounded in social deprivation like Afro-American rhythm-and-blues itself. Then suddenly up she pops, towards the end of the programme, disrupting the line of thought as none of these things. 'A black voice in a white body', Vicki Wickham calls her at this point; but if so, where has she sprung from, where does she belong and how come she had to turn up – apparently out of nowhere – to demolish the carefully reasoned argument which fits Van Morrison, Tom Jones, Eric Burdon and Georgie Fame who are discussed before her? A programme on British soul had to include her[4], but can neither account for her nor contain her within its reference points; and when it moves on, she is left dangling in mid-air – as anomalous and out-of-place in this cultural context as any other.

'What's all that about?' asked Alison Moyet about people's fascination with white women who sound black. In Dusty Springfield's case, perhaps no more than an ongoing recognition of their inability to make sense of her voice and the unusual effect it has on them. 'White', 'coloured', 'blue-eyed soul' – a vocal miscegenation that seems to draw attention to its colour shadings but is only uneasily coded in terms of any of them. 'A black drag queen with the heart of Marilyn Monroe'[5] is what Stacey D'Erasmo called 'the core of this radical mix' of 'what her unique sound imagines'. If rephrased into 'a white drag queen with the heart of Carmen Jones', would it make a difference?

PART TWO

Girls, It Ain't Easy

A woman's work is never done, it never stops – it goes on and on
It ain't easy, girls it ain't easy...

'Girls It Ain't Easy', song by Dunbar and Wayne,
recorded by Dusty Springfield in June 1970

Female roles and stereotypes are far more restrictive, the
standards of perfection so much higher, and the pressures on
women to conform with their bodies, their faces and their
clothes, much greater...

Sue Steward and Sheryl Garratt (1984) *Signed, Sealed and Delivered:
True Life Stories of Women in Pop*, Pluto Press Ltd, p.17

The only person who knows what to do with me is me...

Dusty Springfield to Ben Fong Torres, *Rolling Stone*, May, 1973

Chapter four

Beehive Maintenance and Serial Mascara Excess

A question for possible inclusion on *University Challenge* or Radio 4's *Round Britain Quiz* reads as follows: 'Who links an ex British prime minister; a friend of "Ugly Betty"; a rock navigator with a hang-up about his sex appeal; the wife of a former East European president; a well-known writer and broadcaster; and a toy poodle owned by a 21-year-old pop singer from Devon?' The answer, of course – you've guessed it – is 'Dusty Springfield'. Or at least her hair. Or if not her hair exactly, her wig. Or wigs. Well, one of them anyway. Perhaps the one she called Cilla or the other bit of fluff named Sandie[♮]? At any rate, whether real or fake, Dusty hair styles have been spotted in recent years on the heads of Margaret Thatcher[♮], Ashley Jensen[♮], Rod Stewart[♮], Mira Milošević[♮], Melvyn Bragg[♮] and Joss Stone's dog[♮]. Indeed, in the case of Mrs T, her description as 'the Tories' carefully coiffed answer to Dusty Springfield'[♮] suggests that her current standing as a camp style icon[♮] has a touch of the 'I only wannabe yous' about it. Could the Iron Lady have been a Lady Beehive imitation fashioned by the party faithful to endow her with a user-friendly proxy look of love?

A more improbable political lookalike – Josef Stalin – joins the Springfield hair brigade when a woman called Gina Davidson recalls being intimidated by 'usherettes [who] were Stalins with dyed-blonde Dusty Springfield hairdos'[♮]. So all-pervasive are Dusty's bouffant braids and top-heavy tresses in the public imagination that when a *Time Out* journalist said 'Never has a woman been defined by her hairdo as much as Dusty Springfield'[♮] and Hunter Davies suggested a library could be constructed on the subject of her hair[♮], neither writer could be accused of exaggeration. Dusty, in fact, resides in the collective memory as much for a hairstyle she once adopted as for anything she ever sang. 'I remembered only the beehive hairdo', wrote Max Davidson in 1994, 'not the mighty talent buzzing around inside it'[♮]. Would the memory of her have been

Never has a woman been defined by her hair

late 50s

Courtesy Rex Features

1962

Dusty Springfield: Full Circle, Vision Video Ltd. VHS, 2000 (produced by Initial Film and Television Publication, 1994, originally broadcast 1962)

1962/3

Courtesy Redferns

1962/3

Just For Fun, Columbia Pictures (1962/63)

1963

My Very Best – Love Dusty, Quantum Leap DVD, 2003 (c.1963)

c.1965

Courtesy Redferns

as much as Dusty Springfield

Courtesy Redferns

Dusty Springfield Live at the BBC, BBC DVD, 2007
(from *Dusty*, originally broadcast 15 August 1967)

Courtesy Getty Images

My Very Best – Love Dusty, Quantum Leap DVD,
2003 (c.1968)

Dusty Springfield Live at the BBC, BBC DVD, 2007
(from *Tom Jones Show*, 1973)

Sunday Sunday, LWT (25 November 1990)

as lasting even if she had never opened her mouth? If she had sung not a single note, would the coiffured confections dreamed up by latter-day celebs still be seen as half-baked concoctions falling short of hers♮ in height and aspiration?

But at least Rod, Maggie and the rest have only had their hairdos under scrutiny, and so have not suffered the plight of singer Amy Winehouse. On her rise to fame in 2006–7, in addition to her beehive, Winehouse had such dollops of eye make-up to weigh her down that her cause was taken up by Neil Sowerby when he compared her to Dusty, a 'fellow victim, too, of serial mascara excess'♮. Recommending 'the Practical Manual of Beehive Maintenance, foreword by Dusty Springfield' for Amy's Christmas present but unable, alas, to offer cosmetic consolation, Sowerby was aware that the pressure of ornamental overload could be as cumbersome a burden for the Troubled Britdiva of the Noughties as for her deceased predecessor. Like her heightened hair, Dusty's black-mascaraed eyelids and lashes form such an integral part of her enduring cultural legacy that when BBC TV put together an *A–Z of Light Entertainment* in the early Nineties, 'E for Eyelash' was 'who else but Dusty Springfield?' Her charcoal-eyed look represents the dark end of the spectrum for facial adornment. Thus when Simon Bates on Classic FM wanted to stress the jet-black extremities of Elizabeth Taylor's 1963 Cleopatra war paint, he described it as having 'eye-liner make-up that would have had the late Dusty Springfield green with envy'♮. In posthumous teledocs♮, long and lingering close-ups of the blackened eyes likened by entertainer Beryl Reid to 'twin craters, both extinct'♮ have been short cuts to owner identification; a *Times* headline to a review of one of these tributes, 'Legend in her own Mascara'♮, could mean only one thing. Her eyes, like her hair, have become metonymous for the woman whose body they adorned. With 'Dusty's Hair' already the title of an academic paper presented at an American university♮, the rerecording of the 1981 hit, 'Bette Davis Eyes'♮, with another woman's name in the title, awaits its entrepreneurial moment.

Dusty Springfield is as famous, then, for the look she created as anything she sang, with the words 'beehive' and 'panda eyes' virtually defining her in popular culture. Announcing her death in 1999, television news channels emphasised her appearance. The BBC's 'her defining look of platinum beehive and black eye make-up'♮ became, in Cliff Richard's words on ITV, 'that fantastic image… the great big beehive hair cut, the black-rimmed eyes'♮. Hardly a printed obituary failed to reference her in terms of how she looked from the neck upwards: 'Dusty, with her blonde beehive hair-dos and heavy "Panda" eye make-up was an instantly recognisable celebrity'♮; 'her extraordinary appearance – huge, panda-black mascaraed eyes and excessive gold bouffant hairstyle'♮ were but two of the many. Nearly ten years on nothing changes. Indeed, if anything, the hair and make-up are even more lacquered and caked onto Dusty Springfield in death than in life. It is ironic that someone whose professional raison d'être was the production of sound is equally remembered for her visual image. Indeed amongst those too young to remember her at all, the one thing they may know about Dusty Springfield is the way she looked rather than how she sang or sounded. '[H]er image', as Barney Hoskyns has recently suggested, 'has almost eclipsed the music'[q]. Regularly, the Internet and newspapers mention her when discussing someone else's appearance; her name is prone to turn up whenever an 'oh that's what he/she/it looks like' is required for quick identification or understanding of a visual effect.

The functions of her drop-in visits are many and varied. Like Amy Winehouse, performers can look like her: 'With her peroxide Dusty Springfield bob… Lucky Soul's Ali Howard could be a mannequin'[q]; and Martha Wainwright is 'an appealing figure beneath a Sixties bob, like a brunette Dusty Springfield'[q]. Or her hair can sum up her heyday decade: 'This has a very 1960s feel about it, and why shouldn't a recipe conjure up a decade just as well as plastic furniture, miniskirt or Dusty Springfield hairdos?'[q] When journalist Simon Mills attempts to describe his application of mascara to his own eyes, he uses the name as a short-hand to paint a picture of himself as sooty-eyed and smudgy: 'It wasn't pretty. Think off-duty Dusty Springfield drag queen and you'll start to get the picture!'[q] And on the subject of hair, a *Radio Times* blurb promoting a 2004 Channel 4 programme entitled *Bad Hair Days* plaintively asks 'Who hasn't… had their hair done to emulate the latest celebrity icon, whether it be Dusty Springfield, Farrah Fawcett or Rachel from the sitcom, *Friends*?'[q] Accompanying the text is a photograph captioned 'Dusty Springfield battles with her beehive' as if to sum up the situation and tell potential viewers what they're in for. The mere sight of a beehive styling is enough to put Dusty in mind, as when Sara Nicole Miller can only 'marvel at the number of Dusty Springfield beehive knockoffs in attendance'[q] at a Minnesota 'retrorama'. Whether hirsute or facial, as an instant conduit to a visual image of piled-on-top blonde hair and eyes made invisible through too much mascara, the term 'Dusty Springfield' seems to be filling a semantic gap in Anglo-American culture – so much so, in fact, that its enshrinement in dictionaries as a lexical item may be imminent.

The reasons for this current fascination with a hairdo and facial look from an earlier era are not entirely clear. Why should the Springfield bouffant and heavy use of mascara resonate in popular culture when other once-famous hair and make-up styles seem to generate little interest? It's not as if it is user friendly: judging by Celia Walden's experiences in the *Telegraph*[q] of trying to give herself a beehive and keep it, anything but! So what is it about black on beehive which inspired Amy Winehouse to 'give it a modern makeover'[q], with her 18-inch backcombed hairpiece 'the most copied celebrity hairdo' of 2007–8? The sleek 'Dutch boy' bobbed heads of Twenties flappers like Colleen Moore and Louise Brooks[q] are all but forgotten, and the electric fan rolling pins of the Forties appear in TV and movie period dramas without being billed as featured players in their own right. And if the Joan Crawford face[a] of loudspeaker eyes, hedgerow eyebrows and warrior mouth is not a short-hand means to checking out how other people look, it's because few choose to wear that kind of fortification.

The explanation for the continuing resonance of the look which Dusty popularised may lie in its sheer excess. The hair alone would have been remembered as an example of high hair but not necessarily the highest; the eyes without the hair might have nostalgic allure minus contemporary impact. Together, the abundance of hair and mascara were a beautiful marriage of fashion intemperance and created a style statement lending itself to restylings and reinterpretations. Dusty appropriated a clichéd idea of the blonde, kohl-eyed Glamorous Woman and took it to such extremes that it both honoured and caricatured the pin-ups and Hollywood love goddesses who had inspired it. Over 40 years later, Amy retained Dusty's sleazy grandeur but deglammed the blonde into a slash-black bruiser type with attitude, sneering and snarling like a resurrected Ronette and daring anyone to call her a lady. Whatever glamour the beehive had, it's gone tacky and streetwise. Still, Amy's prick chick owed to Dusty's glam mam a self-indulgent wallowing in overdoing things and a distrust of moderation. 'Other girls might wear mascara', wrote Charlotte Greig, 'but Dusty wore more; other girls might backcomb their hair, but Dusty wore it higher and with more lacquer'[a]. The frequency with which this representation of an exaggerated look-at-me female pops up in contemporary culture suggests that How to Make the Best Use of the Female Head and Face remains as much a subject of interest in the twenty-first century as ever it was in the sixteenth for the first Elizabeth. Indeed, as with Good Queen Drag herself, the look adopted for a few years by Dusty Springfield, and recently adapted and updated by Amy Winehouse, seems to raise questions about what-it-is-to-be-a-woman and the potentials which lie within her grasp for pleasure, guile and masquerade.

The time required to ready the hair and make-up for public view also regularly features in discussion of Dusty Springfield. The beehive and the mascara are of interest not only for their own sakes but for the preparation and application process behind them. Simon Bell, for instance, in 1999's *Definitely Dusty* TV programme, related from experience how 'getting ready to be Dusty took many hours' of long, laborious preparation – a fact the woman herself confirmed in a 1966 filmed extract shown in the programme: 'I find it an effort to keep up appearances 'cause it takes so long'. This interminable make-up procedure – what Jerry Wexler called 'an exercise in lamination'[a] – had, it seems, been going on since the beginning of Dusty's professional life, as brother Tom was complaining soon after the Springfield days that 'it takes her an eternity'[a] to get ready for public perusal.

The many Vladimirs and Estragons waiting for Godot Springfield down the years deserve canonisation for saint-like endurance. Two such stalwart souls[1] were Neil Tennant and Madeline Bell, who have both vouched for the fastidiousness and eccentricity of the beautification procedure. Tennant at her funeral recollected her being 'out of bounds in her dressing room with two make-up artists and three hairdressers'[1]; and the rumour that Dusty slept in her make-up was given credence by Madeline Bell saying that 'she would keep the black on… [E]very night she would… blot it and then keep it on'[1] and 'wouldn't leave the house until she had all her make-up on'. And increasingly, in an age where a celebrity sigh or sulk requires a psychiatric explanation, the reasons such accoutrements were considered necessary in the first place have come to play an increasingly central role in the myth. When Madeline Bell explained, 'everything was all part of a mask'[1] to hide behind, she was merely stating what had long been obvious; the *Daily Telegraph* obituary had been entitled 'Dusty: behind the mask' and Dusty said herself in the mid-Nineties, 'The bigger the hair, the blacker the eyes, the more you can hide'[1]. The matter of *what* was hidden behind the mask need not detain us for the moment.

With all this attention paid to her face and hair by both their owner and her commentators, you might think Dusty Springfield *was* a mask, and that her head had grown so top-heavy under the weight of the wigs and mascara it had crushed the rest of her body to pulp. Had the 'bullet proof… Ancient Greek death mask… [and] blood-red gash of a mouth'[1], which Jean Rook thought gave her a 'terrorist' look in pre-Al Qaeda 1985, 'disappeared' the rest of her as being surplus to requirement? Not entirely. Whilst it is true that the everything-bar-the head part of her can't compete for attention with what was on top, Dusty's body makes a significant, though lesser, contribution to her current image in terms of how she clothed it and what she did with her arms when she sang. The beauty and variety of the gowns were talked about by singer Kiki Dee and designer Eric Darnell on the 2003 TV tribute *Living Famously*[1]: the former recalled them as 'quite a number… you'd have to kind of put her into them' because, in Darnell's words, 'God cursed her when it came to the thighs'. Yet overall the dresses receive less comment now than during the Sixties and are probably referred to more rarely than the hand gestures. Michele Kort in *The Advocate* in 2000 mentioned both 'the glittering gowns and extravagant hand gestures'[1] as being part of the visual iconography and, in affectionate imitation, a group of people filmed outside London's National Film Theatre for *Definitely Dusty* sang to an old hit by waving their arms around as if to say 'we all know who this is, don't we?' These allusions and others notwithstanding[1], no feature of Dusty Springfield's lower body hogs the contemporary limelight like her face and hair; a Betty Grable she is not, nor a Twiggy or an Imelda Marcos, and, though she is often mistaken for her, Sandie Shaw was the one with the bare feet, not Dusty.

Dusty Springfield Live at the BBC, BBC DVD, 2007 (from Dusty, originally broadcast 22 August 1967)

'We all know who this is, don't we?'

The hair and eye fetish has grown over the years. Unlike with the voice, the colours and stylings of these features did not receive undue attention in the early Sixties. Considering the amount of publicity she attracted at this time and in view of what was to follow, it is remarkable how few references there were to her appearance. The hair seems to have been considered nothing unusual. Between 1959 and 1962 the beehive was at its height[h] – literally as well as figuratively. The one on the head of teenage singer, Helen Shapiro[h], for instance, was sometimes of such towering ingenuity it made Dusty's efforts seem slapdash and feeble. Dusty herself knew Brit beehives couldn't compete with their American counterparts: in later life, she recalled those on the heads of the Ronettes and the Shangri-las as 'serious'[h] – hers, she said, was 'only half the size'. In such a context, the Springfield bouffant – later dubbed 'the ultimate beehive'[h] and 'queen of all beehives'[h] – faded into insignificance as just one more Big Hairdo, a bit passé and blowsy perhaps but hardly worth a mention. When there *was* comment, it was on the make-up and the length of time it took to put on. Her brother Tom's 'eternity' remark was confirmed by his sister[h] just before their group disbanded, and in an early interview as a solo singer, the 'black painted rings that encircle her eyes'[h] noticed by Maureen Cleave of the *Evening Standard* and likened by her to 'giant tyres round the wheels of a lorry' had their performative importance emphasised by Cleave's subject, who told her 'without the paint I can't sing: it's like being without teeth'.

Although Dusty's appearance became more overblown during the Sixties, media comments on it did not grow more numerous. A nickname around at the time – Rusty Springboard[h] – was a pun on her name, not the way she

Serious beehives – Dusty with the Ronettes

looked. Ongoing concern with this aspect of her was only expressed in *Disc*; the other three major music papers showed little interest. The make-up of Dusty's music got more coverage than the make-up on her face. Perhaps it was Penny Valentine who was curious. Certainly, in 1965 she asked 'Why does she wear so much eye shadow?'[5] and devoted a lengthy article to both the eyes and the hair in which their owner–creator described the procedure and its results, and confirmed that she was funnier about the ornamentation process than anyone else would ever be.

Whether consciously remembered or not, the article provided the blueprint for numerous subsequent references to Dusty Springfield's idiosyncratic beautification process, its trials and tribulations. She'd borrowed the look from models a few years previously, she said, and although the application and removal procedure varied, she usually smothered her eyelids with kohl and sometimes kept it on 'for five or six days at a time!' On one occasion, she'd wept at the end of a film and got 'black rivulets running all down my face'; on another she had to wear dark glasses because only one of her eyes was made up. As for hair, sometimes it 'makes me furious' because of its inconvenience. Like the time when she'd had to cut herself out of a cashmere pullover because her hair was so lacquered she couldn't get the sweater over her head. As for the basic question 'why?', in the mid-Sixties with her friend Penny Valentine as her interviewer, the reply she gave – 'I just like it' – was answer enough.

However, this state of easy acceptance was not to last. As the Sixties wore on and Dusty's popularity in Britain grew, in Phil Gallo's words, 'just shy of a coronation'[a], with her fame and profile arguably more clamorous than that of any homegrown female pop singer until Amy Winehouse in 2007[a], peaking in 1966 before a slow decline, the cosmetic and sartorial constructions she inhabited began to threaten their tenant with architectural overload. The kohled rings grew blacker; the blonde wigs expanded ever onwards, outwards and upwards with curlier, 'girlier' hairpieces and chignons and more ornamental flowers; the arm and hand gestures signalled alert with greater dramatic abandon; and the dresses sprouted bows, winged sleeves and intricate decorative flourishes before almost trailing the studio floor like bridal gowns. With no sign of a wedding for their more appropriate setting, what was the point of them? And wasn't Dusty getting on a bit now and too old for this larking about? The British had taken her to their hearts for a number of years but, by the late Sixties, they may have been growing a trifle weary and wary of a get-up that was growing more outlandish and oddball with virtually every tele-outing. The advice she'd taken for a while from the producer of her first two BBC TV series, Stanley Dorfman, to tone down 'her leather make-up' and 'get rid of the huge thing she used to wear on her head'[a] was no longer around once Dorfman stopped producing her. 'She didn't really know what she looked like', he said in 2007, which was lucky for her, for by the late Sixties and the coming of colour, she predated The Clash by about ten years[a]. The voice was that of an angel but wherever the look of her was made, it was beginning to seem somewhere other than heaven.

So it was that in 1967–8 tentative attempts were made to 'out' what hid in her eye shadow and the beehives of her hair, rather than just accept this ornamental overkill as what made Dusty look like Dusty. Tony Palmer in the *Observer* thought the 'neon-sign make-up and innumerable blond wigs'[a] served as safety valves which 'she retreats behind'; and in a major article in the same newspaper, Marcelle Bernstein was moved by the toll her 'need to appear beautiful'[a] before the public was taking on Dusty – to the extent that 'if she orders a meal in her room, she'll lock herself in the bathroom while it's served'. With these sympathetic accounts came more abrasive criticism. 'I don't much care for Dusty Springfield'[a] announced Nancy Banks-Smith in the *Sun*. 'That girl', she implied, was a phoney whom she would 'love to scrub… and start again from scratch'. Did anything, she wondered, lie behind her 'piano personality' with 'the gestures… the eye shadow, the immovable hair-do… slapped on from the outside [as]… armour against the audience'?

With this stinging rebuke, Banks-Smith was one of the first to intuit that there was more to Dusty Springfield than met the eye; or rather, that what met the eye was not to be taken at face value. These eyes, this hair could not be trusted.

For this writer, the singer was 'frightened' of what she ominously called 'the many-headed monster squatting out there in the dark'. The unease and suspicion with which Banks-Smith implicitly repeated Valentine's question two years later demanded an answer beyond a glib 'I just like it', that's why. When, the next year, a certain Pauline Lelong wrote a letter to *Disc* mocking Dusty's 'False hair, false eyelashes'[q] and cattily wondering if she also had 'false teeth and a wood leg!' it was the beginning of the end for Dusty's age of innocence. Henceforth more would be required by way of explanation. 'Why does she wear so much eye shadow?' indeed. And what drives the need for the ever-growing panoply of wigs and hair pieces which Penny Valentine thought an indispensable part of her 'Oh look, it's Dusty'[q] appeal and individuality? The motivation behind the compulsion towards visual elaboration would be increasingly probed and prodded.

One reason it had not surfaced earlier was that, from the beginning, Dusty was at pains to make explicit the manufactured nature of the glamour she projected; and to admit that, left to its own devices, her body fell short of conventional standards of female beauty – or at least, of her own Hollywood-derived notion of The Glamorous Star. Lest anyone else should draw attention to the fakery, she would get in first. In 1963–4 she was telling all and sundry that her unbeauty made her an improbable pop star. For a start she didn't have 'a pop face'[q] because it was too old and 'horsy'. Then there were her varicose veins and her short-sightedness, the spots on her face, the fat under her chin – all of which made her so 'hopelessly unphotogenic'[q] that, despite the 'enormously attractive' woman Maureen Cleave saw in front of her, the journalist not surprisingly felt 'a fitting place for [Dusty] is a freak show at a circus'[q]. But, although the artifice was made apparent by the subject herself, there was no talk at this stage of masks to hide behind. Dusty might mention the dark stockings she wore to cover up her varicose veins but that was about as far as the discussion of camouflage went. During the rest of the Sixties, despite an increasing sense of the confessional about Dusty's interviews, masks, disguises and hidings were not part of the vocabulary used in reference to her self-presentations.

Nor was there much talk of masks during the Seventies or Eighties. Indeed, long before the notion of 'Dusty: behind the mask' gained printed currency, another female singer hogged the imagery. 'I was just like a mask'[q] said Julie Driscoll in 1970 'I used to hide… from people. I never wanted to be what they made me. I just wanted to be a musician without all that glamour bit'; and a year later: 'I hid behind that image refusing to reveal my true self'[q]. Although the 'what' of her appearance and the 'how' of its process are followed closely by the 'why' of it in the public myth of Dusty Springfield, the initial pop whistle blower on the impossibility of living with the type of artificial image which threatened personal integrity and proved not worth the candle was the woman known, in those pre-Holland days, as Jools. For a few heady months in 1968, Jools Driscoll had been All The Rage but, by the turn of the decade, that rage was directed at the pressures the pop business had put her under, and the identity fears she now felt so 'incredibly paranoid' about. Wearing the mask had, it seemed, proved too much for Jools. So much so that after all the song and dance of her entry on to the pop stage, she soon limped, sadder and wiser, out of sight. On her near-invisible exit, she bequeathed the idea of a mask[5] and a true self lurking behind it to Dusty and her commentators for use in later decades.

In the meantime, when Dusty resurfaced in Britain in 1978 after going to ground for a while in California, it was the absence of upper-body adornment that came in for comment rather than its presence. While the woman had been successfully staging a latter-day Garbo vanishing act and her music was considered passé and has-been, if indeed considered or even heard at all, her look of painted love had been incubating an embryo which, once hatched, would prove an enfant terrible beyond its owner's control. The memory of a bouffant with panda eyes was now being born as an independent creature with enough robust staying power to ensure a life of its own, whatever the woman's views on the subject. Thus, the lack of obvious make-up and the dispensing of fake hair in favour of her own provoked more reaction than the embellishments of ten to twelve years earlier which, as we have seen, were not then much remarked on. Many who met her in this year couldn't get over the shock of what they saw. Rosalie Shann of the *News of the World* was one such: 'Dusty' she exclaimed in disbelief, 'looked at me through eyes without a trace of mascara'[5] and Jenny Rees of the *Daily Mail* was another: 'It's Dusty with a difference…'[5] That difference being the absence of big hair and heavy make-up. The impact of the change in appearance was even greater on Keith Howes of *Gay News* who wrote that with 'her carefully dryer-blown hair [and] beige on blusher make-up… she just didn't seem to bear any resemblance'[5] to the 'Ol' Black Eyes' he 'clung to' and expected to find at the interview.

TV interviewers too had trouble adjusting to the idea of Dusty Springfield looking different from how she was supposed to look. 'You've quite radically changed your image',[5] *Nationwide* interviewer John Stapleton stated accusingly, prompting Dusty to bemoan peoples' inability to reconcile the 'natural' look staring out from the sleeve of her new album, *It Begins Again*, with the performer they remembered. 'Ooh, it doesn't look like her' she'd heard them say. 'Well, it does look like me', she informed Stapleton, 'it looks like me now'. Oh yes? Well, all right. But if the black-eyed beehive queen wanted to look 'like me now', she had better give up any silly 'comeback' notions, for even though this woman may have had 'the cool elegance of a fashion model'[5], she wasn't Dusty Springfield or even a 'wannabe', just a bargain-basement clone – and 'begin again' it predictably did not. The woman, as usual, knew this anyway: 'once you establish an image… people get that fixed vision of you', she complained in the same interview, 'and no matter how much you change, they expect you to look… that way'.

Although, in another attempt to re-establish herself the following year, there was a little more definition to hair and make-up, the toned-down visual version of Dusty she offered to onlookers remained as ineffectual and lacking in potency as whisky diluted in a barrel of cold water. It was hardly surprising if public indifference caused scheduled concerts to be cancelled across the country. Kind though it was of Mike Mills to think her 'frizzy hair and elegantly casual clothes'[q] made her look 'far more relaxed and natural', if he expected what he called 'the new image of Dusty Springfield' to be accepted by the public, he was going to have to think again. How dare this woman who purported to be Dusty Springfield upset Anny Brackx with her 'conventional and inconspicuous'[q] appearance? What on earth did she think she was up to?

The prospect of Dusty Springfield as ordinary, as – heaven forbid! – *normal*, was not to be countenanced and about the worst marketing ploy anyone had ever come up with. True, her Drury Lane and Albert Hall concerts[q] in London during 1979 proved triumphant and adulatory, and she showed herself to be almost as compelling a performer without the trademark ornamentation as with it. But the woman on stage was only unmistakably Dusty Springfield from the voice which came out of her and the way she moved; there was little evidence to this effect from the look of her. With the hair and cosmetics now natural and muted, the glitzy gowns replaced by smart trouser outfits and the stop-the-traffic arm movements employed more sparingly as if to ward off flies, the Dusty who still sang like Dusty Springfield, though with more control and restraint, and less power and force, only vaguely resembled the household face whose regular visits to TV screens had liberally sprinkled hair spray and eye polish over Sixties living rooms. There was no getting away from it: Dusty Springfield looking natural and normal was the fake[q], the not-real thing, and may be seen in retrospect as a late-Seventies impostor on a 'take in a concert or two' shopping trip from the States. Lurking in the wings, though, was Dusty Springfield, Britpop pantomime dame, awaiting a propitious moment to re-establish her 'authentic' credentials.

That moment came on her next British outing, in the mid-Eighties. After trying to fob off on American audiences[q] as Dusty Springfield an overweight woman with podgy face and sheepy-fringed short hair, she sensibly rang a Sixties retro shop, ordered a Do-a-Dusty-for-the-Eighties kit and proceeded to turn herself back into herself. Although in every other way, this 'comeback' attempt proved the most disastrous of all Dusty's post-heyday forays into the limelight – her professional dealings with Peter Stringfellow[q] were acrimonious and undignified, and hits were unforthcoming – the strong look she came up with made an impact and announced that The Real Dusty Springfield was back – in an amended version, certainly, as befitting a Woman of a Certain Age, 15 years on – but recognisably Her. On a 'can't beat 'em, join 'em' basis, the 'Ancient Greek death mask' with which she 'terrorised' Jean Rook and the rest of the publicity machine had an attack and presence about it which made you sit up and take notice. 'Startling' and 'vivid' were adjectives given it by Andrew Simpson in *Woman*[♮]. If other men like Gordon Biggins and John Peel emphasised the butch aspect by likening the effect to 'the Michelin man in drag'[♮] and, in the silver suit seen by Peel, 'a minicab driver in Bacofoil'[♮], at least she was again inspiring her commentators to remark on what she *was* rather than what she was not.

Unusually, her finest moments during this brief visit to the spotlight were when she wasn't singing – the first talking to Janet Street Porter on *Saturday Night Out*[♮], the second chatting up Terry W on *Wogan*[♮] a few months later. On both occasions she looked stunning in her big-shouldered, spangly jackets, colourful silk tops and long candelabra earrings, her hair thankfully 'big' again – frizzy and brown grey – and her eyes daubed in look-at-me black-red mascara which could easily pass as updated panda with a hangover. With Wogan particularly, her appearance

Picture: Rex features

'Ancient Greek death mask'

had a look of louche love about it that was charming and touching; if this were a 'terrorist', it was one you wouldn't mind meeting on a dark night. So striking was this from-the-shoulder edifice that it has often appeared in print as a kind of mature variant on the look of her prime – in contrast to photo outings of the late Seventies which, unsurprisingly, are sighted rarely, as a bleached-out woman has wandered into them, and no-one knows who she is.

In terms of commercial success, the next resurgence, under the nurturing wing of the Pet Shop Boys, was the highest point in Dusty Springfield's post-Sixties career. During the late Eighties and early Nineties, she maintained a profile

Nationwide, BBC1 (January 1978)

The bleached-out woman of 1978: 'no-one knows who she is'

which was high enough for her to be back in the public eye but low enough to maintain her privacy and take second or even third billing on TV music or chat shows. Her look during this time was a toned down version of the 1985 self-parody; manicured matron rather than butch queen. She looked what she was – a woman in her fifties – though, with near shoulder-length silver grey hair combed into a stylish bird's nest, dangling ear-rings, long scarves, chic smooth trouser suits and high-heeled boots, one for whom attention to the details of her wardrobe remained important.

Press reference to the hair and make-up as masks or disguises became commonplace, with Dusty herself as keen as any of her interviewers not only to confirm but also promote the idea that the ornamentation was there for a reason. 'Was it not a mask?'[a] Jon Savage asked in the *Observer*. 'It was a good thing to hide behind', she replied. Mick Brown in the *Telegraph* referred to the mid-Sixties as the years in which 'she had perfected her disguise'[a]. And when Gloria Hunniford suggested 'You would literally hide behind your make-up'[a], Dusty quietly pointed out to her and the audience 'Oh, I think I still do. Look.' Although more subtly and sparingly applied, she still wore it for purposes of display and concealment, as she wished to make obvious. The numerous mentions after her death[a] of masks and disguises could have been penned by Dusty herself who, in her last years, would readily own the masquerade without discussing its darker motivations or broader implications.

Whether or not currently in evidence, the high hair and/or mascara would be mentioned in interviews and articles as if the mere idea of them were an elixir of happiness. Requesting Dusty to 'get rid of that bloody awful perm'[a], Sarra Manning longed nostalgically

Sunday Sunday, LWT (25 November 1990)

'You would literally hide behind your make-up.' 'Oh, I think I still do. Look.'

for the bouffant that was. Now, however, there was no hope of her seeing it again – unless as a send-up instigated by Dusty herself. For in the decade before the cancer forced her out of the public arena for good, she was back in charge of her own act and reclaiming her original role as the main player in the charade of Dusty Springfield. 'I have special muscles that I developed from years of teasing my hair'[9], she told Brant Mewborn in 1988, '[t]o this day I can hold my hands in the air longer than anyone I know'. And to Rob Hoerburger seven years later she confessed, 'I used so much hair spray that I feel personally responsible for global warming'[9]. On two early Nineties TV outings with the comedians Dawn French and Jennifer Saunders, she mocked her own image[9]. Instead of being exasperated by people's reluctance to accept her as fully herself without the visual apparatus which had come to follow her around like a stalker, she now showed gratitude to collective memory by making fun of herself; after all, although she had come a long way from Dusty Springfield, she could still touch base with her – and if it gave people pleasure, why not show her off every now and then?

When the mid-fifties woman first walks into the room in the 1994 documentary *Full Circle*, French and Saunders pretend not to recognise her – 'She's more beehive' – and, still unsure of her identity, they later attempt to get her to wear a wig and false eyelashes – 'It would just help the viewer at home if you put them on'. Dusty rebuffs them by saying 'No, no, honestly I can't… Not any more'. At the end of the programme, Saunders mocks the fixed image of Dusty Springfield as detached from the woman who bore that name by holding up the wig and lashes and saying, 'I told her if she'd worn this and this, people would know who she was'. But the flesh-and-blood woman has already left the room. On a second French, Saunders and Springfield occasion[9] nearly two years later, in response to offers of 'huge big beehive, yeah?' and 'this eyeliner, it's to die for', Dusty simply smiles, kisses the two women and departs. As these were amongst her last TV appearances, it seems she was telling us that not only was she wise to the fond joke her image had become, but that it was perfectly all right to equate Dusty Springfield with a wig and two lovely black eyes – she had come to terms with the daftness of it all, had a certain fondness for her invention and was happy to bequeath it, along with her music, as her legacy. She now knew that the middle-aged woman had only a tenuous connection with the original concept of Dusty Springfield, and she believed that we knew it too. What she wished us to know also was that the myth could no longer get to her. We had her permission to play with it and have a bit of fun. This, above all, was what her presence in these final programmes seems to have been about.

It is a mark of both the affection Dusty still generated in the press and how little they understood her that, while her own contributions to Full Circle were received with warmth, French and Saunders were attacked[9] for their crass behaviour in her presence. When Craig Brown said he wished they had been 'allowed the night off'[4], he was speaking for several others. Can anyone doubt, though, that the irreverent tone of the script – with lines like 'You're an icon', 'Oh, you make me cry, that's really nice' – received Dusty's full approval, or that even if the concept of the mock-interview was not her idea, she more than willingly went along with it? Rather than the victim of the two comedians as she was depicted in the press, Dusty was working alongside them to 'take the mickey out of myself'[4], as she told Andrew Duncan at the time. Certainly a self-mocking approach was the only way she would have done it. Few performers have been so complicit in both debunking and honouring their own myth, or done so with such mischievous relish or canny sense of entitlement.

Her detached fondness for the old image was also displayed the last time she sang live on TV. Seeing an old Sixties black and white clip of herself, she twists her fingers into a gun, 'shoots' her old self, and exclaims to Jools Holland and audience 'Oh, the hair, I want it'[4]. Again, but more tenderly, on her last visit to the world's TV screens on 17 January 1996, when her old associate Des O'Connor gently detected 'slightly less eye liner'[4], he put her in mind of recently putting on 'the full black eyes' for the first time in years 'and... it felt so good'.

Other factors made this valedictory occasion poignant and appropriate. She had a trio of her beloved black female singers to mime along with her, and she seemed to have found a touch of the serenity which had always eluded her. Telling Des and the viewers how her illness had given her a sense of priorities she hadn't had before, she spoke the last words the public would ever hear Dusty Springfield speak: 'What's important is being alive and being happy'. And as she spoke them, and during her song 'Where Is A Woman To Go?', she looked radiant and glowing and almost – dare one say? – content. Dressed in black as if aware at some level of what was to come while simultaneously reminding viewers, with the silveryness of her hair, of the black and white glory days of what had been, she went out with dignity. The last sighting of the woman who bequeathed an endearing and unforgettable look of garish female bravado to Anglo-American culture, and thereby held up a distorted mirror to that culture's fantasies, was of a Goya-esque Madonna with her hands together as if in prayer. Perhaps, unconsciously, at the very end, she felt able to dress as Dusty Springfield yet at the same time ditch her by bidding farewell to her public as Mary O'Brien, the good Catholic girl who was strictly not come dancing or singing or darkly made-up with blonde bouffant hair.

Chapter five

Oh, You Beautiful Doll

The role Mary O'Brien played with regard to her Dusty Springfield persona and alter ego was that of creator and manipulator, a behind-the-scenes impresario. As the woman remarked in one of her last interviews, she was her own Svengali[a]. Shy and self-doubting though Mary was, the PA job she did with Dusty during the Sixties was a solitary and successful one requiring organisational skills of great determination and shrewdness. She was, in Maureen Paton's words, 'a supremely stylish operator'[a] and manager of her own product. Keeping the high-profile Dusty Springfield show on the road for more than a decade made such demands on her time, energy and resources that it is hardly surprising if she wilted under the strain and took time out in the Seventies. Concocting Dusty was one thing, maintaining her quite another. Such an act of self-invention and promotion is worth exploring, for, as Robert Sandall said in 1989, 'her self-reinvention procedure was as complex as it was original and there is still plenty to be said about it'[a].

For a start, there was no-one else involved. Mary seems to have acted alone and on her own initiative to fashion the star image we have been discussing, and in this sense she is unlike most of the female glamour queens of Hollywood, whose screen images captured her imagination. With the exception of Mae West – whose imperious self-regard brooked interference from others at no stage in her long and bizarre career and whose blonde buxomness was essentially a hangover from nineteenth century burlesque – movie goddesses needed, and invariably got, a little help from their friends before they could be wheeled from the studio make-up room to a film set marked 'available for public consumption'. If they were to make an impact, reconstruction work was often called for on anatomical parts which were thought a little too long or short, big or small or a bit off to one side.

The painful electrolysis programme Eddie Judson inflicted on the hairline of shy, bewildered Margarita Cansino before she could look like Rita Hayworth[a] makes Dusty's hair experiments seem half-hearted and timorous. Margarita was chubby and had to lose weight, and her voice was too high and had to be lowered[♮]; but unlike the singer nearly 30 years after her, the duckling-to-swan transformation process was in the minds and hands of the men around her, not the woman being worked upon. If, as described earlier, Dusty found her body lacking in the 'glamorous star' department and moaned about its shortcomings, she had only her internal critic to tell her to 'fix your hair here' or that 'this bow doesn't look good'[♮]; and unlike (Marga)Rita, she could decide for herself what, if any, 'improvements' needed to be made. A later star persona, that of Rita Hayworth's 'successor' at Columbia, Kim Novak[♮], was similarly manufactured by others – in her case, studio boss Harry Cohn. For starters there was her name – Marilyn – which had to be changed because there couldn't be two of them. And then the rest of her required a thorough refurbishment. In 1958 art imitated life when, under Hitchcock's direction, James Stewart in *Vertigo* redressed and restyled her[♮], dyed her mousy hair blonde and generally moulded her into his Ideal Woman – without, however, needing to cap her teeth as, thankfully for Kim, this had been attended to by Cohn before Stewart laid his hands on her.

There was nothing particularly unusual about these real-life and cinematic shapings of Rita Hayworth and Kim Novak – in life and art men were doing it to women all the time. What *was* unusual in the late Fifties and early Sixties was for a woman to decide for herself, with no exploitative masters to urge her on, that a 'starrification' of her own body was called for, and then to follow thought with deed by implementing a programme of works for the makeover to be put into practice. Drawing attention to the mechanics of the glamourisation process by stressing the artificiality of the enterprise to anyone who would listen was also unusual, and further undermined the established (male) system by which (female) stars were manufactured. No witness to this Trilby transaction would be fooled into believing the blonde, elaborately coiffured, dressed and cosmeticised performer on stage or screen was anything other than a self-made sham. Although details of the hard work which had gone into turning Margarita Cansino into Rita Hayworth[♮] had, surprisingly, been made public, the woman had not been her own spokesperson as with Dusty Springfield. Youth, class and nationality sprinkled even more uncommon ingredients into the O'Brien/Springfield transformation recipe. Sure, middle-class British girls were expected to make the most of themselves in the looks department, but turning your body into a cheap and nasty objet de tart was hardly done or decent.

With Mary the subject and Dusty the object, producer and product one and the same, an original piece of backstage theatrics took place so that, in the words of Lucy O'Brien, 'a mediocre misfit, Mary O'Brien, changed herself into somebody who would impress the world… she created a girl called Dusty'[♮]. Even pop's chameleon prince, David Bowie, would need a little push from the likes of wife, Angie, and mime artist Lindsay Kemp before stardusting himself down as Ziggy[a]. In the Dusty Springfield version of the creation myth, Mary was instrument rather than recipient of divine intervention. As with the other Mary, though, she was sole human conceiver and deliverer of her attention-grabbing chimera of an offspring.

The invention of Dusty Springfield and transformation into her is sometimes mythologised as having occurred virtually overnight. A chubby, bespectacled 16-year-old tomboy named Mary apparently looked at herself in the mirror, scowled at the boring potential librarian gazing back at her and decided that, if she didn't want to be miserable, she would have to become someone else. 'So I became someone else'[a]. Lucy O'Brien gave this account in her 1989 biography, and added that there and then 'on went the tall beehive wig... false eyelashes and heavy black mascara'[a]. Although she amended this instant metamorphosis in later editions to first 'a radical change of style'[a], then 'a radically thought-out change of style'[a], the idea of a Mary-into-Dusty magic act caught on. So much so that, although, as we have seen, each dressing-up-as-Dusty for performative purposes was agonizingly slow and arduous, it is often believed that the initial conjuring up took one expectant rub of the hairspray upon which – hey presto – a beehived, mascaraed genie popped out saying 'Hi, Mary. Bye, Mary. Welcome to Dustyland'. Like all good fairy tales, this has a poetic resonance but distils and distorts reality. Mary may have decided 'in one afternoon to be this other person who was going to make it'[a], but the black dress and French-rolled hair 'with endless pins in it'[a] sound a long way from Dusty Springfield.

What Lucy O'Brien appears to have done – at least initially – is shorten an account given by Dusty on Canadian TV[a] in the early Eighties where she described the decision to change from 'gymslips and hockey-sticks into French pleats' as 'an overnight thing', but crucially added that 'the metamorphosis came long before Dusty Springfield came about'. A time gap is thereby suggested between the initial attempts to change her appearance and the emergence of the Dusty Springfield look. Indeed, there is little doubt that 'years of hard work and pushing got me to be Dusty Springfield'[a] and the look 'grew on me like fungus'[a].

What Dusty wrote in one of three pieces published in *Woman* at the height of her fame in the mid-Sixties emphasised the trial and error element of the process. The make-up, she said, was only got right after hours of 'experimenting' in front of a mirror. '[T]he first time I appeared as a blonde, I looked simply frightful'[a] because the colour – 'bright yellow' – did not suit her at all. The statement made in this article – 'obsessed as I've always been to get the right pop star image' – indicates that far from vanishing in a puff of smoke and rematerialising as Dusty, the young Mary had thought long and hard about how she was going to make it as an entertainer and knew the importance of presenting audiences with a strong, easily identifiable image – the carefully constructed 'radically thought-out change of style' Lucy O'Brien finally came to identify. She would have to shape and play with the image until such time as a look came about which best suited the kind of pop star she wished to be.

Like Eddie with Margarita, and Harry and Jimmy with Marilyn, Mary probably didn't know who Dusty was until she stumbled across her one day and recognised her as the culmination of a long and time-consuming struggle – with many setbacks along the way. Her description of herself in later years as ambitious and single-minded – 'a fairly calculating bastard'[1], 'a seething mass of ambition, ready to claw my way to the top'[2] – makes sense in terms of the attention she gave to the wholesale packaging of herself as a commodity to be successfully branded and sold in the marketplace. Her look was every bit as important to her as her sound for promoting the product she was putting together: 'the reason I worked so hard on my appearance'[3], she informed Maureen Grant in 1978, 'was not to look attractive for my sake but to help my career'. The 'right pop star image' Mary O'Brien 'obsessed' over was the subject of painstaking research and a certain amount of physical discomfort. Madeline Bell recalls her sitting at Vidal Sassoon's 'having her hair bleached, in tears – she went through a lot of pain and aggro to be Dusty Springfield'[4].

Careful study of her public performances in the six-year period between 1960 and 1966 supports the contention that the look was more a lengthy experiment with facial and bodily artistry than a sudden shift from one state to another. During her first professional manifestations in close harmony trios – the Lana Sisters between 1958 and 1960, then the Springfields from 1960 to 1963 – she tried out a number of guises, the one consistent factor being the regularity with which she switched from one type of look to another.

In the Sisters' act her hair was cut short to match the style of the others, with her outfits, like theirs, consisting of shiny silver blouses, wide tulle skirts and silver lamé pants; about the make-up there was nothing unusual. A 1961 publicity still for the Springfields shows all three group members attired in white trilby hats, casual denim-type shirts and dark slacks, and sitting with legs splayed, elbows on knees and hands under their chins. If there were a caption, it would read 'We're a trio of swells'; there is little to indicate that one of the 'swells' is female. The 'tomboy' Mrs O'Brien described her daughter as being[5] is unashamedly to the fore at this early stage in her career. In 1961 virtually every photographic image of British girls in pop sought to emphasise the subject's ladylike femininity by displaying plunging necklines, figure-hugging glittery gowns or ornate balloon-like skirts. This sighting of the 22-year-old Dusty looking – from both the clothes she wears and the 'blokeish' way she sits – like one of the lads after a bit of a razzle in no way suggests Milady

Springfield is waiting in the wings. A few other visual images – including the one on the cover of her first solo album, *A Girl Called Dusty*, with cosmeticised face and lacquered hair above blue denim shirt and black trousers – take us closer, but they still convey a playful sense of a girl who'd be happier climbing a tree than polishing her nails.

Courtesy Redferns

'Happier climbing a tree than polishing her nails'?

The year 1962 appears to have been a very experimental year. Images of full or semi-tomboy alternate with a short-haired, unmade-up pretty young thing looking demure in plain summery dresses – in rehearsal perhaps for the 'natural' somewhere-around-40 stranger who turned up in the late Seventies. A bright-eyed, fresh-faced female type with swept-up darkish hair, huge cravats and pod-like skirts you could shelter under is also around; but the closest thing to the recognisable Dusty comes that May with the sight of a 'sick' girl in a hospital bed, short blonde hair styled and bobbed, lipstick in place and eyes caked in mascara. Her fully fashioned visage and alert expression leave you wondering if the theatre she is off to has stage and curtains instead of a surgical table. Dusty Springfield may be spotted here not just because the eyes and hair are beginning to look suitably ebony and ivory but because this patient has acquired a sense of occasion and the grand gesture to accompany it. Equally ironic is Dusty's appearance with the two boys later that year in the film, *Just For Fun*, when she rolls her eyes to heaven as if to say 'How much longer are we gonna have to sing such rubbish?' The song 'Little Boat' was well put together but the mascara was not; indeed, after the hospital promise, it wasn't much in evidence.

'Short-haired, unmade-up pretty young thing'

Dusty Springfield: Full Circle, Vision Video Ltd. VHS, 2000 (produced by Initial Film and Television Publication, 1994, originally broadcast 1962)

Just For Fun, Columbia Pictures (1962/63)

'Mascara… not much in evidence'

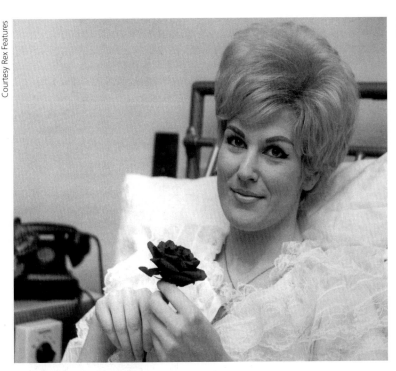

'This person has acquired a sense of occasion'

Although the famous beehive was given a draft outing or two in late 1962, it was the following year which saw its slow build into the tower blocks of 1964 – by which time fashion generally had already moved on to lower levels of effrontery. As with the eyes the previous year, building work on the roofing of the Dusty Springfield edifice progressed slowly: one week it seemed to be coming on nicely, the next there may have been an extended tea break. The trouble was that it couldn't make up its mind[a] whether to go straight up or make diversions to right or left; just when you thought it was going one way, it would take a U-turn and mooch off somewhere else. Granted it was often seen heading in an upwardly mobile direction but its detours were too numerous for any reliable mapping. On many viewings the structure had an oval shape like a barrage balloon rather than the more elongated sausage-look of what generally passes for beehive, while on other occasions odd triangular structures walled in the face like papier-mâché pyramids.

But at least for the Springfields' *Sunday Night at the London Palladium* farewell concert in October 1963, a special effort was made to tone down its avant-garde tendencies and show off the heights it might rise to. Unfortunately, Dusty's first two singles as a soloist were up tempo and, although the eyes showed encouraging signs of sleepless nights dancing around to them, the hair seemed to be awaiting a more dramatic arousal – something operatic would do nicely. A big weepy sort of ballad perhaps? No sooner conceived than delivered, for in the summer and autumn of 1964 along came two slices of pop melodrama calculated to make the hairs on *anyone's* head rise. It had taken a while but finally both hair and eyes knew what was expected of them. The rehearsal was over, their lines were learned, the curtain was up and they were

Dusty Springfield: Full Circle, Vision Video Ltd. VHS, 2000 (produced by Initial Film and Television Publication, 1994, originally broadcast 2 May 1994 on BBC TV)

'Papier-mâché pyramids'

about to step onstage as the main support to their owner's act, little dreaming as they did so that they would come to upstage her altogether.

To provide the grandiose orchestrations of 'I Just Don't Know What To Do With Myself' and 'Losing You' with suitably ornate visual accompaniment, the hair had grown tall with a celebratory bow at its back while the eyes had comfortably buried themselves beneath charcoal. Dusty Springfield – panda-eyed, beehived, blonde – now often chicly attired in natty streetwise dresses – had arrived as Queen of the Mods. Not yet Dusty the full-blown glamour queen of 1965–70, and still inclined to favour horizontal as well as vertical head shapings; but a credible younger and more accessible version of prime-time Dusty. Mary was reaping the rewards of several years' determination and hard work, her vision of blonde ambition finally realised.

Courtesy Rex Features

'A celebratory bow at its back'

With, however, one proviso. There was no *Blonde On Blonde* on the horizon. Why Dusty let Bob Dylan swipe this title for his 1966 album remains as much a mystery as the commercial failure of *Dusty In Memphis* at the end of the decade. Though clearly *her* slogan by right, this was one marketing ploy which unaccountably slipped past her. Unlike Dylan, it was she who turned her carrot roots into full fields of barley; she who provided the black on black of her eyes with blonde on blonde hair dye companionship. Early on it became apparent that Dusty's hair would need to impress, so if at the end of her life she was going out blonde♮, she had better make damn sure she came in as it. There had, of course, been no serious doubts from the age of five that she would settle on blonde. This was the age she saw her first Twentieth Century Fox musical – *Irish Eyes Are Smiling*♮ – and fell in love with its female star, or at least her blonde hairdos. Rita Hayworth? Not a chance. For one thing she was a red-head, for another she had committed the cardinal sin in Mary's eyes of not signing with Twentieth Century Fox♮. Kim Novak wasn't with them either, and not even her dazzling display of *Vertigo* platinum blondeness could get round that one. And though Marilyn Monroe and Betty Grable were at the right studio and with the right hair shading, they were minus the allure of a certain June Haver♮ who quickly became the wannabe of Mary's youthful imagination. 'Glittering and forbidden'♮ is how Lucy O'Brien describes the movie land that June Haver frolicked through; but Haver's cheerleader friendliness was of the girl-next-door rather than goddess type, and Lucy probably mistook the down-home musicals at Twentieth for those over at MGM♮.

Why the eminently forgettable June Haver? No explanation from Dusty was ever forthcoming. The answer, though, is obvious. Incredible as it seems, the character she played in *Irish Eyes* had the *same name* as the girl watching her – Mary O'Brien – and probably left the child thinking it was herself up there singing and dancing on the big screen. Certainly the sight of a blonde woman with her own name hogging the attention made an indelible impression; with her hair a similar colour of eye-catching brilliance, would she too be noticed at last? If the movie-world Mary O'Brien went under the sunshiney name of June Haver when the lights went down, the one watching her could dream of some day finding her own bright name tag; instead of boring 'O'Brien', she could call herself after a month, or, well… a season of the year when the flowers came out. Just as the Mary up there on the big screen had the vitality of her song and dance vindicated by her other name, so might her own future blossom if she called herself something fresh and optimistic. O'Brien on O'Brien, blonde on wannabe blonde – what larks!

In the drab real-life world of the 1950s, of course, Mary was not alone in wishing she could live in a wide-screen, Technicolor Hollywood musical. Nor was there anything unusual about her blonde fantasy, for in the post-war years, being blonde formed 'part of a dream of inclusion'♮, in the view of Joanna

Pitman, and changed the way many women felt not just about their appearances but their very identities. 'Blonde was no longer just a look'[4], Pitman explains, 'it was a whole psychology'. But this child's blonde aspiration consisted of far more than feeling good about itself by turning heads in the high street, getting a husband and raising a family. The blonde bimbo package the child envisaged for herself went beyond the *Oh, You Beautiful Doll*[5] mediocrity of a June Haver and was as much a means to an end as a way of cheering herself up. As it incubated in the child's imagination, the blonde embryo realised what it would be called on to do: illuminate the shadows in its owner's heart, brighten up her stage-struck prospects and lighten the surrounding darkness.

The idea of Dusty Springfield as a single artistic creation may need reviewing. Although in popular myth the visual memory that goes under this name is of an above-the-shoulders look that more-or-less straddles the Sixties, there were, as we have seen, a number of Dusty Springfield representations across the years. It may therefore make more sense to regard the name as a portmanteau brand name – a kind of chain store containing within its organisation a number of different branches, all distinctly Dusty Springfield but each with a visual style and atmosphere of its own. What Mary O'Brien may have been doing, probably unbeknownst to herself, is conducting a personal inquiry into what it means to be a woman – presenting herself, as it were, in a number of guises in a sort of ongoing subject–object gender exploration. In addition to disguise, the wigs, hair-pieces and outfits enabled her to experiment with different visual versions of herself. In this sense, if in no other, she prefigured the more self-conscious image shifts of Madonna or Kylie Minogue; without, however, choosing a brunette makeover or deliberately parodying certain fashion styles of the past. The hair styles especially changed the shape of her face so that with almost every TV appearance during the Sixties and early Seventies, she seemed to show an aspect of herself she had not shown before: in later years, as has been outlined, her appearance veered between 'natural' and outlandish and remained as unpredictable as ever.

As if to half acknowledge this aspect of her presentation style, the sleeve of her 1988 *Silver Collection* hits repackaging album shows the same photograph of a young Dusty Springfield nine times over in varying colour tones. Although her hair remains the same shade of yellow-blonde and the lips are white, the background and shirt colours flash blue and orange one moment, red and green the next, blue and purple, yellow and white, and so on. The artistic style is that of Andy Warhol, with similar use of colour tones and the same concept of facial replication he used in pictorial representations of Marilyn Monroe. Could the Warhol pastiche have been entirely accidental? For as with Mary's cast of scrubbed pretty maiden, rough-and-tumble tomboy, glamour queen, Southern country belle and Amazonian terrorist, Warhol presented himself across 40 years in a multiplicity of roles and stances, looking, in his self-portraits, one moment like a fluttery infant, the next like a terrifying skull, with vampires, drag queens, criminals amongst the roles he assembled from his repertoire of competing sub-personalities. Like Mary too, Andy Warhol became submerged beneath a wardrobe of upper-body accessories like wigs, dyes, cosmetics and sunglasses, and spent a lot of time gazing into mirrors with no clear idea whom he was seeing[4].

The work of another modern American artist, Cindy Sherman, seems even closer to this perspective on Dusty Springfield as an amalgam of personas rather than one fixed image. In what is probably her most celebrated series of photographs, Sherman snapped herself in the role of an early-Sixties blonde actress in a variety of clichéd feminine postures – some of them in her professional persona as film-noir femme fatale or sexy continental siren, others at leisure in domestic settings like kitchen and bedroom. On one occasion she turned herself into a luscious librarian – an adjective–noun combination which might have precluded the need for Dusty Springfield altogether had the librarian-dreading Mary thought of her first. Like Mary with Dusty, Cindy with 'Cindy' drew attention to the phoniness of the femininity under construction through the use of wigs and hair-pieces, costumes and make-up, as well as utilising other tools of the theatre such as props, prostheses, dramatic lighting and vivid colour effects. This description of Sherman could equally be applied to the Dusty creation(s) of Mary: 'They are entirely fantastic constructions with the artifice so extreme that Sherman appears more doll-like than human'[5]. In the sense that she played with versions of herself to parade before the public, and spent as many hours fashioning and perfecting each incarnation as she did producing her records, Mary showed the artistic sensibility of a Cindy Sherman regarding her self-presentations; and, as with the photographer, approached each performance before the camera as if it were a make-believe exhibition entitled, 'Beautification and Beastliness: Aspects of the Female Sublime'.

The cast of female guises Mary assembled under the artistic portfolio of the Dusty Springfield Collection may, in fact, be placed in a wider cultural setting and viewed as enacting certain psychoanalytic theories connected with women and the meaning of femininity. In 1929, a colleague of Freud's, Joan Riviere, entitled an essay 'Womanliness as Masquerade', in which she argued that women often adopt exaggeratedly 'feminine' behaviour to achieve their aims in a male-dominated world. Since the possession of such 'masculine' qualities as ambition and assertiveness would be regarded as threatening, their concealment behind a mask of flirtatiousness and hesitation is more likely to get a woman what she wants than straight-to-the-point direct action. 'Womanliness', Riviere wrote in a much-quoted passage, 'could be assumed and worn like a mask, both to hide the possession of masculinity and to avert the reprisals expected if she was found to possess it'[6]. As with Mae West before her, the figure who stood before audiences as Dusty Springfield was a self-made woman posing as a dreamy glamour queen. The bombshell front served a necessary purpose by diverting attention from the brains behind its manufacture. Like Mae too, Dusty simultaneously revelled in and undermined the vision of seductive womanhood she offered as spectacle. She seemed to be making at least three very different statements. One was, 'I enjoy being a beautiful woman and showing off my femininity for your delectation'; another 'We know, of course, don't we? that my femininity is phoney, but it's not much different from other women's fakery when they doll themselves up'; and – what separated Dusty from Mae and which will be discussed with sexuality issues later – 'I am doing my best to look feminine to convince myself that I really am: I am uneasy about aspects of myself which don't feel feminine to me'.

But whatever statements she may or may not have been making, Dusty Springfield was a fabrication which constantly questioned what 'woman' was all about. By making obvious that their gender roles were performed and malleable, not fixed, innate characteristics, Dusty Springfield and Mae West anticipated the theoretical work of Judith Butler[♮] who argued that femininity and masculinity were actions people *did* rather than once-and-for-all attributes of what they were. For Butler, gender is performatively constructed, with extreme or stereotypical masculinity at one end of a spectrum and 'girly' femininity at the other. According to how 'masculine' or 'feminine' we believe we need to present ourselves as being on any given occasion, we make choices regarding the point on the scale we wish to go in at. With all gender a form of parody, Butler's particular interest in drag queens stems from the fact that they highlight the disjunction between the body of the performer and the gender being performed, thereby revealing the imitative nature of all gender identities. As a performer who has been referenced in terms of drag on numerous occasions – by others and by herself – Dusty Springfield seems especially suitable for interpretation in the conceptual terms proposed by Judith Butler.

Drag, as Butler discusses it and as it is usually understood, involves a man dressed as a woman imitating the gestures and mannerisms of the female personality he seeks to pass himself off as. The enactment, however convincing and concealing of the maleness behind it, comes from outside the lived experience of the 'woman' on show or any other female person, for the simple reason that this is not a woman once the wig, high heels and make-up have been removed. Leaving aside complex transsexual issues, the familiar situation with drag is that of one gender taking on what it observes as being the visual and behavioural aspects of the other – often for purposes of show or entertainment and, virtually by definition, from a perspective external to the gender being exhibited.

If Dusty Springfield was the drag artist she is often regarded as being[♮], she was a rare example of a female-to-female impersonator, and thus, in a gender-disruptive position very different from the usual drag act. When her blonde coiffure was at its highest and her mascara at its darkest – at the *NME* Poll Winners' Concert in May 1966, for example – she not only offered her audience a certain female look sanctioned as desirable by numerous films and magazines during the previous 30 or 40 years but also suggested that, while having little to do with the woman she was in reality, this potential for gaudy seduction still lay within her: she was only looking how she was expected to look if she were to be an object of male desire and female envy. By exaggerating the cliché, she not only showed it up for the fantasy it had always been[♮] but implied that the impossible dream the fantasy represented lay embedded deep in every woman's psyche, however much her reason might protest. No man in drag could have offered this perspective. Even if his intention were to query gender assumptions, he could not, by virtue of his maleness, bring the same informed understandings to a drag impersonation as a female approaching things from a position of internal knowledge and personal experience. Dusty Springfield was thus one of the female performers Jane M. Ussher had in mind 'who are able knowingly to enjoy (and subvert or parody) the very notion of femininity as masquerade'[♮] in a way impossible for men.

Brian Henderson's Bandstand, TCN Channel 9 DVD, 2004 (originally broadcast 22 October 1967 on GTV9)

'*A female-to-female impersonator*'

In the post-war era one of the few acceptable ways a shy girl like Mary O'Brien, with low levels of self-esteem and looks she was unsure about[♮], could command attention was to give the same level of commitment to her body as a young man would give to his career; the fact that she was able to commit to both and conflate them was remarkable. When she took pains to publicise the mechanics of the procedure demanded by the commitment in the way that we have seen, thereby making obvious the gap between the woman on stage and the woman who'd gone into her dressing room hours earlier, she ridiculed the women presented by men in drag by implying that they were simply no more than that – men dressed up in women's clothes with no more connection to any 'real-life' woman than Dusty was to herself. Less, in fact, because at least her dame in drag was of the same gender.

By demonstrating the unnaturalness of female glamour, she took much of the sex out of it, and suggested it was an illusion keeping men happy and women in seeking-to-please drudgery. If, in the words of Charles Shaar Murray, she 'represented… the female sensibility that was struggling to get out'[5], it was one with a keen sense of the accommodations women made to male values and expectations, and a warning rebuke that payback time was

Courtesy Redferns

'*Potential for gaudy seduction*'

imminent. When journalist, Nancy Banks-Smith voiced mistrust of the woman she saw on her TV screen, and wondered what she was about, she came as close as anyone at the time to sniffing out underground activity. For, in terms of what would later be called 'gender-bending', Dusty Springfield was the mole in British popular culture of the 1960s.

On the surface she connived with a gender cliché, even gave the impression that she wished to further its cause on an 'imitation is flattery' basis; but her furtive burrowings from within the confines of corporate institutions like the BBC chiselled cracks in essentialist ways of thinking about gender. 'You pioneered a look'[5], the dame of drag, Edna Everage, told her in 1989. And when she did so, she pioneered a whole way of thinking. It wasn't new exactly, as it owed a debt to Mae West. But coming along when it did as a preface to a key chapter in the story of women's equality, it probably had more influence. The burdens women laboured under in the quest for The Body Beautiful were made visible in performance terms and complained about in interviews; such gender imbalances awaited more socially and overtly politically minded women to include them on their 'liberation' agendas at the end of the decade. Dusty Springfield often implied she felt like a fraud[5] or an impostor, and, in the subversion of her intent, it wasn't just the music she was referring to.

Chapter six

Bitches and Boils

 Dusty Springfield was inaugurated into the UK Music Hall of Fame[♮] in November 2006 by Joss Stone, one of many singer–admirers who were too young to remember her in her heyday. Her brief speech began by referring to neither the voice nor the look but her status as a pioneering woman in the British music industry. It used to be a man's world, said Joss, but 'every so often a woman comes along who is so talented and determined, the men have to sit up and take notice'. One such was Dusty Springfield who 'took control in recording sessions and, in the studio, wouldn't let anybody leave until she was 100 per cent satisfied'. Well, Joss, when some of those people died, including Dusty herself, there were no reports of them expiring midway through the trillionth take of a drum beat, so perhaps she had to settle for, say, 90 per cent. But Joss's points are now part of the Dusty Springfield myth. In addition to the music and the image, there's the perfectionist producer stepping where no Britpop woman had previously dared to tread. So what are the characteristics of her behind-the-scenes musical reputation? And what were other songbirds doing at the time not to be similarly feted as women who took control?

Discussion of Dusty Springfield's music now often acknowledges[♮] that she not only sang the songs on her records but also had more than a hand in producing them – at least those on the Philips label during the 1960s under the credited production aegis of Johnny Franz. Although she thought Franz deserved the credit[♮] – he could read music whereas she could not and she appreciated his understanding[♮], support and patience – she told Aida Pavletich in 1980 and Paul Du Noyer in 1995 that her main reason for not claiming production credit was concerned with the relative status of men and women in the 1960s British music industry. At a time when a woman producer on a pop music record was unheard of – 'it would have been unthinkable for me to have had on the record label, "Sung by Dusty Springfield, produced by Dusty Springfield"'[♮] – she decided to 'swallow [her] pride and let somebody else's name go on the label'[♮]. She calculated too that if the public got to hear that she was producing herself singing, it would look 'too slick'[♮] and put people off – 'women didn't do that… and I wanted to be loved'[♮].

Presumably, she must have decided that it was better to be loved by the many rather than the few, because a session man wanting to get home for his dinner and an hour in front of the telly would have found it hard to like, never mind love, anyone, man or woman, who thought their music took priority[a] over anything as mundane as eating or family life, or simply chilling out over a beer. Although no reports speak of musicians nearly passing out through being asked to repeat simple chords 40 times over as with Phil Spector[a], making a pop record with Dusty in the studio required stamina and endurance, especially for white British rhythm sections[a] trying to produce her beloved Motown sound when they were used to 'How Much Is That Doggie In The Window?' 'To say people found her difficult to work with is an understatement'[a], Lucy O'Brien reported after researching her book. 'Oh my God! It was just a nightmare from start to finish' all her interviewees told her. Dusty herself admitted in the mid-Sixties that she had acquired a reputation for being hard to work with and that, because she liked to 'spend hours working on the arrangements for a record'[a], she was inclined to 'snap sometimes when the musicians don't do it exactly the way I see it'[a]. Later she called herself 'a pain in the neck'[a] and 'a great scowler'[a] and would probably have agreed with Jerry Wexler's view that many of the problems making *Dusty In Memphis* stemmed from her 'stigmata of perfectibility'[a]. Also, in the case of that record at least, someone else was in charge of proceedings rather than (or at any rate, as well as) her – something she hadn't been used to in Britain.

Courtesy Getty Images

'Oh my God, it was just a nightmare'

Considering Dusty's usual tendency for self-disparagement, we need to take seriously her claim that she produced her records, especially since her trombonist and musical arranger for many years, Derek Wadsworth, unhesitatingly endorsed it by telling Paul Howes, 'She produced the whole thing. She was in there with the musicians and wouldn't let a thing slip through'[♮]. 'Seventeen of them I gave over the credit to someone else'[♮] said Dusty, 'I did all the work... I did everything' but 'in those days it looked wrong to be a young woman and producing yourself'[♮], so she chose not to take the credit. 'Somehow it looked too competent'[♮] for a girl pop singer to let it be known that, in addition to acceptable 'girly' things like hair, make-up and wardrobe, she poked her nose into matters like sound engineering, vocal and orchestral arrangements, rhythm and brass section balance, song selections and business schedules[♮]. If the dedication and efficiency with which she handled aspects of her career other than singing itself were to become public knowledge, folk might start asking 'who does she think she is?' and want to take her down a peg or two. With word out from the studios and theatres that she was an 'uppity' career woman, what chance success?

Joan Riviere back in the late Twenties knew what she was talking about, it seems, for here was her 'masquerade' theory being acted out in a 'swinging Sixties' pop setting. This ambitious and accomplished young woman who seemed able to turn her mind and hand to any work area concerned with her professional self-interest chose to let a man's name follow the words 'produced by' in the hope that any hint of her own 'masculine' initiatives and independence of spirit would be submerged beneath her hair and mascara. If in her visual stylistics, she was playing a complex and devious game of questioning gender assumptions, in the matter of deciding it was in her best interests not to push herself forward, she colluded with the very discrimination practices she deplored. 'When a man stands his ground,'[♮] she used to say to Madeline Bell, 'they go, "Yeah, he stood his ground" but when a woman stands her ground, she's a b-i-t-c-h'. Although as 'competent' in the practical and administrative aspects of her job as any of the men she worked with, if not more so, she decided to play down these sides of her character in the public arena.

She might have also liked to tuck away her musical knowledge and intelligence from sight but, unfortunately for her, they held such sway over her that they surfaced in virtually every interview. A teasing question remains, however. At the start of her career, she wrote some of her own songs: both 'b' sides on her first two singles were by her and they showed flair and promise. Although she claimed to 'get so many ideas which I can't or won't finish'[♮] and thus 'it doesn't flow easily', she also described herself as 'determined to try and make it as a songwriter as well'[♮]. Could the main reason she stopped composing be because she felt that this too was an activity that female pop singers in the early Sixties just did not do – at least in Britain? Was her song-writing talent sacrificed to conformity and expediency? Did Mary O'Brien not realise that, if she'd kept quiet about her real name, it could have gone on the credits after 'composed by', without compromising Dusty Springfield's glamour queen 'integrity'?

But – have a heart, you can't have everything. A look at the music industry's attitudes to female pop singers in the years before Dusty branched out on her own tells us what she was up against, and helps us understand how studio frustrations turned into shouting matches and temper tantrums. In the years 1956–63 virtually every pop girl who stepped into a recording studio or stood in front of a microphone to sing put her vital statistics on the line. She may have thought she was 'only singing' but unless – through her looks or her voice or both – she managed to dangle a set of bedroom keys in the mind's eye of her male mentors, she might as well close her eyes, count to ten and take a long nap on the back porch.

Charles Govey's 1957 *NME* piece about a chanteuse named Yana is typical: her gown 'leaves plenty of food for thought… breathing warm sex down the necks of the customers… soon every male is convinced it's just him she's singing for'[a]. Before she had opened her mouth in the interview, the woman who was briefly the most televised female face in Britain was described by Maurice Burman as follows: 'Marion Ryan stretched out her pretty arm… stroked her strawberry blonde hair… and looked at me with her pretty blue eyes'[a] whilst sitting 'very demurely on the edge of the armchair'. When it came to sexy on-stage shenanigans, however, no pop bimbo could compete with Shirley 'it's nice for a girl to have a mink coat'[a] Bassey, whose first concerts seem to have been like vocal strip-tease shows: 'the hottest piece of singing glamour… every gesture, every lyric projected her sex appeal… [she] sent shivers down the spine of every man in the audience'[a]; whilst elsewhere her gold dress 'revealed [her] considerable assets. She looked like a Grecian goddess with sex appeal'[a]. For *NME* reviewer Keith Fordyce, a woman's voice was judged according to how far en route to the bedroom she sounded: '"I Couldn't Say No" [by Connie Stevens] has that small, ultra-feminine voice sending masculine temperatures soaring. Well, with a title like that, what else could happen?'[a] When 'a girl said yes with all of her might'[a], he wrote on another occasion, 'that's the sort of gal I like'. Anything less than a sexy-sounding turn-on had Fordyce and his male colleagues reaching for the turn-off button[a]. The same thing applied to more than a few minutes at a time of *any* female vocalist, however alluring. 'Grouping singers in a higher vocal range together'[a], broadcaster Stuart Linnell wrote, 'was reckoned to produce "listener fatigue"', thus DJs – anxious not to increase stress levels or antagonise their audiences – rarely played women singers back-to-back.

If by any warped chance, pop songbirds aspired to please themselves rather than the men in their vicinity, they would soon be given short shrift. Even in the mid-Sixties, girl singers were expected to appear before their public looking like… well, girls. If, as with Elkie Brooks[♮], they turned up for a Beatles Christmas show in jeans, they would be hastily bundled by the producer into high-heels and a skirt in order to play the game and 'look more feminine'. Even as gowny and girly a performer as Dusty was urged by the producer of her BBC TV shows to look as feminine as possible[♮]. As for any pretensions to knowing what was best for their careers, they had better keep such bolshy notions out of the public eye – as even as loose a cannon as Dusty managed to do. After all, the men around a pop bird were the ones with the know-how and control, and if she had other ideas, she should at least have the grace to keep them to herself so as not to show her men up in public. By claiming not so much as a co-production credit with Johnny Franz, Dusty was only doing what Auntie Pearl of the popular 'Mr and Mrs Music' husband-and-wife act, Pearl Carr and Teddy Johnson, had advised. Dusty had no husband but it was the maleness that mattered: 'Let the husband be the boss of the act and the wife the boss of the home… I think a woman is more able to step down than a man is'[♮]. And, as we've seen, although she later drew attention to the injustice, step down Dusty did.

Most of her contemporaries didn't need to step down because they hadn't stepped up in the first place. However much she may have aspired to sovereignty in her later career as the Queen Mum of British TV[♮], as a Sixties songbird Cilla Black apparently agreed with Mrs Johnson, since in the Nineties she confided: 'I would put my own feelings aside and say, well, they are the experts, and they were. …who am I to tell all these great people otherwise?'[♮] And what did it matter anyway? For, as one of Cilla's 'experts', George Martin, has pointed out, women were regarded as 'an inferior part of entertainment… the world didn't accept them as readily as they did men'[♮].

Indeed, where British women in Sixties music are concerned, it still apparently doesn't. Two recent general histories of Britain in the Sixties[♮] devote pages to men in groups, but mention only one woman – Marianne Faithfull – in her clichéd role as Jag-hag appendage; and cleverly solve the question of 'what to do about Dusty Springfield?' encountered by the makers of *Soul Britannia*, by acknowledging her contribution in invisible ink. Likewise, two TV reviews of Sixties music[♮] in 2008 dealt with women by mentioning Cilla Black as part of the Liverpool scene, but not Dusty (who 'qualified' for both programmes), or Aretha Franklin (who 'qualified' for the second). Thus, two of popular music's most supremely gifted singers are airbrushed out of Sixties musical history like latter-day Trotskys because, as women not obviously toeing the male party line, they serve no useful purpose.

The view of Dusty's friend and manager, Vicki Wickham, that 'it was absolutely easy for women to get ahead in music then'[♮] seems perverse and is shared by virtually no other commentator. The post-war music business is more often considered the man's world Joss Stone referred to, with the success of the women who entered it dependent in large part on how far they were prepared to massage male egos and take a back seat, or at least not sit steering in the front with everyone's eyes on them. For singers, the climate was especially tough. 'Musicians', as Fifties singer, Lita Roza, told Lucy O'Brien, have 'always considered female singers a boil on the face of god knows what, a necessary evil'[.] But as long as she did what was required of her and combined singing with pleasing her men-folk, a girl could lance the boil, make good the evil and never have to worry her pretty little head about anything – especially matters pertaining to boring things like work or career, or even what she sang or where or how she sang it.

Fifties pop princesses, Joan Regan and Marion Ryan showed her how, the first taking the trouble to be 'beautifully dressed' for Doug Geddes[.] 'with the graciousness of a Dresden china doll'; the second presenting herself for Bill Day as a 'strawberry blonde with the curls on top'[.] in 'a gown with a definite He-appeal'. Although neither Joan Regan nor Marion Ryan allowed herself to be pushed around by men, they recognised it was in their best interests to appear unconcerned about anything other than their looks and songs. If, like 'Bobby's Girl' singer, Susan Maughan, they had made it known that they operated 'a business office… and [kept] a careful check on contracts, records, songs, letters, and all that'[,] they would probably not have lasted for even the few years that they did. Every aspect of Susan Maughan's career had been 'carefully planned', *Record Mirror* readers were informed, except the wit to keep the knowledge to herself and thus prevent the 'tremendous future' predicted for her[.] by the 'astute' agent, Dick Katz, from sliding into 'one hit wonder' obscurity. American singers like Peggy Lee and Connie Francis could get away with having bandstands rebuilt, enlarging orchestras, insisting on 20 takes and demanding guitars be toned down in favour of the bouzouki sound[;] but those Yankee women wearing the trousers were all the more reason to be extra vigilant in keeping the homespun dresses as full-blown and pleated as possible. We might not be able to prevent women interfering in matters that didn't concern them, but we could at least see to it that they didn't bang on about their professional multi-tasking in places they might be heard.

A striking case of a pre-Dusty Springfield British female singer whose ultra-feminine image belied a steely resolve to control her career is that of Alma Cogan. The most successful and famous Britgirl singer of the 1950s, Alma Cogan beamed her big face into living rooms the length and breadth of the UK with the remorseless cheeriness of a 'Hi De Hi' hostess overdosing on pep pills. In the Fifties Alma was ubiquitous: you would have had to emigrate to get away from her. Known as 'the girl with the giggle in her voice', she sang catchy confections about twenty tiny-fingered Eskimos confusing waltzes with tangos, wondering where the baby's dimple will be and not surprisingly getting the bell-bottom blues for their trouble. Like Dusty, who was around in the Lana Sisters and the Springfields while Alma ruled the roost, and presumably met her and knew her♮ – *everybody* knew Alma, or thought they did – appearance was as important as voice in establishing and maintaining the package that was known as 'Alma Cogan'. This was perhaps all the more so inasmuch as the bubble-and-squeak personality and fantastic sartorial wedding cakes seemed to upstage the light and insubstantial voice for which they were supposed to be back-up. One of her gowns had 12,964 diamante beads♮ and seven skirts, and needed two men to carry it; another had hundreds of feathers, every one of which was grabbed as a souvenir by fans waiting outside the theatre until not a feather was left on the dress – 'it was like plucking a chicken'♮, her sister wrote. So associated was Alma with these magnificent monuments to fashion intrepidity that when she decided to ring the changes with a plain black dress♮, she had so many letters of complaint that she considered issuing a public apology.

What TV viewers and music fans did not get to see was the businesswoman who controlled virtually every aspect of Alma Cogan's career: Alma Cogan herself. Only since her premature death in 1966, aged 34, have details emerged of Alma Cogan as lighting director, Alma Cogan the dress designer, Alma the photographer studiously arranging her camera angles♮, Alma as choreographer, Alma the publicity officer, Alma the chairwoman of a big business who let no-one – man or woman – tell her what to do or how to do it. Three men who worked closely with her – HMV producer and executive Wally Ridley, journalist Mike McGrath and her pianist companion, Stan Foster – all attest to her business acumen. Ridley talked of how she calculatingly organised press and publicity for herself by cultivating the right people♮; McGrath regarded her as 'a very hard businesswoman'♮; and for Stan Foster, 'she wouldn't let anything stand in the way of her ambition. Whatever she wanted to do, she was going to do it – she did it'♮.

Behind the giggly girl singer in the enormous dresses who became the nation's favourite Big Sister – a kind of pop-singing agony aunt – was this driven, hard-nosed mover and shaker who may well have been as much an inspiration to the young Mary O'Brien as the black singers she enthused over. Not for the way she sang or the styles she sang in, more for the clever way she hid her ambition and competence behind a look of sit-up-and-notice fluffy female exotica. Alma Cogan almost certainly lacked Dusty Springfield's musical literacy and perfectionist need to have the sounds in her head translated into the sound quality of her recordings, and is thus unlikely to have dealt with all the studio details Dusty attended to. She probably took an interest in how her records sounded without concerning herself unduly with how much echo was needed on the drums or whether the fifth violin had played a wrong note at the start of the second verse. Astute businesswoman though she was, Alma Cogan is likely to have had sufficient trust in her recording team to leave the production side to them. But, in both her determination to take charge of all aspects of her professional life and the visual flair of her self-presentations, Alma surely set the tone and influenced Dusty at the start of her solo career.

Like Joan and Marion – and Ruby Murray, Petula Clark, Anne Shelton and the other girl singers in Britain of that era – Alma was always at pains to be well-mannered. Niceness mattered at that time, and you wouldn't get far without it. With the arrival of the Beatles in late 1962 all that changed. At the end of the following year it was suddenly expected that girls would be cheeky. A 'dizzy dame'[♮] wanting a mink coat like Kathy Kirby[♮] or 'a shapely figure wrapped in a pale leopard-motif ensemble with handbag to match'[♮] like Julie Rogers might still feature; but with Shirley Bassey around to corner the market by out-styling, out-yelling and out-gesticulating every bejewelled, man-enticing rival, the conventionally feminine showbiz type went out of fashion. As usual, Dusty led the way. As well as making startling remarks like wanting to be coloured and rattling on about matters musical, the female Springfield had hinted at the zany humour she would later be known for and established herself as 'an interesting personality'[♮]. Thus, she had prepared the ground for newcomer Cilla Black saying in the month the Springfields disbanded that her dislikes were people who slurped their tea[♮] and sling-back shoes which slipped – whimsical nonsense it is hard to imagine earlier girl singers coming out with. More directly signalling the death knell for Alma and the Fifties pop sorority, Cilla suggested a few months later that all 'that flaredy-flaredy stuff… makes me look like the fairy queen on top of a Christmas tree'[♮]. Hers may have been the chirpiest, cheekiest voice but it wasn't the only one. In 1964 there was Lulu who 'bounces and bounds across rooms'[♮], apparently saying anything that came into her head, and a year after Cilla and Dusty's solo debuts, Sandie Shaw told David Griffiths in perhaps her first interview, 'A good job you didn't arrive five minutes ago… You'd have caught me in my underwear'[♮]. And to give the girl newcomers a slightly darker edge, Marianne Faithfull came along with a bit of winsome 'mixed-up girl' soul-searching and outspoken views on pop music's shortcomings[♮].

This 1963/4 girl singer was a new breed – younger, sassier, bolshier and more irreverent than the women who'd preceded her. Only three women in their mid-twenties were able to weather the teenage onslaught and establish themselves as even bigger stars in the 1960s: Shirley Bassey, by wowing the gents in Las Vegas and other casino cities with the reticence of her 'colouredness' and the bulldozer brashness of her ingratiations; Petula Clark, by reinventing herself in France and, with her manager–husband at her side, becoming the most successful British female singer in the USA; and Dusty, by dispensing with the two men either side of her onstage then acquiring token men, like Johnny Franz and 'manager' Vic Billings, to 'beard' her independence and single-mindedness.

If Dusty was alone in attending to the technical niceties of her records and stage act, it was largely because the other female singers were not interested or knowledgeable enough. Apart from Cilla, the new pop chicks were still teenagers when they had their first hit records and happy to concentrate on their singing and performances. In any case, they would have been too immature and inexperienced to concern themselves with the technical and administrative sides of their careers, and would probably have agreed with Judith Durham of the Seekers, who liked 'a man to tell me what to do. I like a strong character'[q]. Although Cilla Black was older, used to 'being in a man's world'[q] because of living with three brothers and 'wouldn't bow down to any man'[q], she too, as we saw earlier, deferred to male 'experts' when it came to making music. Like Alma Cogan and virtually every other woman in Britain at that time, she lacked Dusty's intensely musical ear and obsessive commitment to getting the music right, however many session men's evenings she ruined or marriages she put on the rocks. So when Burt Bacharach put Cilla through take after take[q] on the 'Alfie' session, it just about did her in.

The fact that Cilla could go on stage as an unpretentious, gawky, all-hands-and-legs 'ordinary' young woman indicates that, apart from her boyfriend and a huge hunger for fame[q], there was little going on behind the scenes she needed to keep under wraps. And the experience of so-called studio 'perfectionism' Cilla had endured under Bacharach's production mantle was not one she would have relished repeating – whereas for Dusty this was par for the course. Hence both her fearsome 'Oh my God' reputation and her latter-day standing as arguably the first woman in the country to regard the production of her records as her rightful territory, and not just the way she sang on them. Without wishing to denigrate the contributions of Johnny Franz and musical arranger Ivor Raymonde, the question may be asked: was Dusty Springfield the first woman record producer in Britain[q]? If so, has any woman overseen a more impressive catalogue of recorded pop music?

PART THREE

You Don't Own Me

You don't own me, don't try to change me in any way
You don't own me, don't tie me down 'cause I'll never stay

'You Don't Own Me', song by Madara and White,
recorded by Dusty Springfield in January 1964

The lesbian remains a kind of 'ghost effect'... elusive, vaporous, difficult to spot – even when she is there, in plain view, mortal and magnificent, at the center of the screen... The lesbian is never with us, it seems, but always somewhere else: in the shadows, in the margins, hidden from history, out of sight, out of mind...

Terry Castle (1993) *The Apparitional Lesbian: Female Homosexuality and Modern Culture*, Columbia University Press, p.2

'I don't imagine you on the Grand Canal'
'No, somewhere hidden... It does not matter where, as long as it is difficult to find, with many blind alleys on the way'

Colm Tóibín, *The Master*, Picador, p.248

Chapter seven

An Apparitional Lesbian?

 Few commentators on Dusty Springfield would disagree with Jill Jones' view that 'it was her battle to deal with her sexual preferences that drove her to hide behind all that make-up and the yearning pop arias she sang'[n]. In the decade since her death – and fostered in no small part by Valentine and Wickham's biographical 'revelations' – these 'preferences' concealed behind the image are assumed to have been directed towards women. The odd man might get an occasional sleepover but was more often than not a last resort when she was drunk, drugged or desperate. Despite on no public occasion saying she was any of these things, three words are regularly used to describe Dusty's sexuality: 'gay', 'lesbian' and 'bisexual'[n]. Different opinions are offered as to whether she 'came out' as one or other of these[n], partially 'came out' as one or other[n], or didn't 'come out' at all as any of them[n]. Opinions are offered as to whether she was wise to steer clear of labels[n], or whether attaching herself to one or other of them would have saved her pain and heartache[n]. Moreover, did she have a responsibility to her gay and lesbian fans to declare her true sexual orientation and add her name to the growing list of celebrities making a stand?[n] One writer has her 'openly supporting gay issues'[n], without specifying what these were; while another tantalisingly suggests 'by all accounts she was a voracious lesbian'[n], without providing any evidence for this vampire-like lust.

Working on the assumption that Lilian Faderman is correct to state that the 'criterion for identifying oneself as a lesbian' is 'you are one only if you consider yourself one'[n], I shall assume that since the public record provides no evidence of Dusty Springfield claiming to be 'lesbian', 'gay' or 'bisexual', the only sexuality tag one may safely attach to her is 'not exclusively heterosexual'. However 'not confused about her sexuality'[n] she was in private where 'she knew she was gay'[n], or however many lesbians in the Sixties 'knew that Dusty was gay but… didn't say it to anybody else'[n], 'non-straight' is how she will be referenced and assumed to have been. This anyway seems an appropriate term to describe Dusty Springfield's general personality-in-culture and need not be restricted to sexuality. Although Patricia Juliana Smith believes it is fair to call Dusty a 'lesbian' because, as Terry Castle defines the word elsewhere in her book, this is 'a woman whose primary emotional and erotic allegiance is to [her] own sex'[⁴], I prefer Faderman's perspective – you are what you say you are and not what someone else puts on you. With Dusty never claiming to be anything, it seems easier to go with what she suggested she was not. Publicly unadopted by Dusty though it was, however, the lesbian concept remains as elusive and marginal as in Terry Castle's 'ghost effect', and haunts proceedings with as apparitional a presence as Castle described. Never more uncannily than when, seated before a dressing room mirror in an often-repeated 1966 film extract, Dusty explains her short-sightedness by saying: 'I am constantly peering in mirrors and I'm actually not seeing anything'[⁴], thus unconsciously verifying the lesbian experience described by Adrienne Rich in the memorable phrase, 'you looked in the mirror and saw nothing'[⁴].

My Very Best – Love Dusty, Quantum Leap DVD, 2003 (from *Just Dusty*, originally broadcast 1966)

'You looked in the mirror and saw nothing'

Back in the early Sixties when Dusty Springfield's solo career began, lesbians were certainly conspicuous by their absence – at least from the perspective of the early twenty-first century when we are aware that they are certainly there to be found, however camouflaged. At the time, *any* sexual pairing other than male and female was barely acknowledged in the public arena. Although rumours of individuals being 'homo' or 'lesbian' or 'bisexual' ('gay' was yet to be used in common parlance to denote homosexuality) were whispered in dark corners, preferably at twilight time, everyone was publicly assumed to be heterosexual – inasmuch as the issue of sexuality rarely, if ever, came up in the popular press[5], at least directly. However bizarre the O'Brien family's habits were in other ways, Dusty's remembrance that 'sexuality was never discussed… it didn't exist'[5] made it typical of post-war households and British culture in general. Women who did not bat exclusively with men featured hardly at all on TV or cinema screens, or on the radio. The elderly Mavis played by Cicely Courtneidge in the 1962 British film, *The L-Shaped Room*, was a lonely exception. This was not so much because the mere idea of bedroom embraces between women remained inconceivable or distasteful in itself; but more because any sexual activity which did not involve a man was such a threat to the patriarchal order that it felt like mass psychic castration. Only a sense of terminal dread can explain the neurotic reaction of television and radio companies to any hint of lesbianism in their programmes across a 40-year period after the Second World War. When the BBC very occasionally broke its commitment to its non-sequitur of a 1965 policy – 'the average lesbian will always want to live in the shadows because that is where she wants to be'[5] – there were invariably recriminations and regrets, with backslidings, apologies and cancellations to follow as if encouraging the smallest step out of the shadows was an act of cultural insurrection.

The very absence of men in female couplings created panic, as with the 1958 TV comedy series *Trouble For Two*[5], in which two 'bachelor girls' shared a flat in flagrant breach of the 1950s cultural imperative of man, matrimony and motherhood. Thankfully for the state of the nation, the series was removed after a few episodes – a guest appearance by Nancy Spain, the only visible (to insiders) lesbian on TV, merely adding insult to injury. Four years later, a woman kissing the nape of another woman's neck was predictably cut before the transmission of the play, *Afternoon Of A Nymph*[5] – as was another kiss, that between the writer, Colette, and her lover, Missy, from *The Gentle Libertine*[5] in that liberation year of sex, drugs and rock 'n' roll, 1967. Being free to go to San Francisco with flowers in your hair did not permit you to sit by a vase of roses and a TV set, and watch one woman show affection for another. Flower power's love expectancy depended on where you put the flowers.

At least these were fictions and could be disbelieved. The true horror came when real women-who-loved-women intruded into the family living room by way of documentaries. There were two main such programmes during the Sixties. The first came via ITV's *This Week* in 1965; but if you fled into the garden screaming with the shock of hearing women relating things that had no place in any decent home, at least you couldn't say you'd not been warned. Before transmission a community-minded *Daily Express* writer had the sense to recommend preventative measures, declaring 'you still have time to stop this filth entering your living room'[5] and avoid infection. In the 1967 *Man Alive* documentary[5], warnings cannot be traced. However, the tragic plight of the women featured was warning enough; if you had any suspicion that you too might be 'that way inclined', you'd do better to find yourself a husband pronto, get pregnant and realise that a life without a man ain't no life at all. 'All You Need Is Love', the fab four were proclaiming that year, but if it's love like that, better say 'hello, goodbye' to it and save yourself a lifetime of sorrow.

Things improved only marginally during the Seventies. Although the mid-Sixties success of Frank Marcus's tragic-comedy *The Killing of Sister George* on stage and cinema screen acknowledged the existence of women-orientated women and provided much-needed, if stereotypically unhappy, role models, the media in general remained wary. 'Lesbian… is an ugly word'[h] viewers were told in a 1971 factual piece while a 1975 radio drama, 'the first modern play about lesbians on radio', *Now She Laughs, Now She Cries*, came with this endorsement from the *Radio Times*: 'It seems that most of us find the idea of relationships between two women totally unacceptable'[h] – presumably again because they excluded men. Not surprisingly, the programme was deemed 'unsuitable' to be repeated in the usual Sunday slot – well, with more men at home on that day, measures were understandably thought necessary to prevent digestive problems with the weekly roast. The situation regarding another Seventies radio programme – a pseudo-therapeutic series called *If You Think You've Got Problems*[h] – indicated that male homosexuality, however unsavoury, was preferable to female, and more in the realms of the discussable. An edition on this subject was broadcast with no fuss in 1975, but a similar programme on female homosexuality scheduled for transmission in 1977 was withdrawn and never aired. Even the early Eighties had their share of Sixties angst at the mention of the 'L' word. A *Gay Life* TV programme[h] asked people in the streets for their views on 'those invisible creatures called lesbians', while in 1982 the producers of the long-running series, *Tenko*, followed in the footsteps of the stage version of *Sister George* 17 years earlier by forbidding the utterance of the word 'lesbianism', since it represented 'turn off time' for viewers[h].

This atmosphere of shame, silence and barely disguised distaste provided the cultural backcloth – and possibly raison d'être – for Mary O'Brien to transform herself into Dusty Springfield. Whatever the nature of her non-straight sexual make-up, is it any wonder she preferred to keep it out of the public arena? Or at least, to do her best to do so. But as with other personality aspects which lay behind the singing and the image – the laborious construction and production work that went into the surface presentations – she felt compelled to let us know she was more than just a pretty voice and face. Try as she might, 'I just couldn't be a bimbo'[h] – or refrain from hinting at darker psychic activity. Vicki Wickham thought 'she needed to shut up'[h], but she didn't seem able to help herself. As if we couldn't hear her hurt in the notes she sang, she disclosed her pain and confusion in virtually every interview, and wrote several articles and letters during the 1960s as substitutes for the protest songs she was not composing any more.

The tone was set as soon as she went solo: 'Dusty Springfield's biggest problem is Dusty Springfield'[1] announced *Disc*'s June Harris in November 1963, thereby heralding 35 years of media tea dances which both dabbled with and shied away from self-disclosure. Although much has been made of her victimisation by the press, Jon Savage's analysis is nearer the mark. 'It would be wrong', he states, 'to represent Springfield as an innocent victim. She has enjoyed a flirtatious relationship with the press: often issuing outrageous quotes and seemingly unable to establish the limits of self-revelation'[1]. But whether it was 'revelation' or 'obfuscation' is debatable – and ultimately, is there any difference? Savage's 'flirtatious relationship' was 'enjoyed' as much by the press as by Dusty. Regarding the matter of her sexuality, each side led the other a very merry dance.

In a baffling paragraph from perhaps the earliest of her self-penned writings – in August 1964 – she uses the words 'normal', 'abnormal' and 'sick-minded' to describe a situation where she had complimented a young girl singer on her recent record only to hear later that the girl had thought this 'a bit odd' of her. 'Her sick little mind', Dusty wrote, 'had obviously twisted my compliments into something else'[1]. What else other than… well, the obvious? As Edward Leeson comments[1], the girl had either heard rumours and acted warily, or a pass had been made and been rebuffed. Either way, why was Dusty mentioning the incident if she had no wish for the public to associate her with alternative sexuality? It seems to have little connection with the rest of the article and has to be unravelled to make any sort of sense. There were other early hints that she might not be a boy-centred girl. 'My mother used to say, "Why can't you be like other girls?"'[1] she told readers earlier in 1964; and the following year was writing that she had never had any 'steady boyfriends like the other girls had'[1] or 'cried over' a boy standing her up. A good decade before sexuality was directly on the press agenda – and, in Madeline Bell's words, 'every interview would go to her sexuality'[1] – the urge simultaneously to reveal and conceal operated in Dusty Springfield's relationship with her public, alongside teasing remarks like: 'It would be too much a personal thing to discuss'[1]; 'I shall comment no further'[1]; and – especially calculated to arouse the curiosity of the most soporific journalist – 'I'd like to tell you more but it's very personal, and not the kind of thing you could put in print'[1]. No wonder they considered her fair game.

Perhaps Dusty felt she could hint at bits of the truth at this time because she had spent much of the first six months of 1964 building herself up as a bride-to-be-but-not-quite-yet by denying her imminent marriage to pop singer, Eden Kane, rumours of which were set up and spread by their Philips publicity machine. 'Are they engaged?'[1] headlined the *Daily Mirror* alongside a photograph of the two 'sweethearts' – but with Dusty saying 'It wouldn't be fair… to think about getting married… we have no definite plans', the answer seemed obvious. Dusty later twice denied the 'romance' had been a publicity gimmick: she was first 'furious'[q], then 'hurt when people suggested that it was all cooked up for publicity. I have never done anything like that for publicity'[q]. With Eden Kane confirming in 2005[q] that the whole thing had indeed been a publicity stunt, we may accept one of four options: Eden Kane 'misremembered'; it was done behind Dusty's back; she suffered an immediate attack of amnesia; she told a little white lie. Since the latter is the most probable of the four, it is fair to suggest that the writer Fay Weldon learnt a lesson or two from Dusty Springfield on how to deal with the press: 'I don't always tell journalists the truth', she said in 2006, 'I don't see it as part of my function'[q].

The manoeuvrings of what Edward Leeson calls 'the madrigal and pavane... of the Marriage Question'[q] were convoluted and specious. The 'man in my life' who had been 'frightened off'[q] by a Sunday newspaper in 1965 was probably no more real than either her hope that year 'to announce her engagement soon'[q] or a late-Sixties romance with DJ, Emperor Rosko[q], which seemed to be over and done with in a matter of days. And although the man named Howard with whom she had a relationship that 'lasted a year'[q] in the US during the Seventies seems to have existed – 'he always talked about Dusty and was madly in love with her'[q] – his role in her life was probably greatly inflated, and the 'traumatic' break-up of their 'affair'[q] referred to another separation. Even when she spoke of marriage with no specific man in mind, there was a sense that she was concocting ever more ingenious excuses to account for her single state. As with the artificiality of her appearance, she was skilled at getting in first. The reasons for her matrimonial reluctance varied[q]: her parents had set her a bad example; she was a Catholic and there could be no divorce; happiness could not be found in marriage; she wanted the man to be the boss but also didn't want it at the same time; she was too self-centred to bring up children; a failed marriage would be her failure as a human being; she wasn't mature enough. Whatever the reasons given, she discussed the subject with such regularity, as well as wearing rings to indicate she might already be a wife, that the music papers received letters like 'Please tell us if she has been secretly married'[q] and, even more curious, 'Was Dusty Springfield married on January 18 1969? If so, what is the name of her husband?'[q]

The longing for the security which a happy marriage represented for her came through in print as a deeply felt sadness which no number of fabricated story lines could hide or ease. When she made statements like 'marriage, if it happens, is the most desirable state to be in'[q] or 'this feeling of belonging'[q] which marriage can bring 'is something that I've always yearned for', she spoke from a heart that was wishing and hoping but all too keenly aware that the signs on her particular emotional path pointed in other directions. At least in the 1960s. In the more inclusive early Eighties, Australian TV viewers may have been surprised to hear chat show host, Mike Walsh, congratulate Dusty on 'getting married very soon'[q] to a groom whom she described as 'a Toronto musician. You wouldn't know him'. Her name was Teda Bracci, she turns up as one of the *Demons* Wickham and Valentine have Dusty *Dancing With* and, as if to prove to doubters that the ceremony occurred, subsequently appears in a wedding photo with her bride in a 2006 edition of the *Daily Mail*[♮]. The 'desirable state' did not last long, however, and could hardly have offered Dusty the 'feeling of belonging' which she craved. The wedding was not on 18 January 1969 and the groom was named neither Eden nor Howard – but Dusty Springfield did, however briefly, get 'married'.

Although press discussion of alternate sexuality was taboo in the Sixties, for those who read and pondered on the small print, reasons for Dusty Springfield's reluctance to get married other than those stated were there to be deciphered – often on the back page of the *New Musical Express*. In a section called 'tail', the 'Alley Cat' wrote single sentences about pop people in a kind of 'guess what X was seen doing this week' tittle-tattle way, usually of a fairly harmless nature. In the mid-Sixties three apparently trivial statements were made concerning Dusty and Madeline Bell; 'Singer Madeline Bell one of Dusty Springfield's closest friends'[♮]; 'Close friends: Dusty Springfield and American singer Madeline Bell'[♮]; 'Is Dusty Springfield for whom the Madeline Bell tolls?'[♮] Together they seemed to be telling the reader something. A week after Sandie Shaw had told a *Disc* reporter that she preferred to hear Dusty singing on her own than with other girls[♮], the question appeared, 'Dusty Springfield is puzzled: why doesn't Sandie Shaw like her singing with other girls?'[♮] which, for *NME* readers who had not seen *Disc*, would have been totally meaningless unless they could read between the lines. In 1968/9 insinuating sentences included: 'Close friends – Dusty Springfield and US singer, Norma Tanega'[♮] and 'Flat mates: Dusty Springfield and US singer, Norma Tanega'[♮]. A slight change of wording in 1971 to accommodate 'US tennis star, Billie Jean King'[♮] imparted the same message. At the time of her professional fracas with jazz musician Buddy Rich in the spring of 1967, Dusty must have been sufficiently annoyed to complain because two weeks after printing 'Buddy Rich told London theatre audiences, "Dusty Springfield is my favourite boy singer"'[♮], the Alley Cat issued 'an apology… for printing Buddy Rich's unjustified remarks against Dusty Springfield'[♮].

Reaching a larger and more varied audience than the back pages of a music paper, the *Observer* implied Dusty's alternative lifestyle in two late Sixties articles. Tony Palmer mentioned 'an unhappy series of relationships with girl-friends'[♮] whilst the flat-share friendship between Dusty and Norma Tanega which Marcelle Bernstein wrote about was particularly close, it seemed. 'The double bed', Bernstein wrote[♮], 'looks quadruple at least'. And with Dusty doing one of her 'it's very difficult to be a completely natural woman in the company of a man'[♮] defensive explanations for nothing in particular, readers were left to draw their own conclusions. A typical Dusty half truth – 'I feel almost masculine. It's like being a husband' – ostensibly explaining the unequal financial status between herself and any male partner but ambiguous enough also to refer to her friendship with Norma, further muddied the waters and enhanced the sense that part of her wanted to say things about herself that another part sought to withhold.

When Terry Staunton of *NME* wondered in 1989 'how Miss Springfield coped with the closed closets of the sixties'[4], he would have found some sort of answer by consulting the music papers of that decade. A mere glance at some of the headlines[5] concerning her speaks volumes: '"I Can't Take Any More", Says Dusty', 'Cordell Marks Goes In Search Of The Happy Side of Dusty', 'What Makes Dusty Tick?' and 'What's Wrong With Me', all from 1964; 'I Feel A Bit Of A Fraud' and 'Why Dusty Was Worried', both 1965; 'Dusty's Secret Fear', 'It Seems The Powers That Be Have A Let's Punish Dusty Springfield Period' and 'Sometimes I Hate Being A Star', from 1966; 'Where Is Dusty Going?', 'The Personal Turmoil of Dusty Springfield' and 'Dusty: Searching So Hard To Find Herself', from 1967; 'Dusty Says: I Want To Hit Back' and 'The Penalty Of Being A Star: She Cries Once A Day', both 1968; and 'Dusty Is Still Asking: How Can I Be Sure?', 'Dusty: Fed Up With The Drudgery' and 'Have You Ever Been Afraid Of Losing Your Mind?', all 1970. However angst-ridden the titles of the articles about her, however forlorn the things she said, she seemed to reach the end of her tether in the year she began to fade from sight for a while, 1971, by writing a letter from New York in reaction to a reader's comments. 'What is Dusty Springfield playing at? May I say that I am not "playing" at anything? Unless it's being a human being, and that's bloody hard work!'[6] She coped, it seems, by finally not coping. But though her sexuality went to the core of her and troubled the part of her that had to deal with press and public, her private 'closets' surely contained more than just the sexual material Staunton was referring to – it would be foolhardy and simplistic to attribute all the 'bloody hard work' she experienced in life to these aspects of her nature.

Anyone who has never heard of Dusty Springfield, given a stack of press cuttings of articles and interviews from the 1960s, would surmise that, far from these years being a period of fame, fortune, travel, constant praise, respect and immense popularity, this time in the woman's life was one of struggle and hardship with nothing going right; years when she was trying to work out who she was, what she wanted from life, where she wanted to be, how she was going to turn around her current situation of poor self-image and emotional poverty so that something positive would come of it. Could good fortune ever have meant so little or sounded so bleak and undesirable? It would not be fair to describe what she was expressing as 'one long moan': another headline read 'The Wild, Whacky World of Dusty Springfield', and, given her charm and debunking sense of humour, there were also the inevitable likes of 'Dusty Whoops It Up!', 'Dusty Does The Tweety-Pie Bit', 'Dusty Day Of Giggles' and 'Dusty Gets Bill For Bunfight'. But the overall impression is of a woman for whom money, fame and adoration compensated not at all for some deep hurt which could not be cauterised – except, indirectly, through song. 'Dear Dusty' a 'former love' is reported as saying, 'she could always feel a dead sea beneath her particular crest of a wave'[q].

Whatever caused and sustained the malaise at the heart of her, it almost certainly stemmed from early childhood and held material of great emotional complexity. In Dusty Springfield's case the 'closed closets' were more an interior than external threat and included – but did not consist of – guilt and fear about public exposure around sexuality issues. Reading what she said and wrote in print in the Sixties and across the subsequent 30 years, it is difficult to disagree with her own comment 'I shall only be joyous very fleetingly'[q] or her friend Simon Bell's assessment that 'there wasn't anything that... made her that happy'[q]. Although the wayward wit, absurd sense of humour and sheer verve and power of her up-tempo recordings thankfully prevent Dusty from being typecast as a mere tragedy queen – she herself declared, 'I'm not a tragic person. I don't want to be seen that way'[q] – Billie Jean King's view that much of her conduct was of a manic-depressive nature[q] is probably not too wide of the mark. While some people were understandably shocked and saddened to see displayed in the pages of Wickham and Valentine's *Dancing With Demons* the destructive extremities of self-harm which overtook her in the Seventies and Eighties[q], the surprise factor was negligible for anyone who had read or heard her carefully. And for those like Simon Frith who thought there was 'an air of failure'[q] about her or *Q* magazine's Peter Kane for whom her 'promise [was] tragically unfulfilled... there might have been so much more'[q], the retort must be that we should be thankful – given her hyper-sensitive disposition, low self-esteem and fragile state of mental health – that there was as much as there was. Or even that she managed to sing at all. After all, if Dusty Springfield had recorded only a dozen songs, wouldn't they would be worth more than a hundred tracks by almost any other singer?

Whether or not the main reason Dusty left Britain for the USA in the early Seventies was due to being hounded by the press over her sexuality – she herself gave it as 'one reason why I didn't want to stay here'[q] – the interview she gave to Ray Connolly in the *Evening Standard* in 1970 certainly served as a marker in her cultural history, separating the ubiquitous but asexual Dusty Springfield of the 1960s from the sporadically present, half-remembered sexual outsider of later years. The groundwork for her statement had been laid in the Bernstein article the previous year. 'They say you're either a prostitute or a lesbian'[q] she had complained there – words which presumably helped her pluck up sufficient courage for the mixture of honesty and circumvention which characterised the Connolly interview, and established her reputation as perhaps the first major artist in pop, male or female, to put sexuality on the public agenda. After describing herself to Connolly as 'promiscuous'[q] and 'very unfaithful' and acknowledging that 'a lot of people say I'm bent', which she had 'almost learned to accept', she then came out with one of her most memorable 'outrageous quotes': 'I'm as perfectly capable of being swayed by a girl as by a boy. More and more people feel that way. I don't see why I shouldn't'. You can almost sense the 'Whew! Now I've said it. You've got what you want. Maybe you can leave me alone and I can stop having to make things up.' In 1999 Connolly himself confirmed that she had been 'relieved at finally confronting the gossip'[9]. The trouble for both press and Dusty was that before this announcement, as Connolly also said, 'the subject just wouldn't have come up' in interviews, but once it had been put on the public agenda, it was up for grabs by anyone encountering Dusty Springfield for professional purposes – just as it was for singer k.d. lang after her more explicit lesbian acknowledgment in later years[9]. The matter of Dusty's sexuality pursued her for the rest of her life with a more high-profile tenacity than before 1970; but if it bothered her, she was the one who, however cornered, had made it public property.

Although her words on that occasion have been discussed and reprinted many times, the sadness of them has rarely been remarked on. An exception is Patricia Juliana Smith who finds her fear of being thought 'a big butch lady' and having 'her sense of being a woman' 'undermined' by 'being mixed up in a gay scene', rightly 'indicative of the baleful self-image for which many, if not most, lesbians suffered'[9]. Of course, her statement was brave at a time when, as Connolly said, 'to admit in public to being anything less than 100 per cent heterosexual was considered artistic suicide for a pop star'[9], and her courage should be applauded. But, in the usual Dusty way and for the heterosexual majority, her words teased as much as they communicated, concealed and revealed in equal measure and set things up for a even giddier series of 'will she?/won't she?' cat 'n' mouse skirmishes with the press once she re-emerged from Californian seclusion later in the decade. Simon Bell is probably correct to think it might have been easier for all concerned 'if she had been absolutely clear and gotten the subject out of the way' but 'she couldn't do it for whatever reason'[9].

She thus kept the 'mystique, a sense of belonging outside her own space and time'[9] that Peter Doggett wrote about and which may, in the final analysis, have been more important to her than run-of-the-mill openness and clarity-of-focus; so that she would have said, with Andy Warhol, 'I'd prefer to remain a mystery'[9]. Ironically, at the very start of her life as a soloist, Derek Johnson wrote, 'Last weekend I set about the tricky task of locating Dusty Springfield'[9]. If, with an additional layer of irony, she has still not been found by press and public after a near 50-year search, it is because, at certain levels, she never existed outside the imagination of a girl called Mary. Dusty never sang a song called 'Detour Ahead' but there is a line in it which fits her as artist and celebrity better than almost any song she did sing: 'The further you travel, the harder to unravel the web'.

Chapter eight

Butch Roars and Girlish Shrieks

 In addition to comments on Dusty Springfield's appearance and vocal colourings in the 1999 obituaries, there were several references to her standing as a gay icon. *The Times* said that 'she became something of an icon for gays and lesbians'[ʜ], while for the *Financial Times* 'she earned a status… as a gay icon'[ʜ]. In the *News of the World*, Richard Stott lamented the fact that she 'became saddled with that dreaded "gay icon" tag'[ʜ], whilst A.N. Wilson in the *Evening Standard* considered the same label to have been 'slightly absurdly'[ʜ] attached to her. Considering the regularity with which the words 'gay icon' have been applied to Dusty Springfield across the past 30 years, one can sympathise with these writers' frustration at the gratuitous dumbing down of a unique and original artist to the level of cliché. However, despite recent mentions of her name to conjure up a gay lifestyle – Sean, a gay character in *Coronation Street* receiving one of her records as a present, for instance[ʜ], or a Dusty Springfield record reported as playing on a Philadelphia juke box to indicate gay clientele[ʜ] – calling Dusty a 'gay icon' or using her name as a short-hand for gay or lesbian identification[ʜ] may have had its day. Stott and Wilson need worry no longer.

The inability to take the 'gay icon' label seriously stems as much from her own debunking of the myth in the 1990s with French and Saunders as from any other factor. Dressed as two gay men awaiting the identity of the 'biggest icon ever?'[ʜ], the two comedians guess 'Judy Garland? Not Cilla? Not Dusty?' then scream ecstatically as she appears and knowingly remarks that she's 'performing at Heaven tonight'. Nowadays her 'gay icon' tag tends to be accompanied by an 'oh dear, here we go again' mocking type of humour, as when her old mates, French and Saunders, updatedly include her in a 2007 *Gay Times* interview amongst the 'gay icons' who they're 'totally in love with'[ʜ], or when Amy Lamé jocularly enthuses in *Time Out* two months later, 'If there is anyone that could be the lesbian icon in the world forever and ever amen, it's Dusty Springfield'[ʜ]. This is not to say that she has lost her allure as a lesbian and gay-associated performer but merely to suggest that the connection now needs a slight 'isn't it silly?' tongue-in-cheek tone of voice to sound halfway credible. Twice, in the late Nineties before she died, the magazine *Boyz* pointed the way by declaring 'Yeah, we know. You always thought Dusty Springfield was for... older homosexuals'[9] and then proceeding to suggest that, 'before you start thinking that Dusty is just for old poofs'[9], she deserved a wider audience.

In the decade since her death, journalist Paul Mathur's 1988 wish to 'see her appeal widen'[9] so that she could escape the 'brash solitude' of gay appropriation seems to have been granted. The use of her voice on the soundtracks of two highly popular TV programmes – *Prime Suspect* and *EastEnders* – to bid farewell in 2006–7 to two 60-something iconic female characters, Jane Tennison and Pauline Fowler[9], placed her sound and atmosphere back in UK living rooms with suitably commemorative mainstream impact. And the huge public vote enabling Katy Setterfield's wannabe Dusty to win 2008's BBC1 *The One and Only* contest seemed to confirm Ms Springfield's rehabilitation as a singer for everyone, whatever their class, colour, gender or sexual preference. On this evidence, the general appeal she had in the 1960s may have returned after more than 35 years. Indeed, the signs are that Dusty has come 'full circle' in a way she did not imagine in 1994, and is now undergoing posthumous reinvention as a – dare I say it? – post-gay icon[9]. Or just a great singer for *anyone* to listen to and enjoy.

For a while in the Seventies and Eighties, though, her appeal seemed limited to what she called 'a cult following'[9] and she would often be thought of as one of the newly established 'gay icons' – stars – almost by definition female – whose devoted fan base was assumed to consist of mainly lesbians and gay men. The civil partnership of 'gay' and 'icon' seems to have taken place in the mid-Seventies as an attempt by journalists to account for the feverish scenes of excess and adoration witnessed at certain performances they attended. Like most things gay-iconic, the instigator was the woman Rufus Wainwright has recently called 'beyond a gay icon... a gay saint'[9], Judy Garland. There was nothing new about auditorium theatricals being as over-the-top as occurrences on stage but in the Fifties and Sixties, when reviewers began to notice and attempt to describe the audience's behaviour at her concerts, the paving stones of her pink brick road were laid and the sign posts positioned for other audiences to follow.

One of the first to draw attention to the 'demonstration of mass affection' at a Judy Garland concert was Tony Brown, whose experience at London's Dominion Theatre in 1957 was 'almost frightening', and prompted him to ask 'how could any artist live up to this unstinting adulation?'[9] Ten years later, American journalists did not mince their words. *Esquire* writer, William Goldman complained about the 'flutter of fags'[9] at one of Judy's Palace concerts in New York, while for the reviewer in *Time* an equally disparaging phrase, 'the boys in the tight trousers'[q], served to make the same point. The first such innuendo in the 'No Sex Please Unless It's Male and Hetero' Britain of the Sixties was probably the one tucked coyly away on a 1966 *NME* back page: 'There were more queens at Shirley Bassey's Prince of Wales opening than at a royal wedding'[q]. And it was this singer's audience which incited further comment five-years later when Neil Roberts, reviewing a performance at the Royal Festival Hall, looked on aghast as 'scores of young males hurled themselves at the stage, presenting her with bouquets, kisses and grasping at her hands'[q]. Snorting 'I suppose it'll keep them off the streets', and apparently ignorant of Judy Garland or Maria Callas, Roberts wondered, 'Is this the birth of a new kind of star worship?'

Whatever 'star worship' Dusty Springfield attracted in the Sixties, it was not much remarked on at the time. Apart from the odd line in the months after she went solo, saying that when she 'ran on' stage, 'the girls squealed for her'[q] or, perhaps more tellingly, 'it's a personality which appeals to members of her own sex just as effectively as to boys'[q], comment on the make-up of her audiences or buyers of her records is little in evidence. Patricia Juliana Smith suggests Dusty's *Ready Steady Go!* miming appearances were directed at the girls in the studio and that 'homosocial sensibilities' are 'undeniable' in her early performances[q], but this seems to be a case of generalising from one edition of the programme. Smith goes on to say that her 'court' came to consist of 'predominantly young gay men'[q] but however true this may have been with regard to her manager, hairdresser and other staff members[q], evidence of her fan base being mainly of this ilk during the years of her Sixties stardom is not available. Also, despite accounts of adolescent adoration by Elton John and Dale Winton[q], most of the published memoirs of what Dusty meant to them at that time are written by women[q]. Even if it can be reasonably surmised that many of the men and women who subsequently iconised her were – and are – gay, and became fans of hers in the Sixties, it does not follow that the majority of her fan base at the height of her popularity was gay or lesbian. Indeed, when Dusty was filling concert halls across the UK, gaining sizeable audiences for her TV appearances and selling large numbers of records, the likelihood is that it was not.

Although it may well be the case that Dusty Springfield was intuited by those outside the heterosexual mainstream to be 'one of their own', there is little hard evidence beyond supposition or the fact that her records were played in gay women's bars that she was received as one thing by the straight majority while secretly signalling 'otherwise' to a coterie of knowing followers. While perhaps true at an instinctive level, singer David McAlmont's contention that 'her sexuality was obvious to the gay crowd'[q] has no research findings to back it up. The assessment by Paul Gambaccini that the 'part of the minority of lesbian culture that went out to clubs'[9] and 'gay men who socialised together would have known and celebrated Dusty' is sound enough but hardly suggestive of non-straight people having antennae about her which others lacked. Certain TV performances with hip-wriggling male dancers – those during her BBC series and a show hosted by Liberace[9], for instance, plus a knowing 1979 send-up with Sha Na Na of 'You Don't Have To Say You Love Me' – displayed such a delirious sense of camp that *anyone* could have deduced that her sensibility, if not her actual sexuality, lay in maverick directions. On a 2006 *South Bank Show*, however, Charles Shaar Murray enlightened us with the information that Dusty used 'polari' or 'very specific gay slang'[9] in her interviews. She apparently spoke in this 'coded sense… in a lot of her public utterances'. So what struck the uninitiated as half-truths are now revealed to have been secret messages to be deciphered by those in the know.

'Gay icon', then, had yet to be born as a term of any kind of endearment in the heterodominant Sixties. Its birth occurred in the 1970s a few years after a gay and lesbian stowaway finally wedged open the door of the post-war closet it had been cooped up in, popped its head out, shook off the moth balls, took a few deep breaths and decided it had as much right to strut about in the big wide world as Mr and Mrs Straightways. Hints of what was to come for Dusty Springfield now that gay issues featured more visibly in press and the media surfaced occasionally in the early Seventies – as when she was described as being 'at the top of the gay girls' hit parade' on a 1974 TV play called *Girl*[9]. Generally, though, with Dusty lying low for most of the decade, reference to the type of audience she attracted had no reason to surface until she gave interviews to promote a new album in 1978. The one with Keith Howes in *Gay News* spoke of her 'enormously strong gay following'[9] to whom she was 'grateful'. With the endearment 'I love gay people. I'm comfortable with them. I respect gay people', she established a public bond between herself and a section of the population whose dedication to her and her music she referred to the following year as 'a fantastic show of loyalty'[9]. She had faded from view in 1972–3 as a mainstream entertainer, albeit a grumpy one, and re-emerged five years later as a half-forgotten singer whose appeal was strictly confined to non-straight minorities; she departed as family fare and returned as a Brit gay icon to rival Miss Bassey. Such are the vagaries of pop music.

But, as with Shirley, Judy and Bette Midler at her early Seventies 'health club' concerts, Dusty could hardly become a fully fledged gay icon until she and her fans had demonstrated to the press the passionate extremities of their mutual devotion. Such occasions presented themselves in London during 1979 – firstly at a series of concerts at the Theatre Royal, Drury Lane, then at the Royal Albert Hall in December. Like the American writers with Judy Garland, *NME*'s Ian Birch reacted at Drury Lane with 'stomach-churning embarrassment'[9] to 'the utter devotion' of 'a hefty gay contingent ranging from radical feminists to the more foppish caricature'. When Dusty characteristically forgot the lyrics, this 'ecstatic' 'capacity audience' 'went bananas… and dissolved into a fit of the giggles'; when she 'demanded' a 'butch roar and a nice, girlish shriek', they 'yelped'. Either way, the excitement seems to have left Birch totally confounded. Press witnesses of the Albert Hall occasion had even greater difficulty trying to explain what they saw. For Jeremy Myerson writing in the *Stage*, 'her effect on an adoring audience was quite extraordinary to watch'[q] whilst, in a long review in the *Observer*, Dave Gelly found 'the vehemence, even the hysteria'[q] of what he saw 'quite alarming' – so much so, in fact, that trying to account for the yelling, outstretched arms, throwing of flowers and running to the stage of 'the cloud of adoration' in the audience, he could only ask rhetorically, 'how does one explain such scenes?' Another Albert Hall reviewer, Nick Underwood, talked of her fans' 'undying faith and love'[q]. By 1985, and Dusty's next resurrection, courtesy of Peter Stringfellow, this had come to be taken so much for granted that virtually every interview and article mentioned either her 'strong gay and lesbian following'[q] or the 'fierce loyalty among the gay community'[q] she inspired – a connection that continues to this day, but in the more muted fashion suggested earlier.

There has been no shortage of answers to Dave Gelly's question. Commentators have agreed that Dusty's glamour, drama, hurt, survival instinct, bloody-mindedness, anguish and sheer emotionality held up a mirror in which gay men and lesbians could see themselves. The landscape of cracks, potholes and jagged edges she attempted to negotiate reflected the one they inhabited themselves. This sense of Dusty's vulnerability and being, in her own words, 'always the victim… on a knife edge'[q] like Judy Garland and Shirley Bassey has been especially highlighted by commentators. Echoing perhaps Dusty's explanation, 'I cry a lot, they were there to cry with me'[q], Aida Pavletich dubbed her 'St Jude, to whom the faithful flock when hope is gone'[q] while Kris Kirk thought 'her painfully sad voice… expressed for gay men feelings they felt themselves'[q]. Simon Bell assessed her appeal similarly by suggesting that 'her wonderful heart-rending songs' were the sort that 'a certain kind of gay man – and woman – love to sit and listen to'[q]. Her legacy consists of many types of music and a kaleidoscope of moods and atmospheres but some gays don't want to have fun. Or not, it seems, with Dusty.

However, Dusty's appeal for lesbian and gay consumers is broader than this – and does include fun in plenty. Because of her own sexual ambiguity, she was – is – about the only performer amongst the several women of gay iconic status assumed to have shared her fans' outsider sexuality. Her star atmosphere thus uniquely reflects her followers' feelings of 'not belonging' to the general culture and viewing it from a skewed angle; the knowledge that her lifestyle was neither straightforwardly heterosexual nor family-centred adds a dimension to the attraction missing from other fan–gay icon relationships. Gay-sympathetic songs like 'Closet Man', 'Beautiful Soul' and 'Born This Way', recorded in the Seventies and Eighties at the height of her 'cult' attraction for gay men and lesbians, strengthened the connection. The suggestion made earlier that alternative viewpoints and marginalised perspectives could be detected in the voice itself, and contributed to Dusty being heard as not-like-anyone-else further enhanced her appeal for sexual outlaws and social non-conformists.

Shared too, and probably because of this complicity, was the mocking sense of playfulness which star and fans adopted towards the idea of gay iconicity, with Dusty becoming one of the first to treat the matter of her iconic status as a bit of a laugh. This 'knowing sense of camp' and 'being in on the joke'[q] mentioned by Andy Gill further boosted her appeal, and set the trend for subsequent tongue-in-cheek send-ups by Madonna and Kylie Minogue. What gave Dusty Springfield her singularity as a gay icon was this combination of drama-queen wallowing and in-on-the-joke camp parody. No-one else so skilfully and elegantly walked a tightrope between the two modes, or got such mileage from their conceptual possibilities. For Barry Walters, the 'mix of public exuberance and personal anguish'[q] make Dusty Springfield 'the quintessential pop icon' for gay men and lesbians who experience similar vicissitudes of feelings and attitudes in their own lives.

But all this raises more questions than simply answering the one Gelly asked nearly 30 years ago. Amongst them, in no particular order, are these; they are all rhetorical and point the way for research into areas which, as with the issue of race's relationship to voice, call not just for further research but for any research at all: is there and has there ever been a 'gay sensibility'? what changes have occurred in gay and lesbian reactions to Dusty and other 'iconic' stars over the past 30 or so years? do young gay men and lesbians find Dusty and other female stars alluring or even interesting, and if so, interesting in what ways? ditto of straight youngsters; do young lesbians and gay men create or need icons in the way they were created and needed in less 'liberated' times? the term 'gay icon' is still used, but is it increasingly anachronistic and empty of meaning? what does the term mean anyway, and when, where, how and why did it originate? does the assumption that homosexuals comprise most of the fan base of Dusty Springfield have basis in fact – as Barry Walters implies by writing 'an Englishman professing a love for Dusty is akin to an American declaring his love of Judy Garland – a dead giveaway of serious fagdom'[q]? what proportion of the fan bases of other 'gay icons' like Streisand, Madonna, Kylie and Bassey[q] are lesbian and gay? and what are the gendered and sexuality aspects of musical and vocal performance which signify these things to the listener?

The last question on this list – but not the last potential question about music and gender/sexuality issues – is: would I be writing this book if I were 30 years old and straight? Most of these matters concern fans and what makes them tick. Clive Bloom might think 'there has been much work on fans and fandom'[3] but the entire area is woefully under-researched. About the only music fan base we have any reliable information about beyond conjecture is that of Bruce Springsteen, thanks to Daniel Cavicchi's pioneering work in the Nineties[4].

Although the next section does not seek to fill the gap by adding, to the commentaries documented in these pages, one person's experience as a fan of Dusty Springfield, the interpretation of her as a queer rather than gay/lesbian cultural figure is my own, supported by rationales from queer theory. Some of the material presented in earlier sections is reconfigured in the light of this theoretical perspective.

Chapter nine

Que(e)rying the Icon

 The suggestion that Dusty Springfield resides in culture more comfortably as a 'queer' rather than 'gay' or 'lesbian' icon[1] requires an exploration of the respective theoretical positions occupied by these words. Approaching the discussion from a linguistic angle may be a useful starting point.

As we have seen, Dusty's gay/lesbian standing is unusual inasmuch as the adjectives 'gay' and 'lesbian' may be loosely applied to both her and some of her fan base, whereas with almost every other 'gay icon' the meaning is narrower. The fan base is understood as gay but not, as with Kylie or Shirley Bassey for instance, the icon. Calling Dusty Springfield a gay icon and acknowledging that she herself may be gay or lesbian follows the linguistic norm where an adjective ascribes qualities to the noun it precedes rather than transfers to that noun attributes of those who create or possess it as with the other, more usual meaning of 'gay icon'. With normal usage predicting 'gays' icon' or 'icon of gays and lesbians', most of the labelling of icons as 'lesbian' or 'gay' is linguistically aberrant whereas in Dusty Springfield's case 'gay icon' functions as linguistically normal.

Or rather, with the term operating here at a dual semantic level, it functions as simultaneously normal and not normal. When, as in this instance, both x and not-x – 'normal' and 'not normal' – are valid, we approach a seemingly illogical and whacky world where all notions of reality and rationality are stood on their heads, collapsing in on themselves down a black hole of uncommon sense. In language terms alone, referring to Dusty Springfield as a 'gay icon' smacks of something queer.

But what is meant by 'queer' in the term 'queer theory' (or as Donald E. Hall more aptly would have it, 'theories'[2])? How, conceptually, is it different from the other words used to describe sexuality? Like 'quantum', 'queer' disrupts and destabilises received ideas of fixity and normality, and wriggles out of being pinned down as yet another system of classification. In David Halperin's view, 'it acquires its meaning from its oppositional relationship to the norm. Queer is, by definition, *whatever* is at odds with the normal, the legitimate, the dominant'[ᵇ]. Alexander Doty too sees queer readings or discourses as containing 'a wide range of positions within culture that are... non-, anti- or contrastraight'[ᵇ]; though it is not clear whether he equates 'straight' with 'heterosexual' or 'normal', the ambiguity itself serves queer purposes which are almost always shifting, multivalent and indeterminate.

Unlike 'gay', 'lesbian', 'straight' and 'bisexual', 'queer', as applied to sexuality, questions assumptions that identity can be described by means of labels and categories. Whilst the other words seek to name and affirm identity in terms of sexuality, 'queer' troubles the very notion that identity ever stays still long enough to be positioned or given any name at all – in sexual, or indeed *any* referential terms. Thus, when Alan Sinfield enjoins us 'to entertain more diverse and permeable identities'[ᵇ], he pluralises the word to raise the possibility of several identities for each person rather than a fixed one which is permanent and stable.

From queer perspectives, the very concept of identity becomes suspect; as Annamarie Jagose suggests, 'queer is always an identity under construction, a site of permanent becoming'[ᵇ]. The word 'identity' presupposes that human nature is known, understood, and sorted, but our Freudian heritage insists otherwise – that the more we learn about our behaviour and its unconscious motivations, the more unfathomable we become to ourselves. Does it make sense for any slippery and imprecisely delineated human being to claim and affirm a personal sexual identity? The fact that we believe we are in a position to do so, and are busily sticking this or that label on to ourselves and others, may be thought to confirm the scale of the self-delusion.

Besides, why do twentieth and twenty-first century people believe sexuality aspects are a central part of who they are? Shouldn't we agree with Andrew Bennett and Nicholas Royle that it is 'odd... that our social worlds and our social prejudices are organised around a choice – the sex of our sexual partners'[ᵇ] rather than 'choices about eating, or not eating, meat'? Statements like 'she's straight' and 'I'm gay' may serve necessary social ends and psychological needs but, from more philosophical queer perspectives, they reduce mysterious and complex inner processes to simplistic and superficial slogans, and fail to account for the essential mutability and unpredictability of human nature and desire.

For much of the last century, of course, 'queer' functioned as a term of abuse for homosexuals, and – like the use of 'nigger' by black people – was rarely used outside camp, self-mocking contexts by those it disparaged. Although the word seemed to be dying out in the Seventies and Eighties, in the early Nineties – inspired by thinkers like Foucault, Judith Butler and Eve Kosofsky Sedgwick[ᵇ] – it was recycled by a later generation of sexual non-conformists into a proud and defiant self-affirmation of how they regarded themselves and their positions in mainstream society. In the USA especially, 'queer theory' developed credentials as a term for the academic study of dissident human sexuality.

Since the original meanings of 'queer'[♭] connect with being 'across' or 'athwart' or 'betwixt and between', 'neither one thing nor the other but floating here and there and nowhere', the word fitted in well with deconstructionist ideas of undecidability and estrangement, gaps, fissures and discontinuities. In Suzanne Walters' words, 'queer' is 'the perfect postmodern trope, a term for the times, the epitome of knowing ambiguity'[♭]. With its more recent negative homosexual connotations already associating the word with deviant forms of sexuality, 'queer' has become, over the past twenty years, a resonant semantic questioner and subverter of what Michael Warner has called 'regimes of the normal'[♭].

Because 'queer' is more inclusive of potentials and open to possibilities than 'gay', 'lesbian', 'heterosexual' or even the more open-ended 'bisexual', as well as uninterested in promoting identity categories and disrespectful of boundary markers, it welcomes the border crossings of those who feel they don't easily fit into these types of socially constructed sexuality groupings – people otherwise ignored or invisibilised such as: transgendered, intersexed, asexual, celibate, and sexually self-contained people; those who sense they slip and slide – at different stages of their lives and in varying moods – from one thing to another but don't consider themselves bisexual; or people who say they are 'lesbian' or 'bi' or 'gay' for reasons of social expediency. Even people who are 'straightforwardly heterosexual' in their patterns of thought and choice of partners may consider themselves as functioning queerly if they feel capable – even if only imaginatively – of moving anywhere along the sex and gender, or even class and race, lines of inquiry, and choose to align themselves with those who do so in practice. 'Queer' and 'straight' are not necessarily incompatible bedfellows.

In the end, we are all queer in some sexual way or other for, whatever our object of choice during sexual activity, there may be an incongruity between the events taking place in the bedroom and the pictures which form in our heads. About masturbation fantasy scenarios we know next to nothing. How many of us, indeed, are fully aware of what is happening in our psyches during any kind of sexual arousal, never mind in the shifts and turns of our emotional involvements with others? The inner realm of sexual fantasy – what is going on in our minds when we get turned on – is likely to be almost as queer as sub-atomic movements at the quantum level. And we probably know and understand as little, or even less, about the material scurrying around in those dark and inaccessible recesses of desire.

While we are on terminology, it might be useful to say something about 'camp'[♭], for like 'lesbian', 'gay' and 'bisexual', that word has been used of Dusty Springfield, though with regard to her mocking aesthetics rather than her sexuality. When, for instance, Patricia Juliana Smith or Lee Everett describe Dusty as 'camp'[4], they are referring to those performative aspects which have been discussed – the ways in which the cosmetic, sartorial and stylistic elaborations of her appearance and the heightened dramas of her more melodramatic ballads exaggerated and parodied the looks and sounds which were their inspirations. Like 'queer', 'camp' is open to interpretation, but understood here to denote behavioural aspects like irony, humour and over-the-top artifice for the sake of effect. 'Camp' seems related to what we do or say, and how we act, and usually provokes mirth or laughter; 'queer' is more abstract, diffuse and elusive. While 'camp' does not necessarily disrupt the received social compartmentalising of sexuality and need not threaten the status quo, 'queer' cannot help but unsettle *all* the categories and socially structured frameworks it encounters, even its own conceptual applications as 'queer'. And so we return to Dusty.

As has been discussed, Dusty Springfield never publicly defined her sexuality in any socially sanctioned terms; we look in vain for an unequivocal statement like 'I am a lesbian' or 'I am a bisexual'. Despite – or because of – her refusal to put herself into any box or wear any label, she has had boxes and labels assigned to her. Earlier, in the belief that it was easier to describe her in terms of what she was not rather than what she was or might have been, I decided that the only respectful way to refer to her as a sexual person was with words like 'non-straight' or 'not heterosexual'. However, in doing so, I acknowledged that some people described her in other terms or formed the impression that she had indeed 'come out' about her sexuality, though not necessarily agreeing about what she came out as. Her equivocations led to varying interpretations as to what she had said about herself in public. With biographical tit-bits suggesting she generally preferred women to men, and Shaar Murray's 'polari' comment implying that she communicated in verbal secret code to those on her wavelength, the cultural understanding of Dusty Springfield's sexuality has become a free-for-all potpourri of speculation, with little consensus regarding the category she is best assigned to.

Already, we are treading on queer territory. Inasmuch as people seem to have received what little she said about herself on these matters in such different ways, Dusty resists being given a sexuality label which may be clearly and finally allocated to her like 'straight' to Tom Jones, 'gay' to Rock Hudson or 'lesbian' to k.d. lang. Whatever new 'revelations' lie ahead about her private life via biographies or docu-soaps, and however much her future status blows to and fro on the winds of reputation, as a cultural figure she is likely to remain sexually uncertain. Because of her liking for ambiguity and imprecision, and her inclination to keep the picture blurred, she will probably remain resistant to definition by a prescribed set of references. When she said 'I know that curiosity about my private life is the price I pay for having a public life'[4], she recognised that she would have to put up with questions about matters she would rather not discuss; but in no way did she commit herself to answering them.

The more one reads the remarks she made about her sexuality, and sexuality in general, the more one sees how thoroughly she resisted being fitted into a standard-issue uniform on these matters – and thus the queerer she gets. The motivations behind her statements were, in all probability, defensive[*] and sometimes made when she felt her back was against the wall. Nonetheless, her words told truths about her nature which may not have surfaced in less challenging circumstances. On an everyday, practical level, they could be viewed as the 'half-truths' or 'obfuscations' I earlier suggested they were; seen from the perspectives of this section, however, they read like words of wisdom from the mouth of a queer theoretician.

With the words 'I'm not going to commit myself to being homosexual or heterosexual'[*], she acknowledged the socially sanctioned binary boxes but refused to place herself in either of them. Her statement on another occasion that 'They seem to want me to be either gay or straight – they can't handle it if someone's both'[*] questioned the assumption that the one term excluded the other, raised the possibility of a sexual continuum and resisted being manoeuvred into regarding sexuality as a matter of an either/or choice. Referring to herself as a putative lesbian, her remark, 'That doesn't make me one and that doesn't *not* make me one'[*] was similarly open to the possibility of being both this and that, or possibly either or neither.

As for the process of 'coming out' which Andrew Duncan suggested in the mid-Eighties she would 'have little to lose by [doing]'[*], she asked 'why would I have to?' thereby questioning the assumption that any non-straight person had a social obligation to make an open declaration about their sexual orientation. In saying elsewhere 'it's other people who want you to be something or other – this or that'[*], and 'Who's to say what you are?'[*], she questioned the authority and legitimacy of the compartments she was expected to fit into and resisted making any attempt to satisfy other people's needs, even though she knew that, whatever her view on the matter, she would have labels thrust on her: 'You're bound to get tagged with labels when you don't give any information of a very personal nature'[*].

On one occasion she is said to have made a remark suggesting that heterosexuality was as much a mental straitjacket as any other sexuality packaging. 'What about all those heterosexuals? It must be very unpleasant for them too, having to hide in the closet'[*]. Neither gay nor lesbian, nor bi-perspectives would regard the majority category of heterosexuality as closeted, but from a queer point of view, it could be as much of a confinement as any of the others; those who claim to be 'straight' and nothing else are confining their options to narrow pathways on the wide-open map of human sexuality, and curtailing their right to roam.

Other remarks she made in interviews where her sexuality was being probed could refer to more general issues. Categories she held no truck with. Serena Cross is right to say that 'though many have claimed that she was simply a lesbian, Dusty was adamant that she would not be confined by other people's categories'[q]. 'I hate categories'[q], she stated, 'people have run with trying to categorise me'[q]; but since 'all my life I've fought categories'[q], there was not much hope that she would ever willingly slot into one for the sake of conformity.

Unconsciously issuing her queer manifesto, she proclaimed, 'I don't want normality'[q], 'I question everything'[q], 'I feel neither here nor there'[q], and even 'It has nothing to do with being straight or gay'[q] – but everything to do with being queer perhaps? Although feeling like 'a stateless person'[q], she would rather keep herself in a not 'get-at-able'[q] position where 'I don't take stances'[q] than risk being taken up by any particular group and put her name to bandwagons and causes: 'I don't want to be owned by anyone, by any movement'[q]. Presumably identifying with the woman and the butterflies in a 1985 song she recorded – 'I ain't the kind you can tie down… I got to be free'[q] – she had a need to keep all her options open at all times and was wary of commitment to anyone or anything. Not for nothing, did the playwright Stephen Poliakoff call the sound her voice evoked that of 'a free spirit'[q].

She hardly needed to tell us that 'having a sense of the absurd has kept me going'[q] because it was clear from the early days of her career that she thrived on the ridiculous; bringing incongruous elements together was virtually her personal and professional ground rule. 'Sitting in my living room were my mum and dad, various elderly relatives, four drag queens, three nuns, a couple priests, and half the music industry'[q], she gleefully said on one occasion, with the inevitable punch line, 'Everybody got along great'. Creating something fresh and harmonious from disparate and potentially conflicting elements was a means of normalising the abnormal – an inclination natural to Dusty Springfield. Her urge to demolish the distinction between 'normal' and 'abnormal' and fuse the two together rendered defunct the binary concept referenced by words she mistrusted.

But it is not in sexuality issues alone that Dusty Springfield functions as a queer, rather than gay or lesbian, icon. Over almost *every* aspect of her image an aura of not-quite-normal hovers. Christian Ward, for one, is aware of it. Describing the pop style she created as 'burlesque and bouffant and bitchy and baffling'[q] and calling her 'a strange soul Thunderbirdette [sic]', whose 'decadent pop drama incarnate' signalled 'a disassociated personality', he expressed his consternation with her cultural configurations by exclaiming 'this isn't "normal"… This is where pop starts getting "really" weird'. Susan Shaw thought similarly. 'Struck by the eerie quality to her vocal performance'[h], she called Dusty's 'strange voice, entirely its own theatre', thereby suggesting a solitary, even lonely self-regard which acted independently of outside influence and performed from a script[h] of its own authoring.

Virtually everything written about her in previous chapters lends itself to queer appropriation. The entire reception of her in terms of colour is as disruptive of racial categories as her remarks on sexuality were with regard to those issues[h]. According to Dave Godin, people in the USA 'just couldn't understand why a nice white girl should want to sing like a nigger woman'[h]; while others like Larry Katz didn't know where to file her music except under 'soul', where she was the only white and British singer amongst the black Americans[h]. In both instances, the dividing screen between the separate black and white sectors was pushed aside just wide enough to encourage the artistic and social colour blendings of later years. In 1984, when Julie Burchill asked the question 'Where did beige music begin?'[h] she considered Dusty Springfield the originator, along with a later more self-conscious boundary-blurrer, David Bowie.

Whether or not they heard her as black, the many commentators who have mentioned her in terms of 'white' or 'coloured' have struck a discordant note. When her brother too, in his record review, got tangled up in the colour textures of the voice he grew up with, something decidedly queer was going on. Dusty's own statements to the effect that she felt ill at ease with being white – a black woman in a white woman's body and its variants – blew as much smoke at social expectations regarding how a well-brought-up white girl from the suburbs should think and behave as anything she said or withheld about her sexuality.

In matters of gender too, Dusty Springfield pushed boundaries and suggested the dividing lines between male and female were easily breached because made of such flimsy material. She also, as we have seen, questioned received notions of what it meant to be a woman. Through her performative strategies as a female-to-female drag queen, she merged lesbian and straight representations of the seductive female. By dressing up as a presumably straight woman – at least for the mainstream majority – and teasing straight men into fancying her, while at the same time querying Carole King's notion in her Aretha song that 'a natural woman' was brought into being by a man's ability to 'make [her] feel' that way[h], she at once attracted and deflected the male gaze, and turned herself into what Patricia Juliana Smith calls 'a curious lesbian simulacrum of a "girl"'[h].

Never more blatantly than on an Australian TV programme in 1967[h]. Although in many ways her whole act was a parody of the femme lesbian, and a means of bringing this proscribed representation into family living rooms – playfully revealing and concealing an aspect of her nature she was not prepared to discuss – only on this occasion did she make it obvious. She sang 'Twenty Four Hours From Tulsa' in a long blonde wig which fell over her eyes, and wore a high-collared white blouse and dark trousers. Surrounded by butch female dancers dressed as cowgirls in Stetson hats, she displayed the stereotypical butch–femme scenario to those aware of its existence; but for those who were not, she was simply a sexy broad in a hick bar somewhere en route to Tulsa, Oklahoma.

The probability is that she dared to signal so clearly only because it was on the other side of the world. At home on the beeb this was one type of girly girl she would not have given her public – and it may now be viewed as a rare example of Dusty Springfield performing overtly as a femme lesbian. Curiously, though, this characterisation seems as much of a masquerade as most of the others so that even when Dusty performed as a dyke, she still signalled dame-in-drag, more queer than lesbian in the complex personal and theatrical deferrals involved. This presentation too was just one more costume and persona she took from her wardrobe of girly-woman appurtenances; the deadpan seriousness of her mimed performance turned the hokey setting into a two-minute cameo of lesbian camp.

Brian Henderson's Bandstand, TCN Channel 9 DVD, 2004 (originally broadcast 22 October 1967 on GTV9)

'*A two-minute cameo of lesbian camp*'

By undermining accepted (mostly male) perspectives on woman-as-object-to-be-looked-at, and presenting woman as mutable, indecipherable, and fluid – always becoming yet seldom if ever arriving – Dusty Springfield upset gender apple carts and, whatever sexuality contours she assumed or evoked, poked fun at hand-me-down ideas of the gorgeous glamour girl as a normal or 'natural' woman.

In other aspects of her celebrity too, Dusty Springfield seldom functioned conventionally or conveniently. As we have seen, she ought by rights to have been working class to give the argument made in *Soul Britannia* a neat overall fit; instead of which, she came from an impeccable middle-class background. Through singing 'nigger' music, she rejected what came naturally to a middle-class girl in the Fifties and early Sixties, and indulged her queer inclinations to disturb and disrupt.

In life she is said to have often checked herself into various hospitals and sanatoria[a] because she felt at ease in them, thus blurring the lines between home and elsewhere, sanity and madness. This sense of a woman on the edge of mental disorder – neither sane nor deranged but somewhere in between – may be heard on several recordings: the raging 'Your Hurtin' Kind Of Love' from the Sixties for instance, and also, more movingly, on the menopausal early-Eighties album, *White Heat*, especially the warped erotics of 'Soft Core', or Seventies tracks like 'Love Me By Name', 'In The Winter' or 'Exclusively For Me'. On 'Beautiful Soul', where she could be addressing either a female lover or herself, she sounds in a state of such fragility you feel she could fall apart the moment the song is over. Those who only know Dusty Springfield via the hits know a truncated version of her 40-year public persona, for she sometimes took herself to dark and dangerous places in her recordings, when she was probably just about holding herself together as a person. Although some of these tracks were not originally authorised for commercial release, few singers in popular music have provided such access to private hurts and vulnerabilities, or sent postcards from so close to the edge of breakdown.

And few celebrity–public relationships have functioned at so many levels of paradox. The best-camouflaged, most closely guarded of singers is also the most candid and emotionally naked. The least known or understood of performers is the one whom many of her listeners feel they know well. The more she keeps her distance, the closer she seems to come. She offers solace by insisting there is none to be had, and uses words to communicate the non-verbal fears and longings of unconscious processes. Ten years after her death she seems more alive in culture than she did for 15 or more years when she lived. What she does or is, or did or was, is what she's never done or been.

Last but by no means least, there was the matter of her dual identity as Dusty Springfield and Mary O'Brien. She started talking about the two of them in 1968 when she stressed her schizoid nature to Alan Smith of the *NME* with such conviction that he headlined his article 'Dusty Feels Like Two People'. 'I saw my name up in lights… it seems like a separate person'[q], she told him. 'When I hear my name announced, it also feels to me like it's someone else. There's a great deal of Dusty Springfield in me. But I'm not all Dusty Springfield'. Presumably the 'I' and 'me' of the article are Mary O'Brien whereas the two occurrences of 'my' before 'name' is Dusty Springfield, which is 'up in lights' and 'announced'. A disjunction occurs whereby Mary, the subject–observer and listener, splits off from the seen-and-heard object, Dusty, which then becomes 'a separate person' or 'someone else'.

In the same year, she made it clear that Dusty Springfield was a fabricated personality by complaining that 'it's hard for people to see past the image; they don't see me as anything other than Dusty Springfield pop singer'[q]. Edward Leeson called this 'an extraordinary remark'[q] considering the lengths Mary O'Brien went to in order to make sure nobody did get past it. But with the contradictory and perverse aspects of his 'extraordinary' transmuted into a queerly diffuse and all-inclusive way of seeing things, the remark suggests that Mary understandably resented her own success at building Dusty into such an effective wall of self-protection that she, Mary, got left sulking behind the barrier.

In the early days, however, this sense of personality dislocation was little referred to, which makes it surprising to find Keith Altham of *Record Mirror* asking in 1970: 'What is a Dusty Springfield?'[q] and suggesting that it was a question 'both the press and the woman herself [had] been asking over the past five successful years'. What Altham meant by apparently turning Dusty Springfield into an unidentified object is unknown; yet he is not alone in having difficulty in receiving Dusty as a 'real-life' human being – in taking her seriously as a flesh-and-blood person despite, in his case, often interviewing her. Over 30 years later, Christian Ward regarded her as so 'unique, alien… an enigmatic amalgamation of… fantasy and reality'[q] that he asked, 'Who was Dusty? Did she ever exist? What did it all mean?' Like Altham before him, Ward shaped his bewilderment into a question, and similarly implied that pondering who she was or whence she came called for a suspension of common sense; in dealing with Dusty Springfield, the normal rules of the game – whatever they might be – most certainly did not apply. She could not be contained or accounted for in the conventional terms of reference for a female person who performed on stage or screen, or in a recording studio. Something indefinably strange and other seemed to be going on.

By the late Seventies and early Eighties, the 'two people' idea was well under way, though with characteristic boundary overlaps as to which one was speaking, and who was being spoken about. 'In the end… Dusty Springfield can do what she damn well likes'[q], one of them, presumably Mary, told John Selby in 1978 – 'It's Mary O'Brien who I've got to keep going'. But to Sheena

Easton on TV two years later, the woman implied that, though they went under different names, the two merged into each other: 'I did say at 17 "I'm going to invent Dusty Springfield" but it was an extension of Mary O'Brien, convent girl'[h], adding – presumably from her own experience but here unacknowledged as such – 'Trying to invent something that's not natural to you will be a disaster'.

Dusty was usually recognised as either the problem one, or the manufactured 'other', of the pair: 'If you set out to create a Dusty Springfield [there's that 'a' again], then you ask for problems'[h] (1978); 'I became this monster that I invented for myself to become'[h] (1985); 'To this day… I stand backstage and think myself into her personality'[h] (1988). Yet there was also recognition that it was the creator of Dusty Springfield, the person named Mary O'Brien, who was the source of the woman's anguish: 'My drinking had nothing to do with Dusty Springfield… it was Mary O'Brien I had trouble with. I disliked Mary O'Brien'[h] (1988). But since the 'I' speaking in the last statement is presumably Dusty Springfield, had Frankenstein's monster finally devoured Mary, the creator–inventor? Or was it just business as usual, with the two overlapping and conflating into a Mary Springfield or a Dusty O'Brien? Perhaps, indeed, these were two additional personalities in the woman's inventory?

As muddling of identity as anything the woman herself said is the legacy which she bequeathed to those who knew her personally. Whereas Pat Rhodes, Madeline Bell and Lee Everett all described her on *Definitely Dusty* in similar terms to her 1968 self-description – the latter's 'she was definitely two people'[h] can stand for the others' positions – Simon Bell thought 'it's very easy to decide there were two people – Mary and Dusty – but they were the same person'[h], then confusingly added, as if Mary had been submerged into Dusty as suggested above, or perhaps never existed at all, 'Dusty was most definitely Dusty right till the end'. Perhaps Simon Bell had her funeral in mind. Certainly on that occasion, as we have seen, the glitzy artifice of Dusty Springfield's celebrity gave short shrift to any notions the woman may have had about slinking off the world's stage as low-profile Mary O'Brien.

The Mary/Dusty conundrum suggests that lying at the heart of her psychological make-up was an acute sense of fragmentation and discontinuity. Whatever confusion she, and then others, got into by trying to determine which part of her did what, she regarded herself as only uneasily contained under a single nominal signifier. With another name – Gladys Thong – adopted for session singing and recording, and yet another – Shan – being what she called herself in the Lana Sisters, it is probable that her sub-personalities were many, and that Mary and Dusty were only the ones whom she felt able to name, acknowledge and discuss. Inasmuch as she drew attention to the probability that all of us contain multiple or partial personalities rather than an elusive and unlocatable 'real' or core self, she again figures queerly.

Such fluidity around identity may be heard in her recordings. Not only was she able, in her prime, to send her voice soaring one minute, then hush it to a whisper in the next, but she seemed to have the capacity to become the woman in the emotional situation of whatever song she sang, while still singing from some central place inside her.

Although she did not write the songs, she sang them as if she had; her recorded output thus serves as an autobiographical account of the Dusty Springfield cast-of-characters' fluctuating emotional states across a thirty-year period. In the words of Hiram Lee, she brought 'an enormous amount of subtext and meaning to lyrics'[q], becoming 'the "author" of the work as much as the original composer', and probably able to fold into the song's textures only if she could imaginatively identify with the role she was taking on. Whether or not we can take seriously her claim that 'Lyrics I have a real problem with'[q], or again 'Lyrics mean very little to me'[q], it is hard to imagine her singing anything which did not resonate with some member or other of her psychic repertory company. In the choice of the songs she chose to sing, she was never less than true to herselves.

From *Just Dusty*, a Dutch TV show transmitted in Holland on 4 February 1971

'She was never less than true to herselves'

This chameleon approach to music had as much depth as range. Randy Cordova's words, 'she tried on musical personalities the way some actresses try on different accents. In that sense, she was the Meryl Streep of the recording studio'[ɑ] are true as far as they go but fail to account for this mysterious depth of personal experience she brought to every vocal performance. The more she changes, the more she stays the same; the broader her repertoire of personas and characters, the further into the interior she probes on her self-excavations.

Matt Chayt suggests that Dusty Springfield 'was a reminder of the provisional nature of all our identities'[ɑ]. Black, white, straight, gay, lesbian, female, male, sane, mad, country girl, beehive bird, Southern belle, clown, tragic muse, music-hall artiste, camp supremo, jazz stylist, gospel mama, Shirley Temple impersonator[ɑ], and for Peter Doggett, 'a soul singer, a nightclub torch balladeer, a pop maestro, a dancefloor diva, or simply… a mistress of disguise'[ɑ]. Such persona shifting suggests that when Neil Tennant answered her apparently ingenuous question[ɑ] about how he wanted her to sound on the recording by saying 'like Dusty Springfield', she may have had little idea of what that meant. 'Like Dusty Springfield' probably seemed a straightforward enough reply to Tennant, but, for the woman herself, it was probably too vague and open-ended a response to be helpful. A further question, *'Which* Dusty Springfield should I sound like?'* would have helped sharpen the focus.

Perhaps, after all, Keith Altham knew what he was talking about when he referred to 'a' Dusty Springfield, thereby implying there were several of them, and that specification was required regarding the one under discussion. This notion of there being a number of Dusty Springfield voices within the one voice – multiple aural representations under a single name – echoes my earlier argument for a collection of visual Dusty Springfield images rather than one.

It seems appropriate therefore that the Dusty impersonator on BBC TV's 2008 *The One And Only* talent contest emerged as winner when the TV audience voted to send her off for a posthumous Las Vegas debut. Although many of those who voted for her probably did not know who the original Dusty Springfield was, at some subliminal level they intuited that the name acts as a ghost effect in culture, standing so outside norms of Saturday evening TV entertainment that it cannot *but* be viewed as different from others who put themselves on the same plane. Perhaps the audience sensed too that there may no longer be, nor have ever been, an original Dusty Springfield, and that *all* Dusty Springfields were – and are – wannabes, an infinite series of blondely bewigged, begowned and charcoal-eyed females myopically gazing at themselves in a hall of mirrors, and waving to their reflections truly, madly, queerly through a mist of might-have-beens and potential impossibilities.

Postscript

I can do no more than mention some of the many projects and tributes which have been built around the name of Dusty Springfield in the early years of this century.

A number of people have sung Dusty songs on various occasions, sometimes in imitation of her, at other times in tribute to her artistry. However they approach things, they cannot avoid being also-rans. Whether they try to sound like Dusty, sing the songs much as she did, or try to refashion them in their own image, they are doomed not only to fall short but to expose their own vocal inadequacies. Were they to take on board Jerry Wexler's words at the Hall of Fame ceremony – 'the distance between [Dusty] and [her] nearest competitors is light years' – they would make life easier for themselves and others. Still, with imitation the greatest form of flattery, if these singers send people back to their mentor and inspiration, they are not without a purpose.

Wannabe soundalikes include Emma Wilkinson who won *Stars In Their Eyes* on TV in 2001 singing 'Son Of A Preacher Man', and Katy Setterfield, the winner of a Las Vegas contract from the 2008 BBC TV show, *The One and Only*. Dusty may have described Vegas as 'cornball glamour' and stated 'I don't want to go', but 38 years later, whether she liked it or not, she was carted off to perform there. Another imitator named Karen Noble wanders into concert halls across the country performing Dusty tribute shows. Other stage tributes from the likes of Kiki Dee and Marc Almond, and, on another occasion, Joss Stone and Patti LaBelle, convince their audiences that nobody sings the songs with as much musical finesse as Dusty. Similarly, the female musicians who conceived and recorded the tribute album, *Forever Dusty*, would be glad to learn that their homage has been successful: the listener is certain there is only one voice anyone would want singing Dusty Springfield songs. Only Shelby Lynne and her team of pared-down musicians on the 2008 album of Dusty covers, *Just A Little Lovin'*, manages to hold her own and say something fresh with the music.

Another Dusty wannabe – Tamsin Carroll – was the star of the critically lauded and commercially successful musical, *Dusty: The Original Pop Diva*; but since the show has so far only been staged in Australia, her Dusty performance cannot be commented on. It remains to be seen whether this musical, or another one, the American-based *A Girl Called Dusty*, will transfer to London. Perhaps there could be a double dose of wannabe Dusty in theatreland to remind us of what is missing. The actress who played Dusty in the short Radio 4 play by Ali Smith broadcast as one of three *Letters to An Icon* in 2002 must have been relieved that Dusty herself sang on the soundtrack.

Long is the list of promising young female singers in Anglo-American culture who are compared to Dusty Springfield. (The number currently stands at 25.) As one of them, Dawn Kinnard, asks: 'Why are so many new singers being compared to Dusty Springfield?' She is the benchmark of excellence which haunts and taunts them to the point of exasperation. You can sympathise with Candie Payne, whose *Times* headline in 2007, 'Just Don't Call Her Dusty', reveals the same frustration that Duffy felt after the *Guardian* wrote: 'Duffy by name… sounding Dusty by nature'. Although she regards comparisons with Dusty Springfield (in newspaper after newspaper) as 'something to be proud of', she wants 'to be known as Duffy, not the new anyone'. The fact that neither she nor Candie nor any of the others sounds like Dusty merely adds insult to injury, and confirms the general longing for Dusty Springfield to be reincarnated through the voice of *some* young woman *somewhere*. It is interesting that Amy Winehouse, the most famous and (rightly) praised of these sound-not-a-bit-alike-singers, has made no public mention of the performer she is regularly compared to. Tears dry on their own – with irritation perhaps?

Rumours have circulated about three Hollywood biopics – one to be directed by Ang Lee which came to nothing, the others respectively starring Kristin Chernoweth and Nicole Kidman. But as with many if not most Dusty Springfield projects, the more likely outcome of both is that rumour will get as far as speculation and then slink back into the silence whence it came. As the singing in these movies will probably be done by yet more Dusty wannabes rather than the real thing, we can only live in hope.

London art-house tributes have included two screenings of Dusty televised performances at the National Film Theatre and an evening of artefacts at the National Portrait Gallery. Recently Dusty's ghost has manifested itself in recording studios long enough for both Petula Clark and Anne Murray to duet with it. As neither woman is reported to have collapsed from the strain, it is assumed that Dusty's spirit proved a more benign presence in the studio than her flesh-and-blood counterpart usually did.

Fan events include an annual Dusty Day in April each year – either in London or Henley-on-Thames, and lively, sometimes heated, discussions on Internet web sites. There is also a very good thrice-yearly fanzine, the *Dusty Springfield Bulletin*, edited by Paul Howes who is a mine of information on all aspects of Dusty's music.

Forthcoming publications include books by Sharon Davis (biographical material), Annie J. Randall (a critical assessment) and Jeanette Lynes (a poetry collection).

Interest in Dusty Springfield continues to grow, and the name shows every sign of hanging around in the middle of a cultural nowhere to haunt and challenge British female pop aspiration for the foreseeable future.

Dusty Springfield Live at the Royal Albert Hall, Eagle Vision DVD, 2005 (original concert 3 December 1979)

Notes

Wherever possible, I have given the original source of a statement rather than use a later publication which quotes it. When I quote someone or refer to what they said or wrote, I provide as much information as is available to me regarding writer, publication date and title of book or article. Thus, if I provide the year of an article without giving the exact date, it is because I either know (or can work out from the text) the year but have no more specific information. Occasionally I have used unsourced material rather than not use it, in which case 'source unknown' is written. When I make a quick reference to an article for possible further consultation, I often omit title and/or writer for the sake of brevity.

I shall refer to the music paper that went under the various names of *Disc*, *Disc Weekly* and *Disc and Music Echo* during the 1960s and early 1970s simply as *Disc* for the sake of convenience. For the same reason, the *New Musical Express* is referred to as *NME*.

Missing from the texts consulted are fanzines, web fansites and chat rooms. This was a deliberate decision: the large amount of material contained in these areas is complex, and warrants a separate study.

Introduction – A Fab Funeral

the one which took place in Henley-on-Thames: Information about Dusty Springfield's funeral is taken from newspaper reports of 12 and 13 March 1999.

had regularly been dubbed an icon: For example, Alan Jackson, 'Dusty Settles Down', *Scotland On Sunday*, 18 June 1995: 'A pop icon of the Sixties who can still hack it with the Nineties newcomers'; Ben Elton at the Brit Awards Ceremony, 9 February 1998: 'Dusty Springfield, that icon of music'; Keith West, 'Dusty Springfield Deserves Her Icon Status', *Gay Times*, August 1995; Roger Holland, *Sounds*, 23 January 1988: 'She's an icon, a living metaphor'.

almost as famous for her food and plate demolitions: References to these include Penny Valentine and Vicki Wickham (2000) *Dancing With Demons, The Authorised Biography of Dusty Springfield*, Hodder and Stoughton, pp.70–1; Anton Antonowicz, 'The Day Diana Ross Stormed Out Of Dusty's Party', *Daily Mirror*, 23 September 1991; for an account by Dusty herself, see Penny Valentine, 'The Wild, Whacky World of Dusty Springfield', *Disc*, 19 February 1966. Contemporary newspaper reports of food throwing include the *Sun*, 9 December 1964, and the *Daily Express*, 14 September 1966.

apart from leading 'the mourners…': Helen Weather, 'Dusty Gets A Standing Ovation', *Daily Record*, 13 March 1999

he maintained a low profile: Little is known about Tom Springfield's life since the late 1960s; his attendance at his sister's funeral was a rare public appearance. When journalist Peter Jones wrote in 1969, 'I suspect we'll be SEEING a lot more of Tom in the year ahead' (*Record Mirror*, 8 February 1969), he must have scared him into invisibility.

Pola Negri, an actress who... while hovering over the coffin: Kenneth Anger (1975) *Hollywood Babylon*, Dell Publishing, p.168

The boyfriend of singer, Alma Cogan: *Alma Cogan: Fabulous!*, BBC4, producer and director Merryn Threadgould, first broadcast 10 November 2006. Another 'over-the-top' funeral appears to have been that of Hollywood star Lilyan Tashman in 1932. According to William J. Mann, a riot broke out as thousands of female fans crushed into the Brooklyn cemetery trying to get near her grave (William J. Mann, 2001, *Behind The Screen: How Gays and Lesbians Shaped Hollywood*, Viking, p.119).

bursting 'into tears as soon as she walked in': Tim Cooper, 'Stars Gather For Dusty's Funeral', *ITN Website*, 12 March 1999

drop 'away as she fought back tears': Michael Smith, 'Fans Sing In The Rain As Pop Stars Say Farewell To Dusty', *Telegraph*, 13 March 1999

'hundreds of fans... lined the main street': Tim Cooper, op. cit.

'the whole town was out in the street crying': Liz Highleyman, 'Who was Dusty Springfield?', http://www.gmax.co za/think/history/2005/051209-dustyspringfield.html, 19 December 2005

a mere 10,646 souls: The population of Henley-on-Thames as given in the 1991 census.

she had always insisted that most of her records fell short... For an account of Dusty in the recording studio, see Peter Jones, 'Dusty In The Studio', *Record Mirror* 25 July 1964. In Penny Valentine, 'Why Dusty Was Worried', *Disc*, 17 July 1965, Dusty said: 'I do worry about all my records – I never feel very happy with them'.

neither the samba band nor the Irish tenor she'd requested... Fred Perry, *The Dusty Springfield Bulletin*, Issue 44, July 2001

Dusty's later metamorphosis into a Brighton bus: In May 2003, *Mojo* reported that a bus in Brighton, Sussex, was named after Dusty; her parents used to live in the town.

Dusty's showbiz roots in post-war British variety: As a member of her first professional group, the Lana Sisters, Dusty shared bills in theatres like the Princess, Torquay and the Hippodrome, Birmingham with ventriloquists, comedians, animal acts, acrobats, dancers, etc. On one occasion she was on the same bill as The Sensational Skylons, a trapeze act, and, on another, The Daring Rosinas, though in what way they were 'daring' is unknown. Information from posters displayed during *Definitely Dusty*, producer and director Serena Cross, BBC TV, first broadcast 26 December 1999.

the OBE which she'd recently bestowed on Dusty: Dusty Springfield had been named in the New Year Honours List, January 1999, for an Order of the British Empire (see Valentine and Wickham, 2000, *Dancing With Demons*, pp.287–9, 292–3).

insulted her sister Margaret nearly 20 years earlier: Lucy O'Brien (no relation) (2000) *Dusty, A Biography*, Pan Books, p.167. Dusty's remark at the Royal Albert Hall in December 1979 was 'It's nice to see that the royalty isn't confined to the box'. Princess Margaret was so insulted that she refused to shake her hand after the concert and sent her a typewritten apology for insulting the queen, which Dusty was asked to sign and send back. Surprisingly, she did. HRH's behaviour seems so extreme and inexplicable that one wonders if there is any truth in Richard Brooks's remark in the *Sunday Times*, 20 May 2007: 'There was tittle-tattle about rumoured lovers – ranging from the actor Peter Sellers to the singer Dusty Springfield'. Article: 'MI5 raided bank for sex pictures of Margaret'.

Nor, as with Pavarotti over eight years later: Information about Pavarotti's funeral is from web, TV, radio and newspapers, 8 and 9 September 2007.

he is rumoured to have Dusty on his Ipod: Robbie Williams chose Dusty Springfield's 'I Don't Want To Hear It Anymore' as one of his 'tracks of my years' on Ken Bruce's Radio 2 programme, 14 December 2006.

Robbie had notched a mere 10 million sales worldwide: http://en.Wikipedia.org/wiki/Robbie Williams

the four young women: There were originally five Spice Girls; Geri Halliwell left in 1998.

the Lana Sisters: Dusty was one of the three Lana Sisters from 1958–60.

Marie Lloyd, Edith Piaf: Midge Gillies (2001) *Marie Lloyd: The One and Only*, Orion, p.2, states that 100,000 people attended the funeral, which was called 'the biggest London had seen since the death of Wellington'. Regarding Piaf, Robyn Archer and Diana Simmonds (1986) *A Star Is Torn*, Virago, p.78, wrote 'her funeral was virtually a state occasion'.

a spate of suicides… in the wake of Valentino's demise: Kenneth Anger (1975) *Hollywood Babylon*, pp.166–7

she had reportedly said that she wanted to die as Mary O'Brien: Tim Cooper, *Evening Standard*, 3 March 1999: 'As she fought her lonely battle against what she knew had become untreatable breast cancer, close friends said she was desperate to return to the anonymity of being Mary O'Brien'.

'a private person…': *Oxford Times*, 19 March 1999

Stanley Kubrick whose funeral took place on the same day: Rory Carroll, 'Legends of Pop and Film Mourned', *Guardian*, 13 March 1999

Or, as with John Lennon… Jane Rosen and Paul Keel, 'A Vigil But No Funeral for John Lennon', *Guardian*, 10 December 1980

Raised as a Catholic and unable, quite… Valentine and Wickham (2000) *Dancing With Demons*, pp.37–8, 166, 183

she'd polluted her body with drink and drugs and slashed it… Ibid. (references throughout book)

'She never once asked, "Why me?"': Richard Duce, 'Stars Mourn Dusty, First Girl-Power Icon', *The Times*, 13 March 1999

she is said to have sought solitude there… Andrew Smith, 'Making Tracks', *Guardian Weekend*, 4 August 2007: Betty Taylor who lives in the church grounds recalls her 'sitting alone for hours' in St Mary's.

she had often blamed her middle-class upbringing… For example, David Skan, 'Dusty confesses "I have always wanted fame… I have always wanted to be noticed"', *Record Mirror*, 26 September 1970, where she says 'I live by this totally inhibiting middle-class morality syndrome… Unfortunately I have been trapped by it'.

Henley-on-Thames has a whiter population… The 1991 census gives the white population of the town as 10,404 and states this is 99 per cent of the population. Valentine and Wickham say 'Henley is middle England at its finest and bleached white' (Valentine and Wickham, 2000, *Dancing With Demons*, p.291).

had often seemed ill-at-ease with her own whiteness: The Springfields, 'This is Nashville', *Melody Maker*, 5 January 1963: '"I wish I'd been born coloured", said Dusty'.

claimed she felt more comfortable in the company of black people: Ray Coleman, 'Dusty: Pop Probe', *Melody Maker*, 21 November 1964: 'But I have a real bond with the music of coloured artists in the States. I feel more at ease with them than I do with many white people. We talk the same language'.

the conundrum is not easily resolved: In *Daily Mail*, 4 March 1999, Ray Connolly called Dusty 'a collision of contradictions'.

the wording read '1966–1972': Carole Gibson, 'A Tribute to Dusty Springfield, OBE', *The Dusty Springfield Bulletin*, Issue 44, July 2001

someone as restless and unanchored as Dusty Springfield: O'Brien (2000) *Dusty, A Biography*, p.32. Frankie Culling tells Lucy O'Brien that the young Dusty 'gave the impression she was never going to stay long'. And she didn't.

she liked to be part of the surrounding musical ambience: *Dusty Springfield: Full Circle*, director Roger Pomfrey, BBC TV, first broadcast 2 May 1994. Dusty said: 'I've never thought of myself as being a singer with an orchestra. I am part of the orchestra... part of the ensemble. I'm another instrument... that's why I like surround sound. I like to be part of it'.

'allowed me to get close to her': Tim Cooper, *ITN Website*, 12 March 1999

however well you thought you knew Dusty Springfield... *Definitely Dusty*, BBC TV. Pat Rhodes's actual words were: 'I don't honestly think anybody can truthfully say to you, "I know Dusty Springfield, or I know Mary O'Brien". She always kept part of herself back from everybody'.

biographical information... elsewhere: Lucy O'Brien; Valentine and Wickham; Davis (2008) *A Girl Called Dusty*, Carlton

'Wind Beneath My Wings': 'Midler and Dion Top Funeral Chart', BBC website, 5 August 2002, refers to a report which states that this song is the most-played song at British funerals (http://newsbbc.co.uk/1/hi/entertainment/music/2173544.stm).

Part one – My Colouring Book

Chapter one – White Negress

'No listener could have thought...': Simon Frith (1996) *Performing Rites: On The Value of Popular Music*, Oxford University Press, p.197

as with Elvis Presley or Tom Jones: Elvis is famous for sounding black when he started out – for example, Greil Marcus (1977) *Mystery Train: Images of America in Rock 'N' Roll Music*, Omnibus Press, pp.176–7: 'At the start Elvis sounded black to those who heard him; when they called him the Hillbilly Cat, they meant the White Negro.' And according to Mike Evans (2006) in *Rock 'n' Roll's Strangest Moments* (Robson Books, p.55), he was called 'the White Little Richard' by his record company, RCA. The mid-Sixties music papers made much of Tom Jones sounding 'coloured', for example: 'coloured people... most of them thought I was coloured from the sound of my voice' (Laurie Henshaw, 'Surprise for Tom – The Americans Thought He Was Coloured', *Disc*, 8 May 1965).

'they still have an English accent...': Ian Dove, 'Three Sides of r 'n' b – Pop, Jazz and Folk', *NME*, 9 October 1964

made a point of saying she did not: For example, Charles Shaar Murray reviewing *Dusty In Memphis*, *NME*, 2 November 1985: 'She didn't sound black – or even standard issue British fake-black'; Jerry Wexler and David Ritz (1994) *Rhythm and The Blues: A Life in American Music*, Jonathan Cape, p.222: 'You won't hear much of a black influence in her voice, yet she's deeply soulful...'; Greil Marcus on *Dusty In Memphis* in 1969, quoted in Lucy O'Brien (1999 edition) *Dusty: A Biography of Dusty Springfield*, Pan, p.130: 'Dusty is not a soul singer, and she makes no effort to "sound black"'; Chris Willman,

Entertainment Weekly, 19 March 1999: she 'wouldn't likely be mistaken for black in a blindfold test'; Simon Napier-Bell, *Observer*, 19 October 2003: 'People said Dusty sounded black, but really she didn't. She sounded only like herself'.

'she was just another name in a long list...': 'Dusty Fails To Come Clean', *Daily Mirror*, 3 May 1994

few obituary tributes failed to mention her... For example, Richard Williams, 'A Soulful, Smoky Signature', *Guardian*, 4 March 1999: 'she was the only white woman worthy of being mentioned in the same breath as the great divas of 1960s soul music'; Anthony Thorncroft, 'Maverick Pop Diva from An Innocent Age', *Financial Times*, 4 March 1999: 'her powerful, bluesy, "black" voice'; Sarah Nelson, 'Great White Lady who Had Soul of the Sixties', *Herald*, 4 March 1999: 'broke many now-forgotten barriers between black and white music'.

references to her as a 'white soul singer'... For example, David Hemingway, *Record Collector*, July 2005: 'Britain's greatest white soul singer'; Steven Van Zandt (2005) Introduction, *Rolling Stone – The 500 Greatest Albums of All Time*, Wenner Books, p.94: 'Springfield was a great soul singer hidden inside a white British pop queen'; unnamed writer, *Q*, June 2004: 'the greatest white soul voice of all'; Jerry Wexler at the UK Music Hall of Fame 'Induction' ceremony, 14 November 2006, broadcast 16 November 2006: 'I've called her the queen of white soul'.

'a white woman with a black woman's voice': John Barrowman, *Mojo*, January 2008

the association continues to this day... For example, Andrew Marr writes, 'Dusty Springfield had one of the loveliest voices of the age, but if you didn't know, you could have been forgiven for thinking that she was a black babe from Motown, not a Catholic girl from High Wycombe' (2007, *A History of Modern Britain*, Macmillan, p.280).

calling Dusty Springfield 'white' seems perfectly normal: Sometimes she is called 'white' with no overtly stated musical attribution as in Sarah Nelson's headlined article, 'Great White Lady Who Had Soul of the Sixties' (*Herald*, 4 March 1999).

attribution of white... a reversal of linguistic usage: See for instance George McKay (2005) *Circular Breathing: The Cultural Politics of Jazz in Britain*, Duke University Press, p.94: 'whiteness in a majority-white society with a long history and cultural tradition dominated by white work has become invisible'; and p.95: 'for all white Britons: ours is an invisible ethnicity, all- or once-powerful in, because of, its silence'. Also Mike Heffley (2005) *Northern Sun, Southern Moon: Europe's Reinvention of Jazz*, Yale University Press, p.121: 'whiteness has emerged... as we realized that the unnamed "we" naming all "others" was in fact itself just another "other", however effectively disguised as the neutral, universal touchstone'.

'we don't... mention the whiteness...': Richard Dyer (1997, 2007) *White*, Routledge, p.2

the not-quite-conventional quality of Dusty's voice: For example, Nigel Hunter reviewing a Springfields E.P., *Disc*, 20 July 1963: 'Dusty's voice soars out with a forceful spirit you seldom hear from a girl'; Don Nicholl reviewing the Springfields' 'Come On Home', *Disc*, 13 July 1963: 'with Dusty's voice stabbing through. It'll be inside your skull... before the end of the month'. Two of the first to single out Dusty's voice from the Springfields' mix were Keith Fordyce and singer Helen Shapiro in editions of *NME*: 'she has one of the most enchanting voices on record' (Fordyce, 10 August 1962) and 'it demonstrates perfectly how great a singer Dusty is in her own right' (Shapiro, 30 August 1963).

'THE WHITE NEGRESS – THAT'S WHAT...': Norman Jopling, *Record Mirror*, 6 April 1963. The term 'white negro' had been coined by Norman Mailer in a 1956 essay which was reprinted in *Advertisements for Myself* (Harvard University Press, 1959). The term referred to young white Americans of the 1920s, '30s and '40s who liked jazz so much they adopted black culture as their own.

repetition by journalist Peter Jones: In editions of *Record Mirror* on 13 July, 28 September, 9 November, 21 December 1963

add 'soul-stirring' to the whiteness: 'Springfields to Break Up', *Record Mirror*, 28 September 1963: 'because of her soul-stirring voice…'

Dusty had sung solo on a few bars… *Record Mirror*, 30 November 1963 reports DJ Alan Freeman as saying on TV's *Juke Box Jury* that Dusty's first solo single, 'I Only Want To Be With You', sounded just like the Springfields as a group. Her voice, it seems, is the one that was heard in the Springfields' vocal mix and defined the sound of the Springfields.

already 'become more "black" with her voice': Lucy O'Brien, *Dusty*, p.37

'people started saying I sounded…': Peter Jones, 'Dusty – Don't Be Serious About Music', *Record Mirror*, 15 February 1964

'Dusty gets it… she does get it': Paul East, 'Mann Finds Table-Setting Tough', *NME*, 1 May 1964

'she gets a real coloured sound in her voice': *Disc*, 9 May 1964

while… Dionne Warwick thought… 'My Top Choice – Dionne Warwick chooses', *Disc*, 6 June 1964: 'you know, when I first heard Dusty, I thought she was coloured. She has such a soulful sound'.

'No white person ever sounded so coloured': *Melody Maker*, 14 November 1964

'you couldn't tell the difference…': Penny Valentine, 'Dusty One of the Gang', *Disc*, 14 November 1964. Clive James wrote 'When Dusty sang alongside Martha and the Vandellas, she blended perfectly into their big creamy sound' ('Defenestrated Goggle-Box', *Observer*, 17 November 1985).

virtually all the Britgirl singers… named her: Cilla Black's Top 10 in *NME*, 8 August 1964, includes nine black Americans, then in *NME*, 24 July 1964, she names Dusty as her favourite British girl singer; Lulu in *Disc*, 18 July 1964, chooses in her 'Top Choice' six black American records out of 10, then, in the same paper, on both 3 July ('my favourite singer') and 17 July ('I love Dusty's records') praises Dusty; for Marianne Faithfull, *Melody Maker*, 22 August 1964, 'Dusty's songs are marvellous'; in *NME*, on both 16 October and 23 October 1964, Sandie Shaw names Dusty as a favourite singer along with Ray Charles, and with James Brown, Dionne Warwick and the white Peggy Lee on the first occasion; Helen Shapiro in *NME*, 30 August 1963, says that the Springfields' 'Island Of Dreams' 'demonstrates perfectly how great a singer Dusty is in her own right'; Millie in *NME*, 18 September 1964, says 'Dusty herself is extremely good. She has earned an awful lot of respect from our fellow artists with her great talent'.

'Why doesn't Dusty Springfield leave…': *Melody Maker*, 12 December 1964

'Dusty Springfield comes as near…': *Melody Maker*, 26 December 1964. Bob Gibron too asked, 'How could a gal from Hampstead, London sound so soulful, so full of emotion and torment?' ('Dusty Springfield: Reflections', http://www.dvdverdict.com, 18 March 2005)

'closely identified with that of coloured singers in the States': Mike Ledgerwood, 'What Makes Dusty Tick?', *Disc*, 12 December 1964

why, in 1960s pop music, blackness or 'coloured'ness gave… status: In Britain this situation began to occur about 1963/4 with the endorsement of black music by, amongst others, the Beatles, the Rolling Stones and, of course, Dusty Springfield. Amongst numerous remarks providing the status: Ray Davies, *Melody Maker*, 11

December 1965: 'I always feel a lot better when a Negro likes what I'm playing'; Sandie Shaw on 'Blind Date' listening to new records in *Melody Maker*, 24 October 1964: 'That's the first decent record I've heard today [black American Rufus Thomas's 'Jump Back']. Where are all the records by the coloured singers, then?'; Tom Jones, *Melody Maker*, 18 September 1965: 'she [Dionne Warwick] couldn't believe I was white. I was thrilled to bits'. Music critics too held similar views: George Melly, in *Revolt Into Style* (1971, Penguin, p.35), thought rock 'n' roll had an 'emphasis on white and, by definition, inferior performers…'. 'Uncoloured' music could not be preferred to 'the real thing'.

'we did not have the black music…': Peter Hartz, 'Dusty Springfield Is Back With New United Artists LP', *Cash Box*, 11 December 1978

novelty falsetto hits: In 1960 Jimmy Jones got to numbers 5 and 1 respectively with 'Handy Man' and 'Good Timin''.

smooth mainstream romantic ballads: For example, Johnny Mathis's 1960 Top 10 hit, 'My Love For You'.

showbiz cabaret-type numbers: For example, Nat 'King' Cole's 1962 Top 20 hit, 'Let There Be Love'.

dance tunes in the then-popular Twist idiom: For example, Chubby Checker's 'Let's Twist Again' and Sam Cooke's 'Twisting The Night Away' were Top 10 hits in 1961 and 1962 respectively.

revivals of songs from earlier musical eras: Clarence 'Frogman' Henry had a Top 10 hit in 1961 with 'You Always Hurt The One You Love', originally a hit in 1944 for the Mills Brothers. Ketty Lester revised the mid-Forties song 'Love Letters', which got to Number 4 in 1962 and showed that standard ballads could be given innovative soul readings.

Even black innovators like Ray Charles and Sam Cooke… For example, Ray Charles's 1962 Number 1, 'I Can't Stop Loving You', and Sam Cooke's Number 7 hit of the previous year, 'Cupid'.

groups such as the Shirelles, the Chiffons and Phil Spector's Crystals and Ronettes: 'Will You Love Me Tomorrow?' by the Shirelles was Number 4 in 1961; the Chiffons' 'He's So Fine' was Number 16 in 1963; 'Da Doo Ron Ron' and 'Then He Kissed Me' by the Crystals were Numbers 5 and 2 respectively in 1963; 'Be My Baby' by the Ronettes got to Number 4 in 1963; Little Eva's 'Locomotion' was Number 2 in 1962.

the music critics' tendency to dismiss Tamla Motown acts: For example, the Pop Disc Jury in *Record Mirror*, 11 January 1964 said of the Marvelettes' 'As Long As I Know He's Mine': 'it's still too uncommercial for this country as yet'. And reviewers for much of the Sixties couldn't determine whether the Miracles' (male) singer, Smokey Robinson was male or female. Allen Evans, *NME*, 10 February 1968 is typical: 'Is this Smokey sounding just like a girl singer, or is it a girl?'

like the Beatles at the same time: On their first two albums, the Beatles covered songs by black Americans like Arthur Alexander, Chuck Berry, Barrett Strong, the Miracles and the Marvelettes (both Tamla Motown), the Cookies, the Isley Brothers, and – surprise surprise – the Shirelles (two different songs from Dusty: 'Boys' and 'Baby, It's You').

certain black American vocal styles they were… resistant to: Negative comments on black vocalists by white male reviewers were numerous in the early Sixties. In *Record Mirror*, 30 July 1960, Dick Tatham wrote an article criticising Ray Charles for breaking 'every rule in the book' of 'good singing' by 'phrasing against the sense of the lyrics, producing a hoarse, uncertain tone as distinct from a sustained, lyrical one, cutting short the final notes of phrases instead of hitting them squarely and holding them, shirking the issue with high notes by breaking into falsetto' and thus, unwittingly, defined a vocal style which would come to dominate popular singing for the next half century.

'The sense of isolation in which British culture...': Iain Chambers (1985) *Urban Rhythms: Pop Music and Popular Culture*, Macmillan, p.37

'As for the transatlantic harmonies...': Ibid., pp.37–8

Her stand against apartheid... In *Anti-Apartheid: A History of the Movement in Britain* (2005, Merlin Press, pp.104–5), Roger Fieldhouse writes of 'high profile tours of South Africa by Dusty Springfield and Adam Faith undermining the cultural boycott' undertaken by film makers like Tony Richardson who had banned his films from being shown there. Since he includes the Dusty and Adam tours with those of other singers like Cliff Richard which did take place, he seems not to realise the stands Dusty and Adam Faith took. Although they did not tour South Africa, the Beatles made a stand in USA: 'We will not appear unless negroes are allowed to sit anywhere', they said regarding a concert in segregated Jacksonville, Florida (*Record Mirror*, 11 September 1964).

'I know nothing whatsoever about politics...': Bob Dawbarn, 'Well Done, Dusty!', *Melody Maker*, 26 December 1964

'a host of other truly great entertainers...': Bob Dawbarn, 'Dusty: The Row Goes On', *Melody Maker*, 9 January 1965. A number of other British performers performed to segregated audiences more than once. In retrospect, their remarks can seem both shocking and amusing, for instance, Alma Cogan in *NME*, 24 October 1958: 'The major difference between our two countries is that there is no television in South Africa'; Cliff Richard in *Melody Maker*, 8 April 1961: 'the native servants seemed to be treated well in the homes I visited'; Hank Marvin of the Shadows, *NME*, 22 February 1963 on getting tanned: 'we had a bit of a race to see who would be the brownest'; Brian Poole (of the Tremeloes) in *NME*, 27 March 1964: 'The Zulus were very co-operative – performing, dancing and jumping up and down and everything'. At the end of the Sixties, Tom Jones, for all his black associations and identifications, blamed the Musicians' Union ban for preventing him from touring South Africa, *Melody Maker*, 19 October 1968.

Miriam Makeba: Not American but South African like Jordaan himself.

the only white solo performer on a New York R 'n' B show: Dusty appeared at the Brooklyn Fox theatre in September 1964 on a bill which included four white American groups (the Shangri-las, the Dovells, the Newbeats and Jay and the Americans) amongst a host of black Americans – Martha and the Vandellas, Marvin Gaye, Little Anthony and the Imperials, the Temptations, the Supremes, the Contours, the Ronettes and the Miracles. The other solo act was Millie, the Jamaican whose one hit, 'My Boy Lollipop', is still fondly remembered.

'a real bond with coloured artists in the States': Ray Coleman, 'Dusty', *Melody Maker*, 21 November 1964

'I wish I'd been born coloured': 'This Is Nashville', *Melody Maker*, 5 January 1963; *Daily Express*, 23 October 1963. In a perverse ironic twist, Lucy O'Brien reports that over 25 years later, Dusty was briefly taken up as a heroine by the racist British Movement organisation in their fanzine, *Vanguard*, as a 'white woman expressing a white culture', *Dusty*, p.67. Other whites in pop music before Dusty expressed similar wishes to be black. The Jewish American writer–producer, Jerry Leiber, for instance, recalled his youthful 1940s and '50s yearnings in 1990: 'I felt black. I *was*, as far as I was concerned. And I wanted to be black for lots of reasons' (David Fricke, 'Leiber and Stoller', *Rolling Stone*, 19 April 1990).

'we talk the same language': Ray Coleman, 'Dusty', *Melody Maker*, 21 November 1964

she was probably referring to musical affinities: Dusty was not, of course, the first white popular singer to acknowledge her debt to black vocalists. Frank Sinatra, for example, in *Melody Maker*, 18 October 1958 refers to Billie Holiday as 'the greatest single musical influence on me' and expresses admiration for Ethel Waters, Nat Cole and Ella Fitzgerald. 'My debt to Negro performers can never be repaid'.

'showing the world that Britain can produce…': Peter Thomson's 'New Years Honours', *Disc*, 2 January 1965

her 'legendary popularity in America': 'Lowdown On A Breakdown', *Disc*, 24 July 1965

'the Tamla crowd dote on her': Peter Jones, 'The One They Rave Over', *Record Mirror*, 10 July 1965: 'you should now hear Dionne rave on and on about OUR Dusty… The Tamla crowd dote on her… Doris Troy… rates Dusty tremendously… Martha [Vandella] – there's another Dusty "digger". The coloured R and B exponents do the raving while Dusty does the singing'.

'this talk about Tom Jones and Dusty Springfield sounding coloured…': Norrie Drummond, 'Fortunes Knock Burdon's "Soul" Sound', *NME*, 4 March 1966

'seemingly authentic gospel approach': Derek Johnson, 'Bright and Breezy Dusty', *NME*, 11 June 1965. It is doubtful if many people in mid-Sixties Britain would have been much clearer about 'authentic' gospel than in 1957 when Bob Dawbarn in *Melody Maker*, 30 November, thought members of the audience at Sister Rosetta Tharpe's Chiswick Empire concert 'seemed surprised to find the word Gospel was connected with religion'.

'a real Negroid feel for a song': Ray Coleman, *Melody Maker*, 2 May 1964

'natural coloured sound of her voice': Mike Ledgerwood, 'Dusty Is Dynamite', *Disc*, 25 September 1965

'better [performance] than many coloured…': Tony Hall, *Record Mirror*, 3 July 1965

'intense gospel and soul inspiration': Derek Johnson, 'Dusty – Great', *NME*, 21 January 1966

'she even dances like a coloured girl': 'The Raver', *Melody Maker*, 9 January 1965. In an article 20 years later, 'Return of the White Negress' (source unknown), Anne Caborn wrote: 'Even the way she moved was more fluid than other white singers'.

his 1968 *NME* review of the album *Dusty… Definitely*: 'Tom Springfield reviews Dusty's black and white LP', *NME*, 23 November 1968

her 'interest in rhythm and blues meant…': Mike Hellicar, 'Dusty Talks About "Jury"', *NME*, 8 March 1963. Thirty years later, in 1993, Dusty said she was listening to the Staple Singers' 'Hammering Nails' and 'Will The Circle Be Unbroken?' spirituals when she was with the Springfields. She had identified with their backing singer called Cleotha ('The Ultimate Interview', *The Dusty Springfield Bulletin*, November 1993).

she had wanted to be a blues singer since childhood: *Daily Express*, 23 October 1963. Dusty's words were: 'When I was 10 my teacher asked us what we'd like to do when we grew up. I said I'd like to be a blues singer. I didn't know what that was, but I thought it sounded good!'

As an older woman, Dusty repeated this story… For example, in a 1978 *Woman's World* article, Dusty said, 'And I always used to say the same thing. I want to be a blues singer. God knows what that meant'. She would, no doubt, have been pleased by Bernard Zuel's posthumous tribute, 'At her best her songs were the greatest female blues since Billie Holiday and Bessie Smith' (*Sydney Morning Herald*, 4 March 1999).

'I was fascinated with black faces and black voices': *Tonight in Toronto*, Canadian TV interview, late 1982/early 1983

'praying that one day I can make…': June Harris, 'Separate Careers – and All Booming!', *Disc*, 30 November 1963

was, in Jerry Wexler's word, 'mesmerised'... *Definitely Dusty*, producer and director Serena Cross, BBC TV, first broadcast 26 December 1999

'started out copying every coloured voice I heard': *Music Maker*, author unknown, 1968

she 'knew exactly how to sound like a Vandella...': Sharon Davis, 'Dusty From The Soul', *Blues and Soul*, No.564, early 1990s

She often told stories in later life... For example, on *Dusty Springfield: Full Circle* (first broadcast on BBC TV, 2 May 1994, director Roger Pomfrey), Dusty says: 'The Exciters got me by the throat... in New York... I was going past a record shop... out of the blue comes blasting out, "I know something about love"... That's it. That's what I want to do'. In a Radio 1 interview with Andy Peebles, 5 August 1989, Dusty also tells of the impact on her of 'Don't Make Me Over'.

like the Exciters' 'Tell Him': The Exciters were actually a mixed-gendered group consisting of three women and one man: the lead singer was female, however.

such impassioned gospel groups as... 'Dusty Goes For Gospel Music', *NME*, 12 February 1965

'no matter what people think, I don't...': Peter Jones, 'Dusty – Don't Be Serious About Music', *Record Mirror*, 15 February 1964

her 'singing, I think, has a "coloured" feel': 'Cilla, Kathy and Me', written by Dusty Springfield, presumably in 1964, source unknown

the 'important word' in Cliff Richard's... description: 'Dusty – Don't Be Serious About Music', *Record Mirror*, 15 February 1964

a singer of 'gospel-influenced music...': Derek Johnson, 'Dusty Says, "Life Must Be Less Hectic Now"', *NME*, 24 April 1964

'I only sound vaguely coloured to white people': *Melody Maker*, 26 June 1965

'I used to be called the singer even blacks...': Jean Rook, 'The Truth About Dusty', *Daily Express*, 9 August 1985

'I never claimed to sound coloured': Dusty's letter to *Melody Maker*, 12 December 1964

'I want to do things the coloured singers do': Penny Valentine, 'Dusty: The Future', *Disc*, 18 September 1965

'inside this white body is a black person...': A German TV chat show, probably 1990, exact source unknown. In *Definitely Dusty*, BBC TV, her friend Norma Tanega says she 'found out' she was 'black underneath' her white Irish exterior. Dave Clark is quoted in O'Brien's *Dusty*, p.98, as saying something similar: 'She was a white lady who should have been black. She had black mascara and a black soul'.

'I'm split half down the middle...': *Melody Maker*, 27 June 1970

'in those days [to] sound fairly daring...': Interview with John Sacks, Radio 1, 22 October 1994

she described her singing voice as 'inherently brown': Ibid.

'split up all over the place... schizophrenic vocal changes': 'The Ultimate Interview' given by Dusty in November 1993 prior to recording in Nashville and published in *The Dusty Springfield Bulletin*, November 2003

'Part of me wanted to be Peggy Lee...': Ibid. Dusty has more than once named Peggy Lee as an inspiration. It surely is no coincidence that Lee too was often heard as black, and shared Dusty's perfectionism, her sense of being two people and the air of mystery and unpredictability. See Peter Richmond (2006) *Fever: The Life and Music of*

Peggy Lee, Aurum Press Ltd

'always liked black singers more than white': Ibid.

'I wanted to be a cross-section of it all': Radio 1 interview with Roger Scott, 11 March 1989

Chapter two – White Soul Queen

'I like singers with soul… I like Dusty Springfield': Peter Jones, 'Going Shopping With Dionne', *Melody Maker*, 30 May 1964

'soul' was a relatively new term in music: The term evolved between the late Fifties and mid-Sixties. The music made by the artist now often considered the originator of soul, Ray Charles, presented critics with difficulties of definition in these years: was it blues? jazz? gospel? Numerous articles sought to categorise his musical style. 'Soul' filled the gap.

'The story of soul music…': Peter Guralnick (1991) *Sweet Soul Music: Rhythm and Blues and the Southern Dream of Freedom*, Penguin, p.21

pop star Jimmy Jones thought Doris Day had as much soul… Ren Gravatt, 'Meet The Hit Parade "Handy Man"', *Melody Maker*, 27 August 1960. Although not using the word 'soul', Ray Charles thought Connie Francis sang the blues like a black woman (*Melody Maker*, 14 February 1959).

'In America I'm known as…': Chris Hutchins, 'Little Richard Keeps 'Em Guessing', *NME*, 26 October 1962

'she didn't like the term soul singer': Cordell Marks, 'The Happy Side of Dusty', *NME*, 3 April 1964

'I AM NOT, AND HAVE NEVER BEEN…': David Franklin, 'Dusty Wants A New Format for Live Appearances', *Top Pops and Music Now*, late 1969

'unless you knew better, you could be forgiven…': Penny Valentine, *Disc*, 23 September 1967

'Oh the confusion! …the very best soul record…': Penny Valentine, *Disc*, 6 September 1969

'Soul is an attitude' and… 'It's coming from the soul': *Soul Britannia 1*, BBC4, 2 February 2007, producer and director Jeremy Marre. A black soul/R 'n' B singer, Bettye Lavette, similarly fudged the issue: 'anyone who sings with soul – Pavarotti, Caruso – anyone who can make you cry or make you dance or whatever, they're a soul singer' (Autumn Long, 'Bettye Lavette: The Great Communicator', *Blues Revue*, Oct/Nov 2007).

'a feeling you can only acquire from…': Ian Dove, '"I Don't Know What Is The Real Me" admits Ray Charles', *NME*, 24 May 1963

'Soul is a feeling… a lot of depth': Alan Smith, 'House Proud Aretha Loves To Get Home', *NME*, 15 June 1968

'Negro people use the word…': Max Jones, 'Timi Yuro Hates That Soul Tag', *Melody Maker*, 1 June 1968

'Soul (with a capital S) is, was and ever…': Valerie Wilmer, 'Bout Soul', *Melody Maker*, 21 June 1969

'although white musicians are trying to get…': Michael Smith, 'The Other (More Serious) Side of Nina', *Melody Maker*, 7 December 1968. Regarding Dusty, Nina Simone told Sylvia Hampton 'she sounds a lot like one of our singers, Aretha Franklin' (Sylvia Hampton with David Nathan, 2004, *Nina Simone: Break Down and Let It All Hang Out*, Sanctuary, p.23).

'Black soul'… had a tautological sense… Perverse as ever, Scott Walker called Frank Sinatra 'the greatest "soul" singer in the world' (Keith Altham, *NME*, 11 March 1966).

'white soul' the 'marked' or subsidiary 'other': In a letter to *Melody Maker*, 5 July 1969, Robin Lecore wrote: 'if soul (white soul) is imitative of Black soul (SOUL), then it is a diminutive form'.

'doing a bit of white soul': *Disc*, 25 March 1967

Among the first was American Laura Nyro… *Record Mirror*, 17 August 1968

'the first white soul group': John C. Dee, *Record Mirror*, 7 September 1968

'one of Britain's most admired white soul singers': *Disc*, 1 March 1969

'a phenomenon. She is white soul': Tony Wilson, 'Janis Breaks Through The British Reserve', *Melody Maker*, 26 April 1969

'a white woman with a black woman's voice': Jan Nesbit, 'Feminine View', *NME*, 26 April 1969

'the greatest white female rock singer…': Stuart Maconie, *Radio Times*, 19–25 January 2008

'the ultimate white soul mama': Barney Hoskyns (1991) *From A Whisper To A Scream*, Fontana, p.59

'the finest white blues and soul singer': Phil Hardy and Dave Laing (1990) *The Faber Companion to 20th Century Popular Music*, Faber and Faber Ltd, p.420

she is Dusty's closest cultural associate… Another white-heard-as-black singer is Phoebe Snow, whose black vocal transcodings are discussed in detail by Michael Awkward in *Soul Covers: Rhythm and Blues Remakes and the Struggle for Artistic Identity* (2007, Duke University Press, pp.137–99). The section is entitled 'Miss Snow, Are You Black?'

'one of the finest white soul albums of all time': Richie Unterberger in Bogdanov V., Bush J., Woodstra C. and Erlwine S.T. (eds) (2003) *All Music Guide to Soul*, Backbeat Books, p.847

'landmark white soul session': Jim Irvin (ed.) (2000) *The Mojo Collection: The Greatest Albums of All Time*, Mojo Books, p.170

the album was 'largely overlooked at the time': BBC Radio 2 programme, *Dusty In Memphis*, 14 November 2006

'a stand-out album judged by any standard': Peter Jones, *Record Mirror*, 19 April 1969

'her best yet. Eleven great tracks…': *Melody Maker*, 26 April 1969

'every single track is a perfect little masterpiece': *Disc*, 19 April 1969

'if ever there was a history-making album…': Ibid.

Allen Evans of the *NME* thought the record… *NME*, 19 April 1969

'the queen of white soul': Jerry Wexler used this phrase on Dusty's 'induction' into the UK Music Hall of Fame on 14 November 2006, televised 16 November 2006. At other times he used the phrases: 'the incarnation of the white soul queen' (Radio Merseyside Interview with Spencer Leigh, 26 February 2005); 'The Great White Lady – The Ice Queen' (quoted by Peter Doggett, *Record Collector*, November 2002); 'the queen of white soul' (quoted by Geoff Boucher, *Los Angeles Times*, 4 March 1999).

'the queen of white soul singers': RW, *Melody Maker*, March 1973

'a convincing claim to the title of…': Charles Shaar Murray, *NME*, 1973. A year earlier Lanny Thomas called Dusty 'probably one of the best "white soul" singers around' (*New*

Orleans, The States, 14 April 1972); and a year before that Ray Coleman called a Carole King track 'the most exciting "white soul" from a girl singer since the early career of Dusty Springfield' (*Melody Maker*, 9 January 1971). Neither Thomas nor Coleman crowned or titled Dusty, though.

'among the most funky and mellow…': Phil Hardy and Dave Laing (eds) (1976) *The Encyclopedia of Rock*, Vol.1, Panther, p.329

two attempted 'comeback' albums: *It Begins Again*, 1978; *Living Without Your Love*, 1979

'an effortless "black" voice': Anny Brackx, *Cash Box,* 18 February 1978

'the white girl with the black voice': Dennis Hunt, 'Dusty, Show Biz: Together Again', *Los Angeles Times*, 23 January 1978. Another 'black' reference came via Annie Lennox who, in the *Observer*, 21 August 1988, described Dusty as 'one of the few white singers who, if you shut your eyes, you'd think you were listening to a black singer'.

'the best white soul singer in the world': Penny Valentine, *Disc*, February or March 1978

'the best white woman singer in the world': Barbara Jeffery, *Sunday People*, March 1978

'arguably the finest white soul singer in the world': Thomson Prentice, *Daily Mail*, 27 January 1978

'Arguably the greatest white soul singer…': Chris North, part series, *The History Of Rock*, Number 37, Orbis Publishing Ltd, 1982

Fred Dellar: 'the greatest white soul singer in the world' (Fred Dellar, 1983, *Where Did You Go To, My Lovely?*, Star, p.181).

'a singer's singer, a superlative': Aida Pavletich (1980) *Sirens Of Song: The Popular Female Vocalist In America*, Da Capo, p.154

She sold records again both with the Pets… Three Top 20 hit singles and a Top 20 album in 1990, *Reputation*.

'the finest white female soul voice of all time': Jeff Tamarkin, *Goldmine*, 20 May 1988

'the imperishable white soul voice…': Tom Hibbert, *Q*, April 1989

as many variants on these phrases… For example, Richard Stott, *News of the World*, 7 March 1999: 'She was white soul, British Motown'; *The Times*, 13 March 1999: 'the first white woman with soul in her voice'; Jackie Burdon, *Western Mail*, 4 March 1999: 'Britain's white soul diva'; Jill Jones, *Sydney Star Observer*, 11 March 1999: 'The White Queen of Soul, Britain's greatest female pop singer'.

'Britain's greatest white soul singer': David Hemingway, *Record Collector*, July 2005

'the greatest white soul voice of all': *Q*, June 2004

'a great soul singer hidden inside a white British pop queen': Steven Van Zandt (2005) Introduction, *Rolling Stone: The 500 Greatest Albums of All Time*, Wenner Books, p.94

long before ITV's South Bank Show homage… *The South Bank Show*, ITV, 9 April 2006, producer and director Susan Shaw

the 'white queen of soul': *TV and Satellite Week*, 8–14 April 2006

'white lady of soul': *Radio Times*, 8–14 April 2006

'the once reigning queen of blue-eyed soul': *Los Angeles Herald Examiner*, 25 August 1980

'the original blue-eyed soul singer': *Los Angeles Times*, 27 March 2007

'her brand of "blue-eyed soul"': Lucy O'Brien, 'The White Lady of Soul', *Independent*, 25 February 2006

'refers to soul and R&B music...': (2003) *The All Music Guide to Soul, The Definitive Guide to R & B and Soul*, Backbeat Books, p.viii

'the best female blue-eyed soul singer...': Richie Unterberger, ibid., p.847

'the finest white soul singer...': Jason Ankeny, ibid., p.638

'a very, very soulful voice with no colour': Madeline Bell interviewed on *Dusty Springfield: Live at The Royal Albert Hall*, DVD, director Mike Mansfield, Eagle Vision, 2005

she told Dawn French... 'Vodka': *Full Circle*, BBC TV, 1994

Chapter three – The Sounds of Colour

How can a person's skin colour be deduced from... In the 1940s, English jazz critic Leonard Feather played records without disclosing the artists' identities to musicians in *Metronome* and *Downbeat*. He recorded their comments and, according to Gary Giddons' 1994 *Village Voice* obituary of Feathers, 'Over decades, Feather embarrassed scores of musicians who thought that race and gender were audible...' (George McKay, *Circular Breathing: The Cultural Politics of Jazz in Britain*, p.118).

'What has race got to do with voices?': Chris Welch, 'Soul Scene Going', *Melody Maker*, 12 February 1966. Michael Awkward grapples with this difficult question on various pages of his book *Soul Covers: Rhythm and Blues Remakes and the Struggle for Artistic Identity* (2007, Duke University Press).

'a ridiculous song for a white person to sing...': Mike Hennessey, 'Dionne Defiant: "Authentic Coloured Sound? You Can Only Get It If You're Negro"', *Melody Maker*, 5 February 1966

what was black jazz and what was white: Brian Longhurst in *Blackness/Black Music – Popular Music and Society* (1995,1999, Polity Press, p.128) quotes J. Tagg's contention that, despite the musical characteristics of call-and-response, syncopation, improvisation and 'blue notes' which are often used to define black music, 'none of these can be used to identify a discrete category of black music'. 'Black' and 'white' applied to music, he suggests, are ideological rather than musicological descriptors.

In a tradition going back over a hundred years... Whites blacking themselves up for performative purposes goes back at least as far as the 16th century, as may be seen from viewing the 1972 film *Henry VIII and his Six Wives*.

the phenomenally successful TV series... At Christmas 1962, *Black and White Minstrel* albums were at Numbers 1, 2 and 5 in the *NME* album charts. As early as 7 September 1957 Tony Brown in *Melody Maker* called the Television Minstrels, the B/W forerunners, 'bad taste... an offence to the Negro race'. *The Black and White Minstrel Show* continued on BBC TV until 1 July 1978 and the stage show, 1960–72, established itself in *The Guinness Book of Records* as the theatre show seen by the largest number of people.

'If I hadn't seen them with my own eyes...': Alan Smith, 'You've pleased – pleased us', *NME*, 1 February 1963

Timi Yuro, Del Shannon... were wrongly colour-coded... Bill Wyman on Timi Yuro, *Melody Maker*, 19 September 1964; Dave Clark on Del Shannon, *Melody Maker*, 7 March 1964; Keith Fordyce on Jimmy Beaumont, *NME*, 29 July 1960

The list included: Tom Jones, the Righteous Brothers... T. Jones, *Disc*, 22 May 1965;

Righteous Bros, *Record Mirror*, 23 January 1965; G. Fame, *Record Mirror*, 20 July 1963; Four Seasons, *Record Mirror*, 6 July 1963; L.J. Baldry, *NME*, 12 June 1964; C. Farlowe, *Melody Maker*, 4 December 1965; J. Cocker, *Melody Maker*, 19 October 1968; S. Winwood, *Melody Maker*, 12 February 1966; C. Bennett, *NME*, 13 May 1967; J. Joplin, *NME*, 26 April 1969; E. Burdon, *Melody Maker*, 24 July 1965; Rascals, *Disc*, 22 March 1969; Delaney & B., *Melody Maker*, 18 October 1969; N. Sedaka, *Melody Maker*, 23 November 1963; Sandie S. by L. Barry, *Disc*, 26 February 1966; Sandie S. by G. Fame, *Melody Maker*, 7 January 1967. In the case of the Rascals, their record company, Atlantic, kept their photograph off the record sleeves so that they would sell in both black and white markets (Kevin Phinney, 2005, *Souled American: How Black Music Transformed White Culture*, Billboard Books, p.198).

'When I found out they were…': Kevin Phinney, *Souled American*, p.50

Black performers like Nat 'King' Cole… Johnny Mathis: Sammy Davis Junior is a particularly interesting case of a black singer with aspirations to be regarded as white in the early-to-mid-Sixties. Wil Haygood (2004) *In Black and White: The Life of Sammy Davis Jnr*, Aurum, p.136: 'his nose was pressed against the white world – Frank and Jeff Chandler and Tony Curtis showing him the view' or again, p.134, in the opinion of Helen Gallagher, a girlfriend: 'He wanted, she felt, to talk of whites, of white people, white America. He did so want to be white'.

as if their very lives depended on the release… In *Just My Soul Responding: Rhythm and Blues, Black Consciousness and Race Relations* (1998, UCL Press, p.12), Brian Ward suggests that 'genuine admiration for black music did not necessarily challenge basic white racial beliefs… but frequently served to reinforce them… associated with the unremittingly physical, passionate, ecstatic, emotional, and, above all, sexually liberated black world of their imaginations.' Paradoxically, equating black music with emotionality reduced it to cliché.

likes of Judy Garland and Ethel Merman were not thought to sound black… At the start of her singing career, however, Aretha Franklin was heard by Don Nicholl as having been 'heavily influenced by Miss Garland' (*Disc*, 2 December 1961). Perhaps because she was singing 'Rock A Bye Your Baby' at the time.

Shirley Bassey was initially assumed to be white… Stephen Bourne (2005) *Elisabeth Welch: Soft Lights and Sweet Music*, Scarecrow Press Inc, p.107: 'When she [Shirley Bassey] sang 'Goldfinger' in Las Vegas in 1964, she was shocked by the audience's reaction. They were surprised to find a black woman singing the James Bond theme. They had never seen her and assumed she was white'.

Much, of course, had to do with the material… However, when Sam Cooke sang 'Danny Boy' and 'The Bells of St Mary's' and both Little Richard and Jackie Wilson serenaded their loved ones 'By The Light of The Silvery Moon', they were not heard as white.

the voice… 'is of course the most difficult thing…': Ian Sansom, 'Very Like St Paul', *London Review of Books*, Vol.28, No.5, 9 March 2006

'what actually made him great…': Ibid.

Of the 25 tracks… 18 had originally… In Cordell Marks, 'Dusty Talks About Her Royal Variety Shock', *NME*, 27 November 1964, Dusty said: 'I'm guilty of making cover versions myself and still feel mine aren't as good as the originals'. Did Dusty react to black music as Patricia Juliana Smith suggests here? 'The black woman and her music… symbolised a displaced sexual freedom and power to middle-class white audiences'? (Patricia Juliana Smith, 'You Don't Have To Say You Love Me' in P.J. Smith (ed.), 1999, *The Queer Sixties*, Routledge, p.108)

'Dusty's reputation as Britain's great soul voice…': Jim Irvin (ed.) (2000) *The Mojo Collection: The Greatest Albums of All Time*, Mojo Books, p.42

you feel she could be a 'soul mama': Baby Washington's comment on Dusty's covers was: 'she's very close to the style I sang the songs in, and she's done an excellent job' (*South Bank Show*, ITV, 9 April 2006).

'she surpasses Mitty Collier's sultry original…': Robert Gallagher, *Goldmine*, 31 May 1991

like the Crystals' 'He's A Rebel': An anonymous *Record Mirror* reviewer on 13 October 1962 thought the ending 'a bit too wild for polite English ears. It's also non-understandable'. A pop *Finnegan's Wake* perhaps?

Whereas little of Bacharach's beautiful melody… This is despite Bacharach's presence as conductor on the Hunt recording. Apparently, Bacharach later preferred Dusty's version to the one he made with Hunt (Michael Brocken, 2003, *Bacharach: Maestro! The Life Of A Pop Genius*, Chrome Dreams, p.149). In a 1996 *Mojo*, Bob Stanley thought, 'Tommy Hunt's very fine original is simply annihilated' by Dusty's cover.

a more 'churchy-sounding' backing chorus… Two of the three backing singers were black Americans – Madeline Bell and Doris Troy. The other was Dusty herself. Information from Paul Howes (2001, 2007) *The Complete Dusty Springfield*, Reynolds and Hearn Ltd, p.84. Lucy O'Brien (*Dusty*, p.95) suggests that on this track, Dusty 'takes a leaf from Janis Joplin's book', but in 1965 Joplin had yet to make a record and Dusty would not even have heard of her.

Dusty can not only do without her brother… The same point is made by Patricia Juliana Smith in 'You Don't Have To Say You Love Me' (*The Queer Sixties*, p.108). Although 'Mockingbird' is the only track where Dusty duets with herself, other recordings may be interpreted as interior conversations, for instance 'Bits And Pieces', 'Beautiful Soul', 'I Start Counting' and 'Exclusively For Me'.

Inez Foxx… comes across as an imitation… Some years later Inez Foxx said of Dusty, 'I think she is so underrated. This girl is really tremendous' (*Melody Maker*, 13 June 1970).

she put more of an effort into integrating a black vocal into her own: Dusty's reconstructions of black vocalisations put one in mind of H.L. Gates' concept of 'signifying' – a complex notion concerned with subversive black interpretative strategies of white messages (H.L. Gates Jr., 1988, *The Signifying Monkey: A Theory of Afro-American Literary Criticism*, Oxford University Press). Here the reversed position suggests that imitation is the greatest form of flattery or, in Gates' words, 'signification' or 'refiguration as an act of homage' (p.xxviii).

on the 1965 *Sounds Of Motown* TV Special, duetted with Martha: Annie J. Randall writes, 'while Springfield and the Motown artists scrupulously avoided attaching any political significance to their TV special, no one could have missed the message of solidarity it conveyed, following on the heels of Springfield's front-page deportation from South Africa' ('Dusty Springfield and the Motown Invasion', *Institute for Studies in American Music*, No.1, Fall 2005, Vol.xxxv). According to Tom Danehy, 'Ashes To Ashes, Dusty to Dusty', *Tucson Weekly*, 29 March 1999: 'The broadcast became the stuff of legend. Elvis Costello credits it with sparking his interest in music, and Elton John said it made him join her official fan club the very next day'.

'a bit too polite – dare I say…?': Paul Sexton, *Dusty In Memphis*, Radio 2, 14 November 2006, producer Paul Sexton

Without her enthusiasm or agreement… Dave Godin in O'Brien, *Dusty*, p.61: 'The Motown Revue was sold because Dusty said, "Package me with it and my name will get it on"'.

in Martha Reeves' words, she 'glorified' the music: Martha Reeves on *Definitely Dusty*, BBC TV, 26 December 1999. An anonymous reviewer in *NME*, 7 May 1965, wrote 'Dusty Springfield outshone everybody on Tamla Motown TV show'.

as even some of the Motown artists recognised: Ray Coleman, *Melody Maker*, 26 March 1977 reports Motown singer, Mary Wells, sending him a card in the mid-Sixties 'saying her friends [at Tamla Motown in Detroit] were AMAZED at her discovery of this white girl who sounded more black than some blacks'.

'threatening to lapse into gooey hotel foyer muzak': Lucy O'Brien, *Dusty*, p.113

'even manages to "soulify" the song': Paul Howes, *The Complete Dusty Springfield*, p.107

'spine-chilling... histrionic desolation': Ian Hoare, 'Soul: Singles' in John Collis (ed.) (1980) *The Rock Primer*, Penguin, p.119

'one-woman vocal hurricane': Bruce Huston, 'Linda Jones Remembered', *Soul Survivor*, Vol.1, No.1, 1984

what Roland Barthes called the 'grain' of the voice: Roland Barthes, 'The Grain of the Voice', 1977, in S. Frith and A. Goodwin (eds) (1990) *On Record*, Routledge, pp.297 and 299: 'The "grain" is the body in the voice as it sings, the hand as it writes, the limb as it performs'.

'grain' or timbre is heard or felt at non-verbal levels: In Donna Soto-Morettini (2006) *Popular Singing: A Practical Guide to Pop, Jazz, Blues, Rock, Country and Gospel*, A & C Black Publishers Ltd, p.14, the author writes: 'Particular voices can have particular qualities and capacities, and this is an area of vocal work that desperately needs more research'.

Does Camille Paglia come closer...?: *The South Bank* Show, 9 April 2006

we don't know how the great eighteenth century castrati sounded: In *Castrato*, a BBC4 on BBC2 documentary shown on 26 June 2007, an experiment was made to try to reproduce what a castrato might have sounded like. Guesswork though it was, the technological result sounded nothing like Dusty Springfield.

'a very strange voice': *The South Bank Show*, 9 April 2006. Dusty told Ray Coleman in *Melody Maker*, 11 February 1978, 'I knew from the age of eight or nine that I did have this strange voice'.

or not a 'soul' singer: For example, Jim Irvin, 'Be There Then', *Word*, November 2007: 'I don't believe Dusty was the sixties "great British soul singer" as she's too emotionally guarded'.

BBC4 documentary, *Soul Britannia*: First shown on BBC4, 2 February 2007, producer and director Jeremy Marre

a programme on British soul had to include her... But a programme on British pop in the 1960s could dispense with her altogether. BBC4's *Pop Britannia*, first broadcast on 11 January 2008, failed to even mention her. Why? Partly because she did not fit into the programme's theme of teenagers being managed by entrepreneurs like Epstein, Loog Oldham or Mickie Most; but even more, one suspects, because she remains a one-off cultural figure – simultaneously mainstream and on-the-margins – and has to be dealt with separately from everyone else. In this sense, she is one of the most radical and subversive performers in pop music. Also, as I suggest later, she was an independent-minded woman, and fits uneasily into masculist frames of reference.

'A black drag queen with the heart of...': Stacey D'Erasmo, 'Beginning With Dusty', *Village Voice*, 29 August 1995

Part two – Girls, It Ain't Easy

Chapter four – Beehive Maintenance and Serial Mascara Excess

Perhaps the one she called Cilla or... Valentine and Wickham (2000) *Dancing With Demons*, p.45

Margaret Thatcher: *Cambridge Evening News*, 27 September 2006

Ashley Jensen... Lisa Adams, 'Bright On The Night', *Daily Record*, 18 September 2007: 'with her hair swept up in a glamorous Dusty Springfield style... Ashley Jensen looked a million dollars'.

Rod Stewart... Tim Ewbank and Stafford Hildred (2003) *Rod Stewart: The New Biography*, Portrait, p.211: 'I used to have my hair like Dusty Springfield. It stood six inches above my head. Bottles of hair lacquer: it was like a rock when you touched it'. Perhaps Rod's self-reference was due to Elton John telling him on a David Frost TV interview in 1983 that his hair was 'like Dusty Springfield in a nightmare'.

Mira Milošević... She was referred to in a 17 January 2002 Radio 4 programme as having 'an uncompromising Dusty Springfield hair style'.

Melvyn Bragg... A picture of Bragg is next to one of Dusty in *Radio Times*, 8–14 April 2006 and an anonymous writer comments: 'he seems to have been so heavy-handed with the backcombing and the hair lacquer, it's hard to tell them apart'.

Joss Stone's dog... *Q*, April 2007. Her dog is 'named after a music legend' because 'she looks just like her. See?'

'the Tories' carefully coiffed answer...' *Cambridge Evening News*, 27 September 2006

her current standing as a camp style icon... Thatcher was included in an 'Icons of the Gay Community' photographic exhibition at the Getty Images Gallery in London, 2005.

'usherettes [who] were Stalins with...': *Scotsman*, 15 February 2006

'Never has a woman been defined...': *Time Out*, May 1994

Hunter Davies suggested a library... 'Gold Dusty', *Sunday Telegraph*, 8 May 1994

'I remembered only the beehive hairdo...': 'Dusty Replies', *Daily Telegraph*, 3 May 1994

half-baked concoctions falling short of hers: Amy Winehouse was recently considered a rival in hair ascendancy, as when Valerie Hill wrote: 'The super-duper new Winehouse version is every bit as high maintenance as Dusty's backcombed look of 40 years ago' ('Voice of the Beehive leads the Hair Stakes', *Liverpool Daily Post*, 5 October 2007).

a 'fellow victim, too, of serial mascara excess': *Manchester Evening News*, 26 February 2007

Thus when Simon Bates on Classic FM... 29 June 2008

In posthumous teledocs... For example, *Definitely Dusty*, BBC TV, and *Living Famously*, BBC2, producer Tom Ware, broadcast 22 January 2003

'twin craters, both extinct': Bob Monkhouse (1995) *Over The Limit: My Secret Diaries* 1993–8, Century, p.289

'Legend in her own mascara': Joe Joseph, *The Times*, 3 May 1994

With 'Dusty's Hair' already the title... The paper was given by Annie Janeiro Randall at a conference on Feminist Theory and Music, 23–6 June 2005, New York City.

'Bette Davis Eyes', as recorded by Kim Carnes, was at number 1 in the US charts for nine weeks during 1981.

'her defining look…': BBC1 News, 3 March 1999

'that fantastic image…': ITV, 3 March 1999

'Dusty, with her blonde beehive hair-dos…': Chris Welch, *Independent*, 4 March 1999

'her extraordinary appearance…': Anthony Thorncroft, 'Maverick Pop Diva from an Innocent Age', *Financial Times*, 4 March 1999

Her image, as Barney Hoskyns… 'Both Sides of the Beehive Queen', *Uncut*, August 2006

'With her peroxide Dusty Springfield bob…': Simon Price, *Independent*, 20 May 2007

'an appealing figure beneath a Sixties bob…': Luke Jennings, *Observer*, 29 April 2007

'This has a very 1960s feel about it…': Rick Stein, 'Meditations for the Summer Table', *Telegraph*, 28 July 2007

'It wasn't pretty…': 'Male Cosmetics in the Spotlight', *Daily Mail*, 22 April 2007

'Who hasn't… had their hair done…?': *Radio Times*, 15–21 September 2004

'marvel at the number of Dusty Springfield…': 'Romance On The High Mississippi', *Minnesota Daily*, 26 April 2007

judging by Celia Walden's experiences in the *Telegraph*… Celia Walden, 'The Beehive: Amy honey, how do you stand it?', *Telegraph*, 3 October 2007

'give it a modern makeover'/'the most copied…': Clemmie Moodie, 'The Beehive Is Back – and It's Better Than Ever', *Daily Mail*, 30 September 2007

flappers like Colleen Moore and Louise Brooks: Marjorie Rosen (1973) *Popcorn Venus: Women, Movies and the American Dream*, Peter Owen, pp.75 and 87–8

the Joan Crawford face: For example, in two films of 1955, *Queen Bee* and *Female On The Beach*.

'Other girls might wear mascara…': Charlotte Greig (1989) *Will You Still Love Me Tomorrow?: Girl Groups from the Fifties On*, Virago Press, p.97

'an exercise in lamination': Jerry Wexler, quoted in sleeve notes to *Dusty In Memphis* CD reissue, 2002

'it takes her an eternity': Bill Dayton, 'Dusty Then and Now', source unknown, 1963 or 4. In *She-Bop II: The Definitive History of Women in Rock, Pop and Soul* (1995, 2002, Continuum, p.20) Lucy O'Brien records how over the years Billie Holiday also took longer and longer to apply make-up and get ready for the stage.

Two such stalwart souls… Others were Pat Rhodes, Vicki Wickham and Stanley Dorfman. In interviews for the 2005 DVD, *Live At The Royal Albert Hall Concert 1979*, Pat Rhodes said 'It would take six or seven hours to get her ready', while Vicki Wickham's words were, 'It took an army to get Dusty ready to do anything'. In the March 2007 edition of *The Dusty Springfield Bulletin*, Stanley Dorfman told Paul Howes, 'Dusty would lock herself away in the dressing room, wouldn't come out, and the whole orchestra was sitting there and all the guests were sitting there. And she wouldn't come out'.

'out of bounds in her dressing room…': Peter Hogan, *Uncut*, November 1999

'she would keep the black on…': *Definitely Dusty*, BBC TV

'everything was all part of a mask': Ibid.

'The bigger the hair…': Mick Brown, *Telegraph Magazine*, 27 May 1995

'bullet-proof… Ancient Greek death mask': 'The Truth About Dusty', *Daily Express*, 9 August 1985

on the 2003 tribute *Living Famously*: BBC2, producer by Tom Ware, broadcast 22 January 2003

'the glittering gowns and extravagant hand gestures': 'They're Still The Ones', *Advocate*, 9 May 2000. Fashions change, and in the October/November 2007 edition of *Word*, Jim Irvin dismissed these dresses as 'awfully square frocks' which Dusty was 'constrained by'.

These allusions and others notwithstanding… In early 1988 both the *News of the World* and the *Sun* showed unkind, even lurid interest in Dusty's body in headlines that say it all: 'Lusty Dusty's Battle of the Bulges', *News of the World*, 10 April 1988 and 'Dumpty Springfield', *Sun*, 19 February 1988.

the beehive was at its height… A website – http://www.cnn.com/STYLE/9702/24/beehive.queen – credits a certain Margaret Vinci Heldt of Illinois with the beehive's creation in 1960, but Wikipedia says it originated in the US during 1958: 'the beehive remains an enduring symbol of 1960s kitsch'.

The one on the head of… Helen Shapiro: Seen on *Brit Girls: Girls On Top*, Channel 4, 20 December 1997

she recalled those on the heads… Melody Parker, 'A Girl Called Dusty', *Campaign*, 1990 or 1991

'the ultimate beehive': Gail Kavanagh, 'The Care and Maintenance of a Beehive', http://www.loti.com/beehive_hairdo.htm

'queen of all beehives': Jim Farler, 'Swept Away With Dusty', *Daily News*, 7 September 1997. On a 1989/90 Richard and Judy TV programme, Judy referred to Dusty's beehive as 'the most famous, the most well-known beehive in the country'.

Tom's 'eternity' remark was confirmed by his sister: Nigel Hunter, 'Springfields Are Such A Modest Trio', *Disc*, 3 August 1963. Dusty wants to 'make up while we talk… takes me ages to do this'.

the 'black painted rings that encircle…': 'What's Wrong With Me – By Miss Springfield', *Evening Standard*, 20 June 1964

Rusty Springboard: No printed references found but the name is in oral memory, remembered by at least two others as well as the author.

'Why does she wear so much eye shadow?': *Disc*, 25 September 1965

'just shy of a coronation': *Variety*, 10 January 1997

until Amy Winehouse in 2007: The rapidity with which Amy Winehouse became a household name is worth studying in itself. People who have no interest in current pop music not only know her name but have also heard her sing.

tone down 'her leather make-up' and 'get rid of…': Stanley Dorfman interview, 'The Musical World of Stanley Dorfman', *The Dusty Springfield Bulletin*, March 2007

she predated The Clash by about ten years: Perhaps the most outlandish rainbow effect of Dusty's clothing came on a 1969 French TV Special with Charles Aznavour. Green, purple, pink, blue, white, black and gold all jostle for attention in a bizarre fancy dress parade. At one stage, her face is interposed over a roaring fire as if she is being burnt for sinful 'colouring book' impropriety.

'neon sign make-up and innumerable blond wigs': *Observer*, September 1968

'need to appear beautiful': *Observer Magazine*, October 1968. On a 1980 TV programme called *Big Time* Dusty told Sheena Easton 'It took me six years to let anybody from room service in a hotel see me without my eye make-up'. And in his 1991 novel, *Alma Cogan* (Minerva, p.85), Gordon Burn has his fictitious Alma say, 'If I'd ordered a meal in my room in a hotel, I would hide in the bathroom until it was served to avoid being seen by the staff'. Here Dusty has segued into Alma Cogan.

'I don't much care for Dusty Springfield': 'Let's Not Look Gift Pups In The Mouth', *Sun*, 16 August 1967

'False hair, false eyelashes': *Disc*, 8 June 1968. Between 1966 and the early '70s there were numerous press criticisms of Dusty's appearance. Her dresses were either too long or too short; it was time to change her hair but when she did, the style did not suit her; her gestures were excessive etc. Amongst the 'critical' editions were: *Disc*, 1 Oct 1966 and 4 March 1967; *NME*, 12 Oct 1968 and 2 Nov 1968.

'Oh look, it's Dusty': 'Dusty's Wigs', *Disc*, 17 August 1968

she didn't have a 'pop face'... Peter Laurie, 'I'd love to be pop before I go flop', *Daily Mail*, 18 November 1963

'hopelessly unphotogenic...': *Evening Standard*, 20 June 1964

'a fitting place for [Dusty] is a freak show...': Ibid.

'I was just like a mask...': Michael Watts, 'Jools: Climbing Back Into The Sunlight', *Melody Maker*, 7 November 1970

'I hid behind that image': Roy Carr, 'Whatever Became of Baby Jools?', *NME*, 6 March 1971

she bequeathed the idea of a mask... For example, Chris Welch, *Independent*, 4 March 1999, 'a mask to conceal an awkward, insecure woman'; Jackie Burdon, *Western Mail*, 4 March 1999, 'a mask to preserve her privacy'; Fraser Middleton, *Glasgow Evening Times*, 3 March 1999, 'she also used that mask to keep her privacy'.

'Dusty', she exclaimed in disbelief: 'I've learned the Lonely art of Being a Superstar', *News of the World*, 19 February 1978

'It's Dusty with a difference': *Daily Mail*, February 1978

'her carefully dryer-blown hair...': Keith Howes, *Gay News*, April 1978

'You've quite radically changed your image': *Nationwide*, BBC TV, January 1978. Dusty was obviously feeling particularly sensitive about her image change in 1978. That year she told Chris White in *Music Week*: 'I hate competing with my past image... It is wrong to be constantly compared with what you did'; and Jenny Rees of the *Daily Mail*: 'There will always be people who... much prefer you the way that you were... who don't want you to progress'. But as early as 2 November 1968 she was telling Penny Valentine in *Disc*, 'It bothers me that this panda-eyed, immovable bee-hive image has stuck with me...' Regarding 'Ooh, it doesn't look like her', she referred to someone saying 'My God, I thought she was dead' on seeing a poster advertising her (*The John Davidson Show*, 15 August 1980, US TV).

'the cool elegance of a fashion model': Dennis Hunt, 'Dusty, Show Biz: Together Again', *Los Angeles Times*, 23 January 1978

'frizzy hair and elegantly casual clothes': 'The New Image of Dusty Springfield', *What's On In London*, 20 April 1979

'conventional and inconspicuous': *Cash Box*, 18 February 1978

her Drury Lane and Albert Hall concerts: Theatre Royal, Drury Lane: 19–21 April 1979; Royal Albert Hall: 3 December 1979

Dusty Springfield looking natural and normal was the fake: In her *Daily Express* 1985 interview with Jean Rook, Dusty said: 'I did try to ditch the thick make-up for a scrubbed, tanned look, but to hell with that… I reminded myself of those suntanned women in Miami who look like old handbags'.

After trying to fob off on American audiences… For example, *The Mike Douglas Show*, October 1980; *The Toni Tenille Show*, end of 1980

her professional dealings with Peter Stringfellow: Dusty signed for Stringfellow's newly formed Hippodrome label and released one single, 'Sometimes Like Butterflies'.

'Startling' and 'vivid': *Woman*, 12 October 1985

'the Michelin man in drag': Gordon Biggins, *Nine to Five*, 5 August 1985

'a minicab driver in Bacofoil': John Peel, 'Returning Dusty Answers', *Observer*, 4 August 1985. Around this time too, an anonymous reviewer in *Weekend* said she was too 'formidable looking' to be offered a seat on a bus.

talking to Janet Street Porter on *Saturday Night Out*: BBC TV, 27 April 1985

chatting up Terry W on *Wogan*: BBC TV, 9 August 1985

'Was it not a mask?': 'Brand New Dusty', *Observer*, 14 February 1989

'she had perfected her disguise'… *Telegraph* magazine, 27 May 1995

'You would literally hide behind…': *Sunday Sunday*, ITV, 25 November 1990

numerous mentions after her death… For example, Peter Doggett, 'The Enigma that was Dusty Springfield', *Record Collector*, May 1999: 'hiding herself in… her showbiz disguise'; and on Radio 2, pre-Christmas, 1999, Steve Wright asked Vicki Wickham 'Was that her mask?' to which VW replied 'Yes'.

'get rid of that awful perm': *Melody Maker*, 15 July 1995

'I have special muscles'… 'Wishin' and Copin' with Dusty Springfield', *Us*, 2 May 1988

'I used so much hair spray…': 'Dusty Rides Again', *New York Times Review*, 29 October 1995

she mocked her own image… Even in the Sixties she did this. Warren Mitchell, guesting on her 1967 show, said with her obvious approval: 'You wanna see her close to. Half a pound of boot polish on her eyeballs'.

On a second French, Saunders and Springfield occasion: *French and Saunders*, 4 January 1996

French and Saunders were attacked… For instance: 'What an Insult to Dusty', *News of the World*, 8 May 1994: 'making the country's greatest pop and soul songstress the fall guy in a French and Saunders sketch was irritating and insulting'; Paul Bailey, 'White Queen Keeps Her Place', *Guardian*, 3 May 1994: 'they cracked clankingly embarrassing jokes… they shouted at each other to excess… their self-indulgent routine'; Joe Joseph, 'Legend in her Own Mascara', *The Times*, 3 May 1994: 'an extended French and Saunders sketch… seemed not just distracting but more than a little insulting'.

'he wished they had been "allowed the night off"'… *Sunday Times*, 8 May 1994

'take the mickey out of myself': The Andrew Duncan Interview, *Radio Times*, 30 April–6 May 1994

'Oh, the hair, I want it': *Later With Jools Holland*, BBC TV, 10 June 1995

Des O'Connor, gently detected 'slightly less eye liner': *The Des O'Connor Show*, ITV, 17 January 1996

Chapter five – Oh You Beautiful Doll

she was her own Svengali: Paul Du Noyer, 'Fuck 'em if they can't take a joke', *Mojo*, 1995

'a supremely stylish operator': Maureen Paton, 'Blowing Up A Dusty Storm', *Daily Express*, 3 May 1994

'her self-reinvention procedure was as complex…': Robert Sandall, 'Spirit Of The Beehive', *Sunday Times*, 1989

The painful electrolysis programme Eddie Judson inflicted… Barbara Leaming (1990) *If This Was Happiness: A Biography of Rita Hayworth*, Sphere, p.51

Margarita was chubby and… Ibid., p.49

'fix your hair here'… 'this bow…': Ibid., p.59

A later star persona… Kim Novak: Sam Kashner and Jennifer MacNair (2002) *The Bad and the Beautiful: Hollywood in the Fifties*, Time Warner, pp.197 and 201

James Stewart in *Vertigo* redressed and restyled her… In *Mr Hitchcock* (2007, Haus Publishing, p.141), Quentin Falk quotes Kim Novak telling Anwar Brett in 1998, 'I thought my playing this role was simply meant to be because it seemed to be so much of what I was going through already at Columbia'. She was told, 'we want you but we want you to look like somebody else'.

the hard work which had gone into turning Margarita Cansino… Adrienne L. McLean (2004) *Being Rita Hayworth: Labor, Identity and Hollywood Stardom*, Rutgers University Press, Chapter 1

'a mediocre misfit, Mary O'Brien…': Lucy O'Brien, *Dusty*, p.xii

Even pop's chameleon prince, David Bowie: *Girls and Boys, Sex and British Pop*, BBC2, programme 2: 'Oh, You Pretty Things', first broadcast 30 October 2005

'So I became someone else': *Tonight in Toronto*, Canadian TV, early Eighties

'on went the tall beehive wig…': Lucy O'Brien, *Dusty*, 1989 edition, p.xi

'a radical change of style': Ibid., 1991 edition, p.xii

'a radically thought-out change of style': Ibid., 1999 edition, p.2

'in one afternoon to be this other person…': RuPaul, 'Dusty: The Celt of The Earth', *Interview*, August 1995

hair 'with endless pins in it': Ibid.

an account given by Dusty on Canadian TV: *Tonight in Toronto*

'years of hard work and pushing…': Cathy Couzens, 'If You Want To Know The Truth', *Star*, 18 May 1979. According to Peter Miles, a school friend, on *The South Bank Show*, April 2006: 'Mary had – from the age of, probably 12 – an incredible inner drive to become a successful singer in music'.

'grew on me like fungus': *The Big Time: Sheena Easton*, BBC TV, 2 July 1980

'the first time I appeared as a blonde…': 'The Sound That Grew in The Grass', *Woman*, December 1965

'a fairly calculating bastard': Tom Hibbert, 'Blondes Have Less Fun', *Q*, April 1989

'a seething mass of ambition…': *Girl About Town*, 1989

'the reason I worked so hard on my appearance': Maureen Grant, 'I Won't Be Alone Forever', *Woman*, 22 July 1978. *On Remembering Dusty Springfield*, Part 1, Radio 2, 2 March 2000, Derek Wadsworth confirmed this by saying she 'worked at her beauty just the same way that she worked at her voice and worked at other aspects of her craft'.

'having her hair bleached, in tears...': *Remembering Dusty Springfield*, Part 1, Radio 2, 2 March 2000

The 'tomboy' Mrs O'Brien described her daughter as being: 'Mary Was A Tomboy', *NME*, 2 July 1965

The trouble was that it couldn't make up its mind: Dusty told Jean Rook in 1985 'my hair doesn't know where it's going yet. Or let's say it hasn't arrived at where it wants to be'.

If... she was going out blonde... Valentine and Wickham (2000) *Dancing With Demons,* p.285. Dusty phoned her hairdresser to say, 'Debbie, I've got to be in my coffin as a blonde, please come as soon as you can'.

This was the age she saw her first Twentieth Century Fox musical: David Cuthbert, 'Dusty Says Tardiness Comes From Her Fear', *The Times*, Picayune, New Orleans, 24 April 1972

she had committed the cardinal sin: Ibid.

a certain June Haver who quickly became the wannabe: Ibid. Also, Alan Smith, 'Dusty Goes Back To Own Childhood', *NME*, 15 July 1966: 'June Haver was my idol, and I always dreamed of being like her and dancing and singing my way through a wonderful world of music and Technicolor'.

'Glittering and forbidden...': Lucy O'Brien, *Dusty*, p.xi

Lucy probably mistook the down-home musicals at Twentieth... Dusty's lighting engineer, Fred Perry, said 'the only difference of opinion [he and Dusty] ever had in 25 years was I thought MGM musicals were better than 20th Century Fox Musicals; she thought that 20th Century Fox musicals were better than MGM musicals' (*Dusty Springfield Bulletin*, March 2008).

'part of a dream of inclusion': Joanna Pitman (2003) *On Blondes*, Bloomsbury, p.234

'Blonde was no longer just a look': Ibid., p.235

Oh, You Beautiful Doll: A 1949 movie starring June Haver.

Like Mary too... spent a lot of time gazing into mirrors... In *A Whole Scene Going*, BBC TV, 11 May 1966, Dusty said: 'I'm constantly peering in mirrors... and I'm actually not seeing anything'. Information about Warhol is taken from various sources, especially the film *Warhol On Warhol*, shown on Channel 5, 2 March 2005.

'They are entirely fantastic constructions...': Amada Cruz, 'Movies, Monstrosities and Masks: Twenty Years of Cindy Sherman' in (1997) *Cindy Sherman – Retrospective*, Thames and Hudson, p.9

'Womanliness... could be assumed and worn like a mask': Joan Riviere, quoted in Elizabeth Wright (ed.) (1992) *Feminism and Psychoanalysis: A Critical Dictionary*, Blackwell, p.243

anticipated the theoretical work of Judith Butler: For example, Butler's ground-breaking study of gender and performativity *Gender Trouble: Feminism and the Subversion of Identity* (1990, Routledge).

If Dusty Springfield was the drag artist... For example, Ian Collins, 'The Magic of Dusty Lives On', *Eastern Daily Press*, 4 March 1994: 'Girls copied her appearance. So did drag artists'; Charles Shaar Murray, *The South Bank Show*, 9 April 2006: Dusty was 'a female drag queen'; Kris Kirk, *Gay Times*, September 1985: 'I learned most of my tricks from drag queens... In fact, if the truth were known, I think I'm basically a drag queen myself'.

she not only showed it up for the fantasy it had always been... Pamela Robertson has this to say of Mae West: 'She parodically reappropriates – and hyperbolizes – the image of the woman from male female impersonators so that the object of her joke is not the woman but the idea that an essential feminine identity exists prior to the image: she reveals that feminine identity is always a masquerade or impersonation' (1996, *Guilty Pleasures: Feminist Camp from Mae West to Madonna*, I.B. Tauris & Co, p.34).

'who are able knowingly to enjoy (and subvert or parody)... Jane M. Ussher (1997) *Fantasies of Femininity: Reframing The Boundaries of Sex*, Rutgers University Press, p.58

and looks she was unsure about: *Woman*, December 1965: 'I was obsessed with the thought that I was ugly, and I yearned to be glamorous'.

'represented... the female sensibility...': Charles Shaar Murray, *The South Bank Show*

'You pioneered a look': *The Dame Edna Experience*, LWT, 19 November 1989

Dusty often implied she felt like a fraud... For instance, Mick Brown, *Telegraph Magazine*, 27 May 1995: 'I stayed frozen... with the sheer stress of it because I couldn't be Aretha'; Roger Scott, Radio 1 Interview, 11 March 1989: 'I always sounded like a sad copy of them' (the original records by black singers); *Definitely Dusty*, BBC TV, Dusty's voice on soundtrack: 'There was an element of me that... often thought that I was a sham'.

Chapter six – Bitches and Boils

Dusty Springfield was inaugurated... The event took place on 14 November 2006, broadcast on Channel 4, 16 November 2006.

Discussion of Dusty Springfield's music: For instance, Mick Brown, *Telegraph Magazine*, 27 May 1995: 'Almost alone for the time she was a woman singer who paid real attention to what she sang and how it was arranged and produced'; Tracy McVeigh and David Wigg, 'Bravery of Dusty the pop queen', *Express*, 4 March 1999: 'In the studio she would record a song over and over again if she thought something was wrong with the sound or an arrangement'.

she thought Franz deserved the credit... Paul Du Noyer, *Mojo*, 1995: 'Bless his heart, he'd sit in there and read Popular Mechanics... he'd suddenly look up... and go E flat... the producer's credit... he deserved it and I was grateful'. Also, in 'Dusty: The Ultimate Interview' conducted in November 1993 and published in *The Dusty Springfield Bulletin*, November 2003, Dusty called Franz 'a real gent' and said 'he knew that I knew what I was doing', and was able to translate her non-musical explanations into terminology the musicians could understand and put into practice.

she appreciated his understanding: Johnny Franz had worked at Philips as recording manager with Vera Lynn and Shirley Bassey amongst others. One feels he was unusually placid, for recording sessions with Dusty were not like those with Frankie Vaughan whom he described in *NME*, 18 April 1958, as 'extremely easy to work with... surprisingly few "takes"'. In a later *NME* article, 19 August 1966, Franz said: 'Dusty's sessions are quite hard work. She is pretty serious in the studio, and it's a good thing... we're always pretty much in agreement... we just go on till we're happy with the result'. As early as the sleeve notes to her first album, *A Girl Called Dusty* in 1964, Franz wrote of Dusty's dedication 'to getting the right sound from every musician'. He seems to have had a talent for understanding and nurturing wayward musical loners, as he went on to collaborate effectively with the equally fastidious Scott Walker.

'it would have been unthinkable': Aida Pavletich (1980) *Sirens of Song: The Popular Female Vocalist In America*, Da Capo, p.16

'swallow [her] pride and let...': Ibid.

it would look 'too slick'... 'Fuck 'Em', *Mojo*, 1995

'women didn't do that and I wanted...': Ibid.

who thought their music took priority... Accounts of Dusty's studio perfectionism are many. For example, Johnny Franz, *NME*, 19 August 1966, reported that the previous night's session had gone on until 4.50 am; and Ivor Raymonde, her musical arranger, told Lucy O'Brien 'She'd got quite a reputation for being a hard case... Bad musicians would annoy her, the tempo had to be set so it wasn't too high or low. She was a perfectionist...' (*Dusty*, 1999 version, p.52).

repeat simple chords 40 times over as with Phil Spector: *Phil Spector's Demons*, Channel 4, 16 October 2007, producer and director Jeremy Marre

especially for white British rhythm sections: Stanley Dorfman in *The Dusty Springfield Bulletin*, March 2007 said 'Rhythm sections really suffered with Dusty because she wanted the Motown sound... and she went at them, went at them, went at them'.

'To say people found her difficult'... Lucy O'Brien, *Living Famously*. Photographers also found Dusty hard to deal with. In 'Harry Goodwin, the uncrowned king of pop photography', *The Times*, 31 May 2008, Goodwin reports: 'She threw a shoe at my head after I'd burst into her dressing room and set my flash off. Five pictures in five years I got off her. She was an absolute nightmare. But what talent!'

'spend hours working on the arrangements': 'Fame Has A Flipside Too', *Woman*, December 1965

'snap sometimes when the musicians...': Ibid.

'a pain in the neck': Peter Evans, 'I'm a Piece of Living History', *Woman*, 1975 or 1976

'a great scowler': Jon Savage, 'A Brand New Dusty', *Observer*, 14 February 1989

'stigmata of perfectibility': *Definitely Dusty*, BBC TV

'She produced the whole thing': Paul Howes (2001) *The Complete Dusty Springfield*, Reynolds and Hearn Ltd, p.8

'Seventeen of them I gave over the credit...': Interview included in *Remembering Dusty Springfield*, part 2, BBC Radio 2, 9 March 2000

'in those days it looked wrong...': Alan Jackson, 'Madam Butterfly', *Melody Maker*, 17 August 1985. Even in 1978 when she was prepared to publicly acknowledge her role as producer, Dusty said 'I had to fight quite hard to get a production credit on my new album' (Ray Coleman, *Melody Maker*, 11 February 1978).

'Somehow it looked too competent': Alan Jackson, op. cit.

matters like sound engineering, vocal and orchestral... For example, Marcelle Bernstein, *Observer Magazine*, 1967; Peter Jones, 'Dusty In The Studio', *Record Mirror*, 25 July 1964; Derek Wadsworth to Paul Howes, *The Complete Dusty Springfield*, pp.7–8; Caroline Boucher, *Disc*, 25 January 1969: 'Once during a rehearsal she stopped a whole orchestra to point out to the bass player that he was flat'.

'When a man stands his ground...': *Definitely Dusty*, BBC TV

'get so many ideas which I can't...': Derek Johnson, 'Dusty's Disc Surprise', *NME*, 7 February 1964. In 1978 Dusty told Dave Lee Travis: 'I'm really not a natural songwriter at all' (Radio 1 Interview, 2 February 1978).

'determined to try and make it...': Nigel Hunter, *Disc*, 1 February 1964

her gown 'leaves plenty of food for thought': 'Yana at the Prince of Wales Theatre', *NME*, 8 February 1957

'Marion Ryan stretched out...': Maurice Burman, 'I Don't Try To Be Sexy', *Melody Maker*, 15 March 1958 'it's nice for a girl to have a mink coat': Tony Keniston, *NME*, 26 December 1958

'the hottest piece of singing glamour': Dennis Detheridge, 'Saucy Shirley Turns On The Heat', *NME*, 3 May 1957

'revealed [her] considerable assets... a Grecian goddess...': Laurie Henshaw, 'I Never Expected To Make The Top Twenty', *Melody Maker*, 28 February 1959

'"I Couldn't Say No" has that small...': *NME*, 24 August 1962

'a girl said yes with all of her might': *NME*, 2 March 1962

Anything less than a sexy-sounding turn-on... For example, Keith Fordyce heard a Mary Wells' song, 'Two Lovers', as 'a rather miserable sound. And Miss Wells sounds like she's never heard the word, "smile"... the singer utterly fails to sound like a girl that one would ever want to get to know'. So what point could there be to the record? (*NME*, 15 February 1963)

'Grouping singers in a higher vocal range...': Stuart Linnell, *Sunday Mercury Special Edition*, p.11, March 1999

If, as with Elkie Brooks... '"They Told Me To Look More Feminine" says Elkie Brooks', *Record Mirror*, 9 January 1965

Dusty was urged by the producer... Stanley Dorfman Interview, *Dusty Springfield Bulletin*, March 2007

'Let the husband be the boss...': Charles Govey, 'Edna Savage Says Yes To Terry Dene', *NME*, 4 July 1958

later career as the Queen Mum of British TV... But apparently her earlier pop music time is more important to Cilla, as she said on *The Story of Light Entertainment*, BBC4, 7 January 2008: 'On my headstone... I would rather have, "Here lies Cilla Black, singer", rather than "Cilla Black, TV entertainer"'. Isn't there anyone who has the heart to tell her?

'I would put my own feelings aside...': *Brit Girls: Cilla*, Channel 4, 22 November 1997

'an inferior part of entertainment...': Ibid.

Two recent general histories of Britain in the Sixties... Shawn Levy (2002) *Ready, Steady, Go! The Smashing Rise and Giddy Fall of Swinging London*, Doubleday; and Dominic Sandbrook (2006) *White Heat*, Little, Brown. Yet another Sixties history – Gerard DeGroot (2008) *The 60s Unplugged: A Kaleidoscopic History of A Disorderly Decade*, Macmillan – discusses British male groups but ignores British female singers altogether.

two TV reviews of Sixties music... BBC4's *Pop Britannia* and *The 1960s: Pop On Trial* were shown in January 2008. Doris Day was mentioned and film of her shown – apparently because DJ Tony Blackburn fancied her; he said he didn't care about how she sang. By such standards were the likes of Dusty, Aretha and Janis Joplin measured, and considered dispensable.

'it was absolutely easy for women...': Caroline Sullivan, 'Ready, Vicki, Go', *Guardian*, 30 November 1999

'Musicians... always considered female singers...': Lucy O'Brien (1995, 2002) *She Bop II: The Definitive History of Women in Rock, Pop and Soul*, Continuum, p.40

'beautifully dressed' for Doug Geddes: *NME*, 28 September 1956

'strawberry blonde with the curls on top': 'Meet That Ryan Gal', *NME*, 28 June 1957

operated 'a business office...': Peter Jones, 'But Susan Maughan is happy, very happy', *Record Mirror*, 3 November 1962

and thus prevent the 'tremendous future' predicted for her... Ray Coleman, 'Bobby's Girl To Go Solo', *Melody Maker*, 27 October 1962

American singers like Peggy Lee and Connie Francis: Leonard Feather, 'Peggy Lee, Perfectionist', *Melody Maker*, 8 July 1961: 'she had the whole bandstand rebuilt... the orchestra enlarged'; Mike Hellicar, 'Connie Francis Is Boss When She Records', *NME*, 6 July 1962: 'It took 20 takes' and she wanted 'to tone down the guitar to allow the bouzouki sound to be featured more'.

and presumably met her and knew her: And 'knew her very well'? Michael Thornton, 'John Lennon's Secret Lover', *Daily Mail*, 7 November 2006: 'the young Dusty Springfield... with whom Cogan was said to be closely involved'. Tittle tattle. Of course?

One of her gowns had 12,964 diamante beads... Sandra Caron (1991) *Alma Cogan: A Memoir*, Bloomsbury, p.81

'it was like plucking a chicken': Ibid., p.84

ring the changes with a plain black dress: Ibid., p.78

Alma the photographer studiously arranging her camera angles: *Alma Cogan: Fabulous*, BBC4, 10 November 2006, producer and director Mervyn Threadgould

Ridley talked of how she calculatingly organised... *Alma Cogan: The Girl With The Giggle In Her Voice*, BBC TV, 1991, director Michael Poole

'a very hard businesswoman': Ibid.

'she wouldn't let anything stand...': Ibid.

A 'dizzy dame': Chris Hayes, '"I'm Such A Dizzy Dame!" Says Kathy Kirby', *Melody Maker*, 28 September 1963

wanting a mink coat like Kathy Kirby: *NME*, 17 January 1964

'a shapely figure wrapped in a pale...': Allen Evans, 'Julie Weaves An Exotic Image', *NME*, 18 September 1964

'an interesting personality': Mike Hellicar, 'Dusty Talks About Jury', NME, 8 March 1963

her dislikes were people who slurped their tea... *NME*, 18 October 1963

'all that flaredy-flaredy stuff...': Ian Dove, 'Suddenly Cilla Becomes "Fashion Expert"', *NME*, 6 March 1964

Lulu who 'bounces and bounds...': Penny Valentine, 'Lulu Can't Stop Singing', *Disc*, 3 July 1965

'A good job you didn't arrive...': 'Sandie's Fashion Trials', *Record Mirror*, 17 October 1964

Marianne Faithfull... 'mixed-up girl' soul-searching: For instance: Cordell Marks, *NME*, 4 September 1964; Ray Coleman, *Melody Maker*, 22 August 1964

liked 'a man to tell me what to do...': *NME*, 7 January 1966. Ironically, the man referred to was probably Tom Springfield who was the Seekers' producer and songwriter.

used to 'being in a man's world': 'They Spoil Me', *Disc*, 14 March 1964

'wouldn't bow down to any man': David Griffiths, 'Cilla – Off The Cuff', *Record Mirror*, 18 April 1964

Burt Bacharach put her through take after take... Ibid. Bacharach met his match in Marlene Dietrich, however. Her perfectionism in the recording studio rivalled his own, judging from Steven Bach's account, 'Falling In Love Again' in Gerd Gemunden and Mary R. Desjardins (eds) (2007) *Dietrich Icon*, Duke University Press, pp.29 and 36. One of the great collective sighs of relief from session musicians must be that Burt Bacharach and

Dusty Springfield only worked in a recording studio together on one occasion. As Dusty said herself on TV's *Pebble Mill*, 18 October 1995: 'We'd probably have killed each other' if there had been more.

and a huge hunger for fame: Cilla Black said 'Since I was a baby… I wanted to be a star' (*Brit Girls: Cilla*, 1997).

the first woman record producer… Dusty told Veronica Groocock (*Record Mirror*, 3 September 1966) that if her career faltered, she'd stay in music 'probably on the production side'.

Part three – You Don't Own Me

Chapter seven – An Apparitional Lesbian?

'it was her battle to deal with…' Jill Jones, 'Goin' Away', *Sydney Star Observer*, 11 March 1999

three words… 'gay', 'lesbian' and 'bisexual'… For example, Peter Sheridan, 'The Love Affair With Women Dusty Springfield Kept A Secret From The World', *Mail On Sunday*, 7 March 1999, quotes Norma Tanega: 'Everybody in the music business knew Dusty was gay'; John Burtlett, 'Wishin' and Hopin'', *Sydney Star Observer*, 23 March 2006, quotes Tamsin Carroll: 'Dusty was a lesbian'; and on *Top 10 Easy Listening*, Channel 4, 21 April 2001, Pat Rhodes says: 'I still say Dusty was bisexual'.

whether she 'came out': For example, 'Springfield came out publicly in 1971', *Sydney Star Observer*, 12 August 2005

partially 'came out': For example Boze Hadleigh (2001), *In Or Out: Stars On Sexuality: A Selection of Celebrity Quotes*, Fusion Press, p.127: 'she never came out all the way'.

or didn't 'come out' at all: For example, *Scotland on Sunday*, 15 February 1998: 'Springfield has never officially come out'.

as to whether she was wise to steer clear… For example, Rufus Wainwright, *Observer Magazine*, November 2006, 'Because she wasn't open about it, she gave herself the right to enjoy being a lesbian in private'.

or whether attaching herself to one or other of them… For example, Simon Bell, *Definitely Dusty*, BBC TV: 'she would have been a happier person if she had been absolutely clear…'

did she have a responsibility…?: Especially in an interview with Keith Howes, *Gay News*, April 1978

'openly supporting gay issues': Sheila Whiteley (2000) *Women and Popular Music: Sexuality, Identity and Subjectivity*, Routledge, p.24

'by all accounts she was a voracious lesbian': Kieron Corless, *Time Out*, 5 April – 12 April 2006

the 'criterion for identifying oneself as…': Lilian Faderman (1992) *Odd Girls and Twilight Lovers: A History of Lesbian Life in Twentieth Century America*, Penguin, p.5

'not confused about her sexuality': Vicki Wickham, *Sydney Star Observer*, 12 August 2005

'she knew she was gay': Ibid.

'knew that Dusty was gay, but… didn't say it to anybody else': Jill Gardiner (2003) *From The Closet To The Screen: Women At The Gateways Club, 1945–85*, Pandora Press, p.87

'a woman whose primary emotional and...': Patricia Juliana Smith, 'You Don't Have To Say You Love Me' in (1999) P.J. Smith (ed.) *The Queer Sixties*, Routledge, p.106 and 123

'I am constantly peering in mirrors': *A Whole Scene Going*, BBC TV, 11 May 1966

'you looked in the mirror and saw nothing': Adrienne Rich, quoted in Colm Tóibín (2002) *Love In A Dark Time: Gay Lives from Wilde to Almodovar*, Picador, p.9

sexuality rarely, if ever came up... Snide innuendoes about Liberace were common, however, as in: Les Perrin, 'Liberace, Purveyor of Musical Popcorn', *NME*, 11 August 1956: 'the fairy godson of the two-way stretch brigade... Lee had been normal enough to say he might marry. He didn't... his gay little eccentricities'.

'sexuality was never discussed...': Dusty, quoted in Lucy O'Brien, *Dusty*, p.180

'the average lesbian will always want...': Keith Howes (1993) *Broadcasting It,* Cassell, p.867

the 1958 comedy series *Trouble For Two*: Ibid., p.864

the play, *Afternoon Of A Nymph*: Ibid., pp.12–13

from *The Gentle Libertine*: Ibid., p.433

'you still have time to stop this filth...': Ibid., p.841

In the 1967 *Man Alive* documentary: Extract shown on *The Gay Decade*, 2004, repeated BBC4, 2007, director Emily Kennedy

'Lesbian... is an ugly word': *Broadcasting It*, p.456

'It seems that most of us find...': Ibid., p.561

a pseudo-therapeutic series called *If You Think*... Ibid., p.375

A *Gay Life* TV programme... Ibid., p.895

by forbidding the utterance of the word... Ibid., p.828

'I just couldn't be a bimbo': Ray Rogers, 'Dusty Days Are Here Again', *Out*, December 1995–January 1996

'she needed to shut up': *Sydney Star Observer*, 12 August 2005

'Dusty Springfield's biggest problem is...': June Harris, 'Separate Careers – and All Booming', *Disc*, 30 November 1963

'It would be wrong... to represent...': Jon Savage, 'Brand New Dusty', *Observer*, 14 December 1989

'Her sick little mind', Dusty wrote...' 'Some Men Are Almost Afraid Of Me Because I'm Famous', *News of the World*, 30 August 1964

As Edward Leeson comments... Edward Leeson (2001) *Dusty Springfield: A Life In Music*, Robson Books, p.113

'My mother used to say, "Why can't...?"': Peter Dacre, *Daily Express*, 8 March 1964

she never had any 'steady boyfriends...': *Woman*, December 1965

'every interview would go to her sexuality': *Girls And Boys: Love Me Do In The 1960s*, Programme 1, BBC2

'it would be too much a personal thing...': Peter McGill, 'Under the Pop Spotlight', *Pop Weekly*, 1964

'I shall comment no further': Rod Harrod, 'The Honest Truth', *Disc*, 5 June 1965

'I'd like to tell you more but...': Alan Smith, *NME*, 3 June 1966

'Are they engaged?' headlined... *Daily Mirror*, 24 February 1964

she was first 'furious'…: 'Some Men Are Afraid Of Me…', *News of the World*, 30 August 1964

'hurt when people suggested…': 'The Sound That Grew In The Grass', *Woman*, December 1965

With Eden Kane confirming in 2005: *Girls And Boys: Love Me Do In The 1960s*, Programme 1

'I don't always tell journalists the truth': *Guardian*, 16 May 2006

'the madrigal and pavane…': Edward Leeson (2001) *Dusty Springfield: A Life In Music*, Robson Books, p.109. For a decade which is often regarded as sexually liberated, the Sixties seemed to assume that everyone would get married – and the sooner the better. Virtually every pop singer, male or female, was asked repeatedly about their marriage intentions. The sound of wedding bells was the most relevant music of all. What was true for gay film actor George Nader of Fifties Hollywood – 'Either one is married or wants to be' (William J. Mann, 2001, *Behind The Screen*, Viking Penguin, p.318) – was equally true of British pop music for much of the Sixties.

the 'man in my life' who had been 'frightened off': Alan Smith, *NME*, 15 October 1965

her hope that year 'to announce her engagement': Jack Bentley, 'The Perils Of Pop', *Sunday Mirror*, 4 April 1965

a late-Sixties romance with DJ, Emperor Rosko: Caroline Boucher, *Disc*, 25 January 1969

a relationship that 'lasted a year': Judith Simons, 'Men and Me by the New Dusty', *Daily Express*, 3 February 1978

'he always talked about Dusty…': Lucy O'Brien, *Dusty*, p.157

the 'traumatic' break-up… Rosalie Shann, '"I've Learned The Lonely Art of Being A Superstar" says Dusty Springfield', *News of the World*, 19 February 1978

The reasons for her matrimonial reluctance varied: The reasons given may be found as follows: *Woman*, 22 July 1978; *Evening Standard*, 20 June 1964; *Sun*, 19 February 1985; *Woman*, December 1965; *Woman*, 1977; *Observer*, 26 January 1969

'Please tell us if she has been…': *Disc*, 27 July 1966

'Was Dusty Springfield married on…?' *Disc*, 17 May 1969

'marriage, if it happens, is the most…': Penny Valentine, 'Dusty: Searching So Hard To Find Herself', *Disc*, 9 September 1967

'this feeling of belonging' which marriage… *Woman*, December 1965

Mike Walsh, congratulate Dusty on 'getting married…': *The Mike Walsh Show*, Australian TV, April 1981

a 2006 edition of the *Daily Mail*: Clemmie Moodie, 'The Day Dusty Vowed "I Only Want To Be With You"', *Daily Mail*, 5 August 2006

'Singer Madeline Bell one of…': *NME*, 26 March 1965

'Close friends: Dusty Springfield and…': *NME*, 9 April 1965

'Is Dusty Springfield for whom…?': *NME*, 11 November 1966

Sandie Shaw had told a *Disc* reporter… *Disc*, 23 October 1965

'Dusty Springfield is puzzled…': *NME*, 29 October 1965

'Close friends: Dusty Springfield and US singer…': *NME*, 27 January 1968

'Flat mates: Dusty Springfield and…': *NME*, 1 February 1969

'US tennis star, Billie Jean King': *NME*, 25 September 1971

'Buddy Rich told London theatre...': *NME*, 8 April 1967

'an apology... for printing Buddy Rich's unjustified...': *NME*, 22 April 1967

'an unhappy series of relationships...': Tony Palmer, *Observer*, 1968

'The double bed', Bernstein wrote... Marcelle Bernstein, *Observer*, 26 January 1969

'it's very difficult to be...': Ibid.

'how Miss Springfield coped with...': *NME*, 25 November 1989

some of the headlines: These headlines come from *NME*, *Melody Maker*, *Record Mirror* and *Disc* (and *Music Echo*).

'What is Dusty Springfield playing at?': *Record Mirror*, 3 July 1971

'Dear Dusty' a 'former love' is reported... Peter Evans, 'I'm A Piece of Living History', *Woman*, mid-Seventies

'I shall only be joyous very fleetingly': David Skan, *Record Mirror*, 26 September 1970

'there wasn't anything that... made her...': *Living Famously*, BBC2, 22 January 2003

'I'm not a tragic person': Mick Brown, 'You Don't Have To Say You Love Me', *Telegraph Magazine*, 27 May 1995

Billie Jean King's view... *South Bank Show*, ITV, 9 April 2006

While some people were understandably shocked... Even in 2008, singer Shelby Lynne was saying 'I hate to even say what I read because I don't want people to think I believe it' (*Los Angeles Times*, 10 January 2008).

there was 'an air of failure': Simon Frith, *20/20?*, 1990

'promise [was] tragically unfulfilled': Peter Kane, *Q*, May 1999

'one reason why I didn't want to stay here': Kris Kirk, *Gay Times*, September 1985

'They say you're either a prostitute...': Marcelle Bernstein, *Observer*, 26 January 1969

describing herself to Connolly as 'promiscuous': *Evening Standard*, 5 September 1970

she had been 'relieved at finally confronting...': Ray Connolly, 'Dusty', *Daily Mail*, 4 March 1994

just as it was for singer k.d. lang: *Observer Music Monthly*, November 2006

'indicative of the baleful self-image...': Patricia Juliana Smith, 'You Don't Have To Say You Love Me', *The Queer Sixties*, Routledge, p.117

'to admit in public to being anything less...': Ray Connolly, *Daily Mail*, 4 March 1994

'if she had been absolutely clear and...': *Definitely Dusty*, BBC2, 26 December 1999

'mystique, a sense of belonging outside...': Peter Doggett, 'In Private', *Record Collector*, May 1999

'I'd prefer to remain a mystery': *Warhol On Warhol*, Channel 5, 2 March 2005

'Last weekend I set about the tricky task...': Derek Johnson, *NME*, 20 December 1963

Chapter eight – Butch Roars and Girlish Shrieks

'she became something of an icon...': *The Times*, 4 March 1999

'she earned a status... as a gay icon': *Financial Times*, 4 March 1999

'became saddled with that dreaded...': Richard Stott, 'Pure StarDust', *News of the World*, 7 March 1999

the same label to have been 'slightly absurdly'... A.N.Wilson, *Evening Standard*, 8 March 1999

Sean, a gay character in *Coronation Street*... 16 September 2007

a Dusty Springfield record reported as playing... Paul Farber, 'Guerillas In The Midst', *Philadelphia Weekly*, 17–23 May 2006. A *Guardian* blog relates that the relationship in *Hollyoaks* between John-Paul and Craig was played out to 'an entire Dusty Springfield soundtrack' (Gareth McLean, 'Give us a song', 9 June 2008).

using her name as a short-hand for gay or lesbian identification... Her voice with the Springfields on 'Island of Dreams' was used at the beginning and end of Radio 4's 'The BBC and the Closet', broadcast on 29 January 2008. The listeners were presumably expected to make the connection between singer and subject matter.

the identity of the 'biggest icon ever?': *French and Saunders*, 4 April 1996

the 'gay icons' who they're 'totally in love with': Rupert Smith Interview, *Gay Times*, September 2007

'If there is anyone that could be...': Amy Lamé, 'My Favourite Londoner', *Time Out*, 7–13 November 2007

'Yeah, we know. You always thought...': *Boyz*, 1996

'before you start thinking that Dusty...': *Boyz*, 15 February 1997

wish to 'see her appeal widen': Paul Mathur, 'The Look Of Love', *Melody Maker*, 23 January 1988

***Prime Suspect* and *EastEnders*:** *Prime Suspect*, ITV 1, 15 October 2006; *EastEnders*, BBC1, 1 January 2007

post-gay icon: The term 'post-gay' is used by Alan Sinfield in his *Gay And After* (1998, Serpents Tail, p.5).

what she called 'a cult following': Melody Parker, 'A Girl Called Dusty', *Campaign*, 1990

'beyond a gay icon... a gay saint': *Observer Music Monthly*, November 2006

'almost frightening... how could any artist...?': Tony Brown, 'The Famous Came To Cheer Judy', *Melody Maker*, 19 October 1957

'flutter of fags' at one of Judy's Palace concerts: Gerald Clarke (2001) *Get Happy: The Life of Judy Garland*, Warner Books, p.389

'the boys in the tight trousers': Ibid.

'There were more queens at Shirley Bassey's...': *NME*, 21 July 1966

'scores of young males hurled themselves...': *Melody Maker*, 14 November 1970

'ran on' stage, 'the girls squealed for her': Peter Laurie, 'I'd Love To Go Pop Before I Go FLOP', *Daily Mail*, 18 November 1963. Cilla Black said in *NME*, 27 March 1964, 'I sit in my dressing room and say, "Oh, the girls screamed, and they shouldn't, you know, because girls don't scream at girls"'.

'it's a personality which appeals to members...': Derek Johnson, 'Dusty Does It Solo', *NME*, 22 November 1963

Patricia Juliana Smith suggests Dusty's *Ready Steady Go!*... 'You Don't Have To Say You Love Me', p.110

Smith goes on to say that her 'court'... Ibid.

her manager, hairdresser and other staff members... Richard Smith, 'In Private', *Gay Times*, October 2000: Mike Gill says 'she surrounded herself with gay people: managers, male and female, press agents, moi'.

accounts… by Elton John and Dale Winton: Philip Norman (2000) *Sir Elton: The Definitive Biography*, Sidgwick and Jackson, p.33; *Dancing With Demons*, p.107; Dale Winton (2002) *My Story*, Century, different parts of the book – each chapter is named after a Dusty Springfield song.

most of the published memoirs… For example, Veronica Groocock, 'Memories of Dusty', *Diva*, May 1999; Valerie Moffitt in *Diva*, May 1999; Stacey D'Erasmo, 'Beginning With Dusty', *Village Voice*, 29 August 1995

'her sexuality was obvious to…': David McAlmont, *Observer Music Monthly*, November 2006

'part of the minority of lesbian culture…': Paul Gambaccini, *The Sex Lives of Us: Gay Times*, Radio 4, 13 September 2007

those during her BBC series and a show hosted by Liberace: *Dusty*, BBC TV, 1 September 1966; *Liberace*, ATV, 25 May 1969

Dusty used 'polari' or 'very specific gay slang': *South Bank Show*, ITV, 9 April 2006

on a 1974 TV play called *Girl*: Keith Howes (1993) *Broadcasting It*, Cassell, p.456

'enormously strong gay following': Keith Howes, *Gay News*, April 1978

'a fantastic show of loyalty': Cathy Couzens, 'Dusty refers to her "gay following"', *Star*, 18 May 1979

'stomach-churning embarrassment': Ian Birch, *NME*, May 1979

'her effect on an adoring audience…': Jeremy Myerson, *Stage and Television Today*, December 1979

Dave Gelly found 'the vehemence, even the hysteria': Dave Gelly, 'Mother's Best', *Observer*, December 1979

her fans' 'undying faith and love': Nick Underwood, *Cash Box*, 12 May 1979

'strong gay and lesbian following': Gordon Biggins, 'The Resurrection of Dusty', *Nine-to-Five*, 5 August 1985

'fierce loyalty among the gay community': Andrew Simpson, *Woman*, 12 October 1985

'always the victim… on a knife edge': Cathy Couzens, *Star*, 18 May 1979

'I cry a lot, they were there…': Ibid.

'St Jude, to whom the faithful flock…': Aida Pavletich, *Sirens Of Song*, p.154

'her painfully sad voice…': Kris Kirk, quoted by Sarah Nelson, *Herald*, 4 March 1999

'her wonderful heart-rending songs': *Definitely Dusty*, BBC2, 26 December 1999

'knowing sense of camp' and… Andy Gill, *Independent*, 4 March 1999

'mix of public exuberance and personal anguish': Barry Walters, 'Dusty In Heaven', *Village Voice*, 10–16 March 1999

'an Englishman professing a love for Dusty…': Barry Walters, 'Dusty Rides Again', *Advocate*, 13 June 1995

Streisand, Madonna, Kylie and Bassey: One can only hope that the last-mentioned star has overcome the aversion she apparently felt when watching two men kiss in the film, *Sunday Bloody Sunday*. Vito Russell reports that 'screening the kiss had made her sick to her stomach, forcing her to leave the theater' (1981, *The Celluloid Closet: Homosexuality In The Movies*, Harper and Row, p.211).

'there has been much work on fans…': Clive Bloom, 'An Alternative Voice', *Times Higher Education Supplement*, 7 September 2007

thanks to Daniel Cavicchi's pioneering work: Daniel Cavicchi (1998) *Tramps Like Us:*

Music and Meaning Among Springsteen Fans, Oxford University Press. Other serious studies of fans and fan psychology (though not of specific music fan networks) are: Matt Hills (2002) *Fan Cultures*, Routledge; and Cornel Sandvoss (2005) *Fans: The Mirror of Consumption*, Polity Press.

Chapter nine – Que(e)rying the Icon

'gay' or 'lesbian' icon... A good short guide to 'icon' as in 'gay icon' or 'lesbian icon' is to be found in Robin Baker and Briony Hanson (1996) *Celluloid Icons: A Celebration of Lesbian and Gay Icons in Film and Television*, Channel Four Television. William J. Spurlin considers 'a cultural icon as that legible grid onto which our fantasies, desires and aspirations are projected as a means to their conscious expression' and agrees with Wayne Koestenbaum that 'an icon is more an idea than a person'. The latter is very much my own understanding of Dusty Springfield as an icon. Spurlin's essay 'I'd Rather Be The Princess than the Queen! Mourning Diana as a Gay Icon' is in *Queer Theory*, edited by Iain Morland and Annabelle Willox (2005, Palgrave Macmillan, p.159).

as Donald E. Hall more aptly... Donald E. Hall (2003) *Queer Theories*, Palgrave Macmillan

'it acquires its meaning from its oppositional...': David Halperin (1995) *Saint Foucault: Towards A Gay Hagiography*, Oxford University Press, pp.61–2

'a wide range of positions within culture...': Alexander Doty, 'There's Something Queer Here' in C. Creekmur and A. Doty (eds) (1995) *Out In Culture: Gay, Lesbian and Queer Essays on Popular Culture*, Cassell, p.73

'to entertain more diverse and permeable identities': Alan Sinfield (1998) *Gay and After*, Serpent's Tail, p.5

'queer is always an identity under construction...': Annamarie Jagose (1996) *Queer Theory: An Introduction*, New York University Press, p.131

'odd... that our social worlds and our social prejudices...': Andrew Bennett and Nicholas Royle (2004) *An Introduction to Literature, Criticism and Theory*, Pearson Longman, p.193

Foucault, Judith Butler and Eve Kosofsky Sedgwick... Queer theory may be found in: Michel Foucault (1978) *The History of Sexuality Vol.1, An Introduction*, Vintage Books; and Eve Kosofsky Sedgwick (1994) *Tendencies*, Routledge. A good introduction to Judith Butler's work is Sarah Salih (2002) *Judith Butler*, Routledge.

Since the original meanings of queer... This information is taken from Kosofsky Sedgwick's *Tendencies*, p.xii.

'the perfect postmodern trope, a term for the times...': Suzanne Walters, quoted in Julian Wolfreys (2004) *Critical Keywords in Literary and Cultural Theory*, Palgrave Macmillan, p.202

what Michael Warner has called 'regimes of the normal': Michael Warner, quoted in Donald E. Hall, *Queer Theories*, p.15

it might be useful to say something about 'camp': Three useful books on 'camp' are: David Bergman (ed.) (1993) *Camp Grounds: Style and Homosexuality*, University of Massachusetts Press; Pamela Robertson (1996) *Guilty Pleasures: Feminist Camp From Mae West to Madonna*, I.B. Tauris & Co Ltd; Mark Booth (1983) *Camp*, Quartet Books Ltd

Patricia Juliana Smith or Lee Everett describe Dusty as 'camp': Patricia Juliana Smith in the title of her essay 'You Don't Have To Say You Love Me: The Camp Masquerades of Dusty Springfield'; Lee Everett on *Definitely Dusty*, BBC TV

'I know that curiosity about my private life...': *Woman's World*, 1978

The motivations… were, in all probability, defensive… Richard Smith, 'In Private', *Gay Times*, October 2000. In this article Keith Howes remembers his *Gay News* interview with Dusty Springfield in 1978. Before the interview, he says, 'She burst into tears, sobbing that she couldn't talk about being gay, it was impossible'. He says they reached a compromise – they would discuss homophobia in the USA and touch indirectly on her sexuality. After Howes left her hotel room, he said he began crying. 'It had been like talking to someone awaiting the assassin's bullet in some police state'.

'I'm not going to commit myself to being…': *Gay News*, April 1978

'They seem to want me to be either gay or straight': *News of the World*, 10 April 1988

'That doesn't make me one and that doesn't *not*…': *Gay News*, April 1978

she would **'have little to lose…':** Andrew Duncan, *Woman*, 12 October 1985

'It's other people who want you to be…': *New York Times*, 29 October 1995

'Who's to say what you are?': Ibid.

'You're bound to get tagged with labels…': *Woman*, 12 October 1985

'What about all those heterosexuals…': Dusty, quoted in *Mail On Sunday*, March 1999

'though many have claimed that she was simply a lesbian…': *Definitely Dusty*, BBC TV

'I hate categories': *Telegraph*, 27 May 1995

'people have run with trying to categorise me': Ibid.

'all my life I've fought categories': Ibid.

'I don't want normality': Ibid.

'I question everything': *News of the World*, 23 August 1964

'I feel neither here nor there': *NME*, 19 September 1970

'It has nothing to do with being straight or gay': *Gay News*, April 1978

'a stateless person': *Record Mirror*, 26 September 1970

'get-at-able': Madeline Bell reports Dusty as saying 'Never let yourself be too get-at-able' (*Definitely Dusty*, BBC TV).

'I don't take stances': *Gay Times*, September 1985

'I don't want to be owned by anyone…': *Telegraph*, 27 May 1995

'I ain't the kind you can tie down…': Song 'Sometimes Like Butterflies', written by Bruce Roberts and Donna Summer, recorded by Dusty Springfield, May/June 1985

'a free spirit': Stephen Poliakoff on *Desert Island Discs*, 13 March 2005. Poliakoff said he had been listening to Dusty Springfield most of his life.

'having a sense of the absurd has kept me going': *Gay News*, April 1978

'Sitting in my living room were my mum and dad…': *Us*, 2 May 1988

Christian Ward… is aware of it… 'burlesque and bouffant and…': 'Dusty Springfield: In The Land Of Make Believe', notes to booklet for *Simply Dusty* CD, 2006

'struck by the eerie quality to her vocal performance': Kieron Corless in *Time Out*, 5–12 April 2006

The entire reception of her in terms of colour is as disruptive… Pamela Robertson, amongst others, suggests a link between queerness and blackness. 'Queer and camp representations, though non-normative in terms of sex and gender, are still consistently defined through categories of racial difference, and especially blackness' (*Guilty*

Pleasures: Feminist Camp from Mae West to Madonna, p.20).

'just couldn't understand why a nice white girl...': Dave Godin, quoted in Lucy O'Brien, *Dusty*, p.98

others like Larry Katz didn't know where to file... Larry Katz, *Boston Herald*, 4 March 1999

'Where did beige music begin?': Julie Burchill, *Time Out*, 22–8 November 1984

Carole King's notion in her Aretha song: I refer to the Goffin, King and Wexler song '(You Make Me Feel Like) A Natural Woman', recorded by Aretha Franklin in 1967.

'a curious lesbian simulacrum of a "girl"': Patricia Juliana Smith, 'Icons and Iconoclasts: Figments of Sixties Queer Culture' in *The Queer Sixties*, p.xviii

an Australian TV programme in 1967: The programme was *Brian Henderson's Bandstand.*

In life she is said to have often checked herself into... Information regarding Dusty's mental health may be found in Valentine and Wickham's *Dancing With Demons* (2000).

'I saw my name up in lights... it seems like...': Alan Smith, 'Dusty Feels Like Two People', *NME*, 3 August 1968

'it's hard for people to see past the image...': *Melody Maker*, 21 December 1968

'an extraordinary remark': Edward Leeson, *Dusty Springfield: A Life In Music*, p.125

'What is a Dusty Springfield?': Keith Altham, *Record Mirror*, 24 January 1970

'unique, alien...': Christian Ward, *Simply Dusty* CD notes

'In the end... Dusty Springfield can do what she damn well likes': John Selby, *Woman's World*, 1978

'I did say at 17 "I'm going to invent Dusty Springfield"...': *The Big Time*, 2 July 1980, BBC1

'If you set out to create a Dusty Springfield...': *Gay News*, April 1978

'I became this monster that I invented for myself...': *Saturday Night Out*, 27 April 1985, BBC1

'To this day... I stand backstage and think myself...': *News of the World*, 10 April 1988

'My drinking had nothing to do with Dusty Springfield...': Ibid.

'she was definitely two people': *Definitely Dusty*, BBC TV

'it's very easy to decide...': Ibid.

'an enormous amount of subtext and meaning to lyrics': Hiram Lee, Review of Shelby Lynne's 'Just A Little Lovin', World Socialist Web Site, 18 March 2008, http://www.wsws.org/articles/2008/mar2008/cove-m18.shtml

'Lyrics I have a real problem with': *The Mike Douglas Show*, American TV, October 1980

'Lyrics mean very little to me': Source unknown, October 1989

'she tried on musical personalities the way...': Randy Cordova, 'Dusty Made It By Making It Real', *Arizona Republic*, 7 March 1999

'was a reminder of the provisional nature...': Matt Chayt, *The Declaration*, 25 March 1999

Shirley Temple impersonator: Dusty memorably impersonated Shirley Temple at her Talk of the Town cabaret show in London, July–August 1968.

'a soul singer, a nightclub torch balladeer, a pop maestro...': Peter Doggett,

'Simply… Dusty', *Record Collector*, October 2000

when Neil Tennant answered her apparently ingenuous question… *Dusty: Full Circle*, BBC TV

Postscript

The Candie Payne, Dawn Kinnard and Duffy quotes are from British newspapers during 2007 and early 2008.

Index

Index of people mentioned in the main text

Writers, journalists, commentators on Dusty Springfield and others

Behind the scenes in the music industry

Queer/Cultural theorists

Others